Swinburne
A Study of Romantic Mythmaking

Swinburne
A Study of Romantic Mythmaking

David G. Riede

University Press of Virginia

Charlottesville

THE UNIVERSITY PRESS OF VIRGINIA
Copyright © 1978 by the Rector and Visitors
of the University of Virginia

First published 1978

Library of Congress Cataloging in Publication Data
Riede, David G
  Swinburne: a study of romantic mythmaking.
  Includes index.
  1. Swinburne, Algernon Charles, 1837–1909—
Criticism and interpretation. 2. Myth in literature.
PR5517.M82R5   821'.8   78–4940   ISBN 0–8139–0745–4

Printed in the United States of America

For Cecil Lang

Contents

Acknowledgments

I am indebted to Professor Stephen Maxfield Parrish of Cornell University, my first mentor on the subject of romanticism, and to Professors Robert Langbaum, E. D. Hirsch, and Leopold Damrosch of the University of Virginia for supplying the background information that made this study possible. More specifically, I am grateful to Professors Deborah Gutschera and Julian Hartt of the University of Virginia and to Professor George M. Ridenour of CUNY for reading the manuscript and offering many helpful suggestions. I would also like to acknowledge my debt to Professor Jerome McGann of Johns Hopkins, who read part of the manuscript and made several useful suggestions. Professor McGann's book *Swinburne: An Experiment in Criticism* has received less credit in my notes than its influence on my thinking deserves. All students of Swinburne owe an immense debt of gratitude to Professor Cecil Y. Lang, foremost of Swinburne scholars, whose superb edition of the letters and meticulous scholarship have largely been responsible for redeeming a great poet from oblivion. My own debt to Professor Lang, both intellectual and personal, is beyond my power to express. Finally, I would like to thank Raymond G. and Betty A. Riede, Clarence M. Tyler, Jr., and Natalie C. Tyler for their generous assistance and infinite patience, and my wife, Natalie, for her boundless faith, encouragement, and moral support.

I would like to thank Oxford University Press for permission to quote from the Oxford Standard Authors editions of Wordsworth, Byron, Shelley, and Arnold. I am also indebted to the Trustees of the Hardy Estate and the Macmillan Company, London and Basingstoke, for permission to quote from "On a Fine Morning" and "A Singer Asleep" from *The Complete Poems of Thomas Hardy: New Wessex Edition*, edited by James Gibson, and to Random House, Inc., for permission to quote from "In Memory of W. B. Yeats," in *The Collected Poetry of W. H. Auden*, Copyright W. H. Auden, 1945.

Swinburne
A Study of Romantic Mythmaking

Introduction

THE WORD 'ROMANTIC,'" as Arthur O. Lovejoy has observed, "has come to mean so many things that, by itself, it means nothing."[1] The same can be said for the word *myth*, and consequently for *mythmaking* or *mythopoeic*. To understand the radically ambiguous term *romantic mythmaking*, then, it is necessary to define briefly how both terms are used in this study. Mythmaking may be simply understood as the generation of verbal constructs to embody the experience of the life of man confronting the greater life beyond him. The mythmaker may personify the life in nature, create gods, or describe the metamorphoses of natural forms or of man into nature. If he rejects or is indifferent to the natural world, he may even exalt and possibly deify man himself or any of man's works—from society, to civilization, to his creative energy as represented by tradition. In any case the language of mythopoeia is highly metaphorical, since, to use the dated but still useful terms of the New Criticism, the metaphoric vehicle perfectly reflects a metamorphic tenor. The transmutation of language perfectly reflects the transmutations of external nature. The poetry of mythmaking, or mythopoeic poetry, is not to be confused with mythological poetry, for while the former describes the actual experience of the life beyond the self, the latter simply recounts myths generated in the past, in the experience of someone other than the poet. Thus Ovid, though writing of metamorphoses, is primarily a mythological, not a mythopoeic, poet.

[1] "On the Discrimination of Romanticisms," in *English Romantic Poets*, ed. M. H. Abrams (New York, 1960), p. 6.

Mythmaking, by its very nature, can only take place when the external world is perceived as animated by some unifying power, whether of an immanent, pantheistic deity or of the esemplastic imagination of the poet. It cannot take place when man and an objective, external nature are regarded as separate and distinct entities because it demands an interaction of the spirit within man and the spirit without. As Nietzsche explains in *The Birth of Tragedy*, the unified intellect and imagination of man are necessary to create myths. Aeschylus could generate myth in pre-Socratic Greece, but Euripides, coming after Socratic philosophy had sundered thought from emotion, could not. Similarly, medieval and Renaissance poets, for whom all the faculties of man were in harmony, were able to create myths, while those of the Enlightenment, who separated the rational from the emotional faculties, were not.

English romanticism of the early nineteenth century was, among other things, a return in spirit to the ages of romance, the ages preceding the eighteenth-century rationality that hierarchically arranged nature, man, and a distanced, transcendent God. Robert Langbaum, defining romanticism as a modern tradition, has described it as a reaction against the separation of fact from values that characterized the Enlightenment:

the scientific and critical effort of the Enlightenment . . . in its desire to separate fact from the values of a crumbling tradition, separated fact from all values—bequeathing a world in which fact is measurable quantity while value is man-made and illusory. Such a world offers no objective verification for just the perceptions by which men live, perception of beauty, goodness and spirit. It was as literature began in the latter eighteenth century to realize the dangerous implications of the scientific world-view, that romanticism was born.[2]

The separation of fact from value parallels the general separation of life from religion in the eighteenth century. Deism placed God outside of and above man and nature as a rational, Socratic judge who established moral codes and bade men follow them. It is a turn to deism that distinguishes Job from his "Comforters": Job insists on and gets a personal interview; the Comforters are essentially deists. Man could not expect to experience God directly—the word *en-*

---

[2] *The Poetry of Experience* (New York, 1957), p. 11.

thusiasm, meaning to have a god within the self, was a term of denigration to the deists of Dr. Johnson's day. And enthusiasm, in this root sense, is the basis of the mythopoeic experience.

In returning spiritually to the ages of romance, the English romantics were returning to a world view in which religion and life, fact and values, were not divorced. To too many enlightened eighteenth-century thinkers the cosmos was a rigid hierarchy in which nothing could be dislodged from its proper place and in which "facts" were immutable truths. Renaissance Neoplatonism, on the other hand, saw "facts" as merely the mutable embodiments of an eternal ideal, and consequently saw that external reality could be altered. Renaissance beliefs in theology, philosophy, and the sciences, from astronomy to astrology to alchemy, all put man at the center of the universe and attributed to him the power to alter external nature. The established truths of religion and science perfectly reflected the truths of common sense, of experience, which necessarily place man at the center of what he perceives. The lack of a radical disjunction between experience and imposed belief enabled the Renaissance artist to constantly reinterpret and reshape the cosmos in the terms of his own creative perceptions.

In *The Tempest*, for example, Shakespeare, the greatest of all English mythopoeic poets, showed how the imagination of the artist could penetrate the mysteries of nature and could create meaning from the experience of constant change and transformation. The play creates a miniature cosmos in which man, from the subhuman to the superhuman, from Caliban to Prospero, exists in moral harmony with nature and with spirits. The extremely metaphorical language—including, in fact, a great deal of alchemical imagery— reflects the mutability of nature just as the remarkable range of human characters reflects the extent to which the soul of man may metamorphose and find its appropriate place in the cosmic hierarchy.

But even more than to Shakespeare, the romantics looked back to Milton, the last great mythopoeic poet of the age of romance. Even in explicitly Christian poems such as "On the Morning of Christ's Nativity," "Lycidas," and *Paradise Lost*, Milton felt free to assimilate pagan mythology with Christian doctrine and in other ways to create his own myths. Poems like "L'Allegro" and "Il Penseroso," moreover, are essentially mythopoeic—the spirit of man meets the spirit of nature, and from this interaction myth is generated. Both poems begin with mythic genealogies of personified abstractions, both are highly metaphorical, both explore the effects of emotion on the perception of nature, and both, in fact, end with a request for the power of mythopoeic creation, for

> The melting voice through mazes running
> Untwisting all the chains that tie
> The hidden soul of harmony. . . .[3]

In the prose treatise *Areopagitica* Milton suggested that all learning contributes to man's search for ultimate truth, that all perceptions are fragments of "Truth" which "came once into the world with her divine Master, and was a perfect shape most glorious to look on." Even in a prose argument, the language is mythopoeic, metamorphosing the abstraction into a personified deity, and Milton did not restrict himself to Christian terminology: since the ascension of Christ, "the sad friends of Truth, such as durst appear, imitating the carefull search that *Isis* made for the mangl'd body of *Osiris*, went up and down gathering up limb by limb, still as they could find them."[4] The pagan myths, rightly understood, are a part of the eternal Truth, the "divine Master."

The poets who followed Milton, and in a sense Milton himself, in his famous rejection of myths outside of Christian dogma in *Paradise Regained,* were unable or unwilling to recreate the mythic impulses of earlier ages. Poets began to concentrate on "knowledge," on dogmatic beliefs about the structure of a fixed and rigid cosmos. The verse of Dryden and Pope is perfectly balanced and controlled, avoiding any hint of enthusiasm. Mythopoeia was, effectually, denied as a possibility, for according to Pope,

> 'Tis but a part we see, and not a whole.
>   . . . . .
> Then say not Man's imperfect, Heav'n in fault;
> Say rather, Man's as perfect as he ought;

[3] "L'Allegro," ll. 142–44, *The Poetical Works of John Milton*, ed. David Masson (London, 1894), I, 372.

[4] *Complete Prose Works of John Milton*, ed. Ernest Sirluck, II (New Haven, 1959), p. 549.

> His knowledge measur'd to his state and place,
> His time a moment, and a point his space.[5]

The meeting of the whole soul of man with the whole soul of the cosmos is quite inconceivable when the soul of man, divided into component parts of reason and emotion, can see only fragments. The balanced, antithetical, wholly reasonable couplets with which Dryden and Pope translated Homer measure the distance of Enlightenment poetry from the original impulses that generate myth.

Even the lyric poets of this period were, as a rule, incapable of imaginatively fusing the life of man and nature, as a glance at one of the many eighteenth-century imitations of Milton's "L'Allegro" and "Il Penseroso" will serve to indicate. William Collins's "Ode to Pity" and "Ode to Fear" are self-conscious attempts to invoke the "wild enthusiast heat" that makes truly imaginative poetry possible, and both are self-conscious failures. Collins, invoking the inspiration of Shakespeare, closes the "Ode to Fear" with an echo of Milton:

> O thou whose spirit most possest
> The sacred seat of Shakespear's breast!
> By all that from thy prophet broke,
> In thy divine emotions spoke,
> Hither again thy fury deal!
> Teach me but once like him to feel;
> His cypress wreath my meed decree,
> And I, O Fear, will dwell with thee![6]

The emotional life cannot overcome the dominance of rationality; the poet cannot feel. Even the cult of sensibility that emerged in the later eighteenth century could not heal the radical division of the spirit because sensibility was itself a highly self-conscious cultivation of the feelings, and self-consciousness, of course, prevents the mergence of the self in external nature. The closest most eighteenth-century lyricists could come to mythopoeic creation was a facile and sterile personification. Thomas Gray's "Sonnet on the Death of Mr. Richard West," condemned by Wordsworth as illustra-

---

[5] *Essay on Man*, I. 60, 69–72, ed. Maynard Mack (New Haven, 1947), pp. 20, 22.

[6] "Ode to Fear," ll. 64–71, *The Poems of William Collins*, ed. Walter C. Bronson (Boston, 1898), p. 39.

tive of the vicious poetic diction of his predecessors, is a perfect example of the age's inability to meaningfully relate man and nature in verse:

> In vain to me the smileing Mornings shine,
> And redning Phoebus lifts his golden Fire:
> The birds in vain their amorous Descant joyn;
> Or chearful Fields resume their green Attire.[7]

Elements of nature are arbitrarily personified—Wordsworth might well ask what feeling within the poet or within nature justifies the attributes "smileing," "chearful," and so on. Though he missed Gray's point in ostentatiously separating form and content to heighten the sense of loss by illustrating the emptiness of the traditional elegiac comfort in nature, Wordsworth was nevertheless essentially correct in recognizing Gray's poetic difficulties. In his grief Gray recognized the utter disjunction between nature and man—the heightened emotional perception led him away from, not toward, mythopoeia.

The division of feeling from reason, experience from objectivity, is essentially antireligious since it allows no direct perception of God. Most eighteenth-century rationalists nevertheless had a religion, considering themselves deists. Paradoxically, those enlightened rationalists who were not religious, atheists like David Hume, may have prepared the way for a rebirth of truly religious feeling. Following the Nietzschean pattern, the Socratic division of thought from feeling is destroyed from within by its own premises—rationalism must ultimately destroy religion. All of the major romantic poets were essentially religious in temperament, but all, in the sense that they were reacting against deism, were antitheists during their most creative periods. In order to experience nature directly and creatively, the romantic poets had to rid themselves of inherited dogma; in order to experience religion, to know the life beyond them, they had first to be agnostics or, like Blake, heretics. M. H. Abrams, speaking of Wordsworth, succinctly describes the spiritual return of romanticism to pre-Enlightenment times, the rejection of "all hereditary symbols," and the return to mythmaking:

[7] *The Works of Thomas Gray*, ed. Edmund Gosse (London, 1884), p. 110.

in some of his most effective passages he not only vivifies the natural scene, but seems to revert to the very patterns of thought and feeling memorialized in communal myths and folk-lore. Coleridge explicitly maintained that Wordsworth, in the power of imagination, "stands nearest of all modern writers to Shakespeare and Milton; and yet in a kind perfectly unborrowed and his own." This characteristic and unborrowed power is found, not in Wordsworth's formal mythological poems, but in the many passages (of which several are cited by Coleridge) in which his imagination, rejecting all hereditary symbols, and without violence to the truth of perception, operates as myth in process rather than on myth in being.

Furthermore, Abrams goes on to note, the personifications and metamorphoses in Wordsworth's poetry, unlike those of Gray, result from genuine emotions. Abrams sums up in one pregnant sentence: "Symbolism, animism, and mythopoeia, in richly diverse forms, explicit or submerged, were so pervasive in this age as to constitute the most pertinent single attribute for defining 'romantic' poetry." [8] Though Wordsworth's pantheism is not as typical of his age as has often been supposed, his "symbolism, animism, and mythopoeia" are. Blake, for example, rejected nature utterly but found a basis for mythopoeic creation in his belief that the synthetic imagination can recreate the primal unity of man in society, can recreate the spirit in which "all religions are one." Similarly, Coleridge, the most orthodox of the romantics, struggled all his life to explicate the felt analogy between the creative *fiat* of the infinite "I AM" and the creative imagination of the poet. Even Byron, Shelley, and Keats, though unable to accept either the "nature-worship" of Wordsworth or the Christianity, however radical and creative, of Blake and Coleridge, all insisted in various ways that the individual mind orders and is therefore coextensive and in unity with the cosmos. Romantic mythmaking is, then, a sort of religion without dogma. Man's fall into division during the Enlightenment, to put the matter in mythic terms, was a felix culpa, for in returning to the age of romance he was redeemed, but he was redeemed at a higher spiritual level. Once again man became aware of the essential unity of the cosmos, but he became aware also that he created the unity. The artist, as creator of meaning, effectually displaced God in the cosmic hierarchy.

[8] *The Mirror and the Lamp* (New York, 1958), p. 296.

With the exception of Coleridge, all of the major romantic poets attempted to rival and surpass Milton on his own grounds, attempted to embody in epic form a conception of man's relation to God and nature which would supersede that of *Paradise Lost*. All of these poets shared the ideological persuasion that by discarding the old forms and perceiving the world anew they could, in effect, create a new world. Blake insisted that he must create his own system or be enslaved by another man's—Milton's, for example—and he insisted on the identity of fresh perception and creation. We are trapped by the handed-down knowledge of the ages, perceive as we are told to perceive, yet every man should be a prophet, should see into the life of nature. In *The Marriage of Heaven and Hell* he asks: "How do you know but ev'ry Bird that cuts the airy way, / Is an immense world of delight, clos'd by your senses five?" [9] Blake's first epic, *Milton*, describes a deliberate revision of Milton's version of Christianity. In it, the spirit of Milton returns to earth entering into the person of Blake—entering, in fact, into Blake's left foot (Pl. 15, ll. 46–50)—and revises his theology. In *Paradise Lost* he had separated man and God; now he realizes that God is none other than the Divine Humanity and that humanity deifies itself by virtue of the creative imagination. The real hero of *Paradise Lost*, according to Blake, had been Satan, who represents the will to continued creation rather than submission to received doctrine. Asserting the power of mind over matter, Satan was, in a sense, the first romantic: "The mind is its own place, and in itself / Can make a Heav'n of Hell, a Hell of Heav'n." [10]

Wordsworth, as emphatically as Blake, challenged comparison with Milton while asserting the necessity of renewed perception rather than of submissive acceptance—in Abrams's terms, of "myth in process" rather than "myth in being." In his "Prospectus" to *The Excursion* he challenged Milton even more aggressively than did Blake. Praying "fit audience let me find though few," Wordsworth invokes Milton's muse, Urania, "or a greater Muse," and declares his intention of seeing above Milton's heaven, to "breathe in worlds /

---

[9] *Blake: Complete Writings*, ed. Geoffrey Keynes (Oxford, 1966), p. 150.
[10] *Paradise Lost* I.254–55, *Poetical Works*, II, 181.

To which the heaven of heavens is but a veil" and of seeing below Milton's hell. The main region of his song, in fact, is the cosmos not of Milton's God but of his Satan; it is the "Mind of Man." Wordsworth's great theme is to be, in effect, a discussion of man's mythopoeic power; he proclaims

> How exquisitely the individual Mind,
> (And the progressive powers perhaps no less
> Of the whole species) to the external World
> Is fitted:—and how exquisitely, too—
> Theme this but little heard of among men—
> The external World is fitted to the Mind;
> And the creation (by no lower name
> Can it be called), which they with blended might
> Accomplish:—this is our high argument.[11]

Similarly, Shelley's *Prometheus Unbound*, Keats's *Hyperion* and *Fall of Hyperion*, and even Byron's *Don Juan* all self-consciously recall Milton to show that they surpass him in vision, all evolve a myth in which man displaces God as the creative power, and all repudiate secondhand doctrine in order to be left free to create their own meaning. In the eighteenth century, rationalism and deism had destroyed the harmonious interaction of man and nature, and man had ceased to perceive the cosmos creatively, realizing that, as Pope said, "The proper study of Mankind is Man."[12] The romantic poets accepted much from the eighteenth century—they studied man, but they studied him as the creative center of the cosmos, not as one link in a cosmic chain.

The romantic epic clearly illustrates the central importance of mythmaking in romanticism, but epic is not essentially a mythopoeic form—its purpose is rather to enshrine myth than to create it. The constant growth in prestige of the lyric from the beginnings of romanticism in the eighteenth century is actually more illustrative of romantic mythopoeia. The establishment of the lyric as a poetic norm, as a standard of excellence, was, as M. H.

---

[11] "Prospectus" to *The Excursion*, ll. 29–30, 62–71, *Wordsworth's Poetical Works*, ed. Ernest de Selincourt, V (Oxford, 1949), 3, 5.

[12] *Essay on Man*, II. 2, p. 53.

Abrams has shown, associated with the typically romantic elevation of personal feelings and emotions.[13] The lyric, considered the purest expression of the language of the passions, expresses the emotional side of man's nature rather than the strictly rational. Under the influence of the passions, the romantic aestheticians believed, nature is perceived in a new light, and the language used to express this new perception is consequently highly original and highly figurative. In short, as the expression of the impassioned mind in the process of creative perception, the lyric is the most mythopoeic of literary forms. In this connection it may be noted that the epics of two of the romantics, Blake and Shelley, are essentially lyrical, that in *Milton, Jerusalem,* and *Prometheus Unbound* narrative line is almost entirely subordinated to lyrical effusion. With the exception of Byron, in fact, all of the romantic poets are at their best as lyricists, for the lyric is perfectly adapted to mythopoeic perception, which is not logically sequential and therefore is not communicable as narrative. The lyric, moreover, can sustain a highly figurative, metaphoric language better than other forms and can therefore linguistically fuse two separate realms—those of man and nature—without breaking down into logical allegory. Because it has no obligations to plot, the lyric can accommodate the experience of the whole soul of the poet without the mediation of the shaping, controlling intellect.

The romantic lyric is not, of course, the highly spontaneous outpouring that the romantics themselves would have us believe. Rather, as has been frequently shown, these poets took great pains over their work—the critical intellect contributing at least as much to the final product as the original perception. Yet the attempt to make the poems appear spontaneous is in itself indicative of the romantic concern to show the mind in the process of creating and to show myth in the process of becoming. The romantic lyric, as Abrams, Wimsatt, and others have shown, is radically different from the eighteenth-century lyric in its perfect fusion of the object perceived, the perceiving poet, and the poetic imagery.[14] The pur-

---

[13] *The Mirror and the Lamp,* pp. 84–88.

[14] See W. K. Wimsatt, "The Structure of Romantic Nature Imagery," in *English Romantic Poets,* pp. 25–37, and M. H. Abrams, "Structure and Style in the Greater

pose of such poetry is to show the power of the imagination and the essential unity of man, nature, and God. Shelley's "Ode to the West Wind," Coleridge's "Eolian Harp," Wordsworth's "Lucy" poems, and Keats's odes all explore the liminal areas where cyclic nature, time, and the elements meet and merge in the mind of man.

Despite Wordsworth's healing power and Shelley's passionate political concerns, however, mythopoeic poetry, because it eschews overt doctrinal commentary, is essentially amoral and soon fell from favor in the evangelical, progressive climate of Victoria's reign. Keats, in the "Ode to May," had declared his willingness to praise nature and the mythic gods in song, claiming he was content to be "Rich in the simple worship of a day,"[15] but by the middle of the nineteenth century a new Puritanism was having its impact on the arts. Carlyle deplored Keats's "weak-eyed maudlin sensibility," Ruskin unfavorably compared romantic and classic mythopoeia in *Modern Painters*, and Arnold condemned romanticism as feeling without thought.[16] In general the Victorians were beginning to insist that art serve society; they were, in a sense, returning to Milton, but to the orthodox Puritan Milton of doctrine—such doctrine as his Christ expressed in *Paradise Regained*:

Romantic Lyric," in *From Sensibility to Romanticism*, ed. Frederick W. Hilles and Harold Bloom (New York, 1965), pp. 527–60.

[15] "Ode to May," l. 14, *The Poems of John Keats*, ed. Miriam Allott (London, 1970), p. 354.

[16] *Thomas Carlyle's Collected Works* (London, 1869), VII, 25; see John Ruskin, *Modern Painters*, Vol. III, Pt. IV, Chaps. xii, xiii, xvi; Ruskin repeatedly contrasts the mythopoeia caused by emotional distortion, or the "pathetic fallacy" of such writers as Keats and Coleridge, with Homer's natural perception of divinity in the landscape; Matthew Arnold, "The Function of Criticism at the Present Time," in *Lectures and Essays in Criticism*, ed. R. H. Super (Ann Arbor, Mich., 1962), pp. 258–86; Arnold maintained that "the burst of creative activity in our literature, through the first quarter of this century, had about it in fact something premature; and that from this cause its productions are doomed, most of them, in spite of the sanguine hopes which accompanied and do still accompany them, to prove hardly more lasting than the productions of far less splendid epochs. And this prematureness comes from its having proceeded without having its proper data, without sufficient materials to work with. In other words, the English poetry of the first quarter of this century, with plenty of energy, plenty of creative force, did not know enough" (p. 262).

> When I was yet a child, no childish play
> To me was pleasing; all my mind was set
> Serious to learn and know, and thence to do,
> What might be public good.[17]

By the time Algernon Charles Swinburne began to write poetry, the achievements of the English romantics were fading into the past. In 1837, the year of his birth, all the romantics were dead but Wordsworth—and he was dead to romanticism. Society, as in the eighteenth century, was divided—the rationalism of Bentham, which had never died out, was still strong, and the cult of sensibility had been resurrected in the spasmodic school of poets. The fusion of soul and sense, of man and his cosmos, which the romantics had achieved seemed no longer possible. Tennyson, the greatest poet of the age, was perpetually torn between the urge toward the emotions, the "simple worship of a day" symbolized by "The Lotos-Eaters," and the duty to serve society. Reason and duty, to Tennyson as to most Victorians, seemed to be divorced from the emotional life. Mythopoeia, once again, seemed impossible.

In the important respect that he began to write during an age that saw little possibility of mythopoeic creation, Swinburne was in a situation precisely analogous to that of the earlier romantics. Like them, he returned in spirit to the mythopoeic ages of pre-Socratic Greece and Elizabethan England. All of his tastes and critical judgments reflect his fundamental romanticism. He worshiped Sappho and Aeschylus but despised the Socratic Euripides; he idolized Shakespeare but had reservations about Spenser. He was, moreover, a quintessentially lyric poet. Even when ostensibly imitating Aeschylean drama, as in *Atalanta in Calydon* or *Erechtheus*, and when imitating Elizabethan drama, as in *Chastelard, Bothwell,* and *Mary Stuart*, his style is lyrical rather than dramatic. Swinburne, however, did not have to return to the Greeks or Elizabethans for inspiration—he had the good fortune of living after two generations of romantic poets and could look to them for inspiration. He greatly admired Blake, Wordsworth, and, particularly, Coleridge and Shelley. Though not an uncritical admirer of Keats, he considered the highly mythopoeic odes to be masterpieces and praised

---

[17] *Paradise Regained* I.201–4, *Poetical Works*, II, 515.

the "Ode to May" as a "divine fragment." [18] In a sense, the earlier romantic poets were to Swinburne what Milton had been to them—their poetry had thrived in an earlier day, but new evidence had come in and, to an extent, discredited them. Swinburne had to revise the first romantics as they had had to revise Milton.

Like his romantic predecessors, Swinburne had a fundamentally religious cast of mind without adhering to religious doctrine. Though an agnostic—and, in the sense that he abhorred the worshipers of a removed, transcendent deity, an antitheist—Swinburne perceived the life in nature and wrote poetry of the experience. Despite the recent reemergence of respect for Swinburne (thanks largely to the efforts of Cecil Y. Lang, whose superb edition of the letters has inspired something of a Swinburne renaissance),[19] the old judgment that in Swinburne's poetry "there was no progress because there was no central thought" has not yet been shaken.[20] The purpose of this brief, vastly oversimplified history of English mythopoeia has been to show something of the background in which Swinburne went to work, for his career does indeed progress—from the point of alienation, which inspires romanticism, his work proceeds to, through, and beyond romanticism. As the chapters that follow will show, Swinburne's major works show a continuous grappling with the works of the earlier romantics, and his career shows a steady progression to a more and more truly imaginative mythopoeic mode, eventually culminating in a unique, personal, fully articulated myth. His book-length essay on William Blake, with which this study begins, shows him in the process of coming to grips with the greatest preromantic dilemma—the problem of finding a unifying meaning in an apparently fragmented cosmos.

[18] Quoted by Georges Lafourcade, in *Swinburne's Hyperion* (London, 1927), p. 48.

[19] Cecil Y. Lang, ed., *The Swinburne Letters*, 6 Vols. (New Haven, 1959–62).

[20] H. J. C. Grierson, *Swinburne* (New York, 1953), p. 23.

CHAPTER 1

Swinburne's *Blake*:
Criticizing the Critic

FIRST CONCEIVED BY October of 1862 and not fully completed until February of 1867, *William Blake: A Critical Essay* occupied Swinburne throughout the period of his greatest artistic and intellectual development, the period of *Poems and Ballads, Chastelard,* and *Atalanta in Calydon*.[1] Though its main purpose was, as Swinburne said, to "do something durable . . . for Blake" and though it was an extremely important pioneering study, particularly of the prophetic books, the essay has become dated as a study of Blake.[2] One of the main reasons for this, in addition to the grand march of intellect, is simply that, as Ian Fletcher has said, the Blake presented is a Blake "made in Swinburne's image"—that is, there is too much Swinburne and not enough Blake.[3] The very quality that limits the usefulness of the essay for the study of its ostensible subject makes it invaluable for the study of its author. All of the most important ideas of this fruitful period of Swinburne's life find their way into the essay, sometimes in the form of digressions inspired by sup-

[1] In a letter of 6 Oct. 1862 to William Rossetti, Swinburne declined an offer to add a commentary on the prophetic books to the *Life of Blake*, which was left unfinished by Alexander Gilchrist at the time of his death, but he said he intended to set about "this year . . . the making of a distinct small commentary of a running kind but as full and satisfactory as it could well be made, on Blake's work" (*The Swinburne Letters*, ed. Cecil Y. Lang, I [New Haven, 1959], 60); a lengthy note written by Swinburne but described as from an "anonymous source" was sent to the publisher in February 1867. See Swinburne's letter to William Rossetti of 20 Feb. 1867, ibid., p. 228.

[2] Ibid., p. 94.

[3] *Swinburne* (London, 1973), p. 49.

posed resemblances between the creeds of Swinburne and Blake, sometimes in the form of thinly disguised "anonymous" notes, and sometimes unconsciously, in the form of misreadings of Blake's poetry. Even the language of the essay, the prose style, and the choice of metaphors contribute significantly to an understanding of Swinburne's mind and provide insights into his poetry.

The prominence of the author's own ideas and aesthetic theories in the book should not be surprising, since the epigraph, a quotation from Baudelaire, indicates that the emphasis will be as much on the poet who is writing the essay as on the poet he is writing about:

Tous les grands poëtes deviennent naturellement, fatalement, critiques. Je plains les poëtes que guide le seul instinct; je les crois incomplets. Dans la vie spirituelle des premiers, une crise se fait infailliblement, où ils veulent raisonner leur art, découvrir les lois obscures en vertu desquelles ils ont produit, et tirer de cette étude une série de préceptes dont le but divin est l'infaillibilité dans la production poétique. Il serait prodigieux qu'un critique devînt poëte, et il est impossible qu'un poëte ne contienne pas un critique.[4]

Clearly the epigraph is about Swinburne, not Blake, and it indicates that a primary purpose of the study will be to discover the hidden laws of art. Swinburne obviously viewed the essay as an opportunity to explore his own mind and thoughts as well as Blake's. His subject, however, was not art but Blake, and all of his discussions of art have some relation, however tenuous, to his understanding of Blake's life and poetry.

The longest of these discussions, an excursus upon art for art's sake, proceeds from a rather willful and perverse belief that Blake was an early apostle of that doctrine, a belief based primarily on the notion that Blake disdained worldly success, or, as Swinburne ironically put it, "the just aims of life, duties of an earnest-minded man, and meritorious nature of practical deeds and material services" (p. 85). The discussion is strategically placed at the beginning of Part II, at the beginning, that is, of the critical section of the essay and is

---

[4] Algernon Charles Swinburne, *William Blake: A Critical Essay*, ed. Hugh J. Luke (1868; rpt. Lincoln, Neb., 1970), p. 1. All subsequent references appear in text.

plainly intended as the central aesthetic doctrine of the book, the central exploration of "les lois obscures" of poetry.[5]

Swinburne believed that Blake's splendid artistic isolation was the inevitable result of a radical division in society between two perpetually conflicting cultures: the analytic, scientific culture of Urizenic moral repression and the imaginative, artistic culture of creative freedom. His discussion of the two cultures is based not only on his observations of Blake's lack of conventional practicality but also on his analysis of Blake's works, particularly *The Marriage of Heaven and Hell.* Harold Bloom, among others, has accused Swinburne of misunderstanding Blake's contraries, claiming that the "usual misinterpretation of Blake's contraries (stemming from Swinburne) is that they represent a simple inversion of orthodox moral categories," whereas in actuality Blake "is denying the orthodox categories altogether, and opposing himself both to moral 'good' and moral 'evil.'"[6] If it were true that Swinburne misread Blake in this fundamental manner, it could be convincingly argued that his strong disposition toward inverting moral values, as he did in *Poems and Ballads*, is unconsciously revealed by his predisposition toward this faulty reading. But in fact Swinburne did not think the contraries represented a simple inversion of moral good and evil. Bloom's misreading of Swinburne may indicate, among other things, that we need to be wary of our own critical predispositions, based perhaps on a misunderstanding of *Poems and Ballads*, toward Swinburne.

Swinburne actually saw the contraries of heaven and hell as equally necessary elements in a historical dialectic. Like Blake, he was prepared to respect energetic adherents of either position and to reject only those who tried to bring about a false reconciliation through compromise. Because they took a side and upheld it with fierce conviction, even though it was the side of Urizenic oppres-

[5] See Georges Lafourcade, *La Jeunesse de Swinburne (1837–1867)* (Oxford, 1928), Bk. II, p. 326. Lafourcade points out various biographical facts and deduces the thematic centrality of the aesthetic doctrine: "Quelles que puissent être ses autres qualités, je vois surtout en l'*Essai sur William Blake* l'affirmation d'une attitude artistique."

[6] *Blake's Apocalypse: A Study in Poetic Argument* (New York, 1963), p. 77.

sion, Swinburne called Savonarola and Cromwell great men, though one burnt Boccaccio and the other proscribed Shakespeare (p. 87). Swinburne is rhetorically, if not intellectually, convincing in arguing that no compromise between the two cultures is possible:

The betrothal of art and science were a thing harder to bring about and more profitless to proclaim than "the marriage of heaven and hell." It were better not to fight, but to part in peace; but better certainly to fight than to temporize, where no reasonable truce can be patched up. Poetry or art based on loyalty to science is exactly as absurd (and no more) as science guided by art or poetry. Neither in effect can coalesce with the other and retain a right to exist. [P. 98]

Swinburne's perception of Blake's contraries as representing the necessary poles of a continual cultural struggle is, of course, inadequate to describe Blake's final vision as expressed in *Jerusalem*, but it is not a wholly inaccurate account of the relations between the "prolific" and the "devourer" set forth in *The Marriage of Heaven and Hell*. It is true, nevertheless, that though Swinburne recognizes Blake's celebration of the energy expended by both sides in intellectual warfare, he falsely ascribes moral value to Blake's contraries. Blake is, as Bloom says, denying both moral "good" and moral "evil"; Swinburne is affirming both. Just as Bloom's idea of Swinburne's error in interpretation would have implied a significant fact about Swinburne's mind, so Swinburne's actual misreading demonstrates a predisposition toward truly dialectical modes of thought rather than a mere inversion of conventional terms. As we shall see in our examination of *Poems and Ballads*, this tendency results both in the establishment of dualistic and antithetic structures in his language and in a dialectical view of history. And just as he opposes any reconciliation of opposites, any compromise between the two cultures, so in *Poems and Ballads* he rejects any notion of the dialectic of history coming to a final apocalyptic resolution.

The inevitable result, as Swinburne saw it, of a split in society between art and science was that art must have nothing to do with science. He adopted the dogma of art for art's sake, which he inherited primarily from Gautier and Baudelaire. He may also have been encouraged to adopt the doctrine by the current, though mistaken,

notion that his idol, Victor Hugo, had espoused it.[7] To over-
simplify, Swinburne's conception of l'art pour l'art was that art cannot set out to have any moral purpose, cannot "humble herself,
plead excuses, try at any compromise with the Puritan principle of
doing good" or "she is worse than dead" (p. 92). Art must maintain
its own position in the cultural dialectic. Therefore all that matters
about art, all the artist need be concerned with, is the technical
perfection of his craftsmanship: "The one fact for her which is worth
taking account of is simply mere excellence of verse or colour,
which involves all manner of truth and loyalty necessary to her
well-being. That is the important thing; to have her work supremely
well done, and to disregard all contingent consequences" (p. 92).
This is not to say that art is necessarily amoral, but only that its
purpose must be, for "accidentally of course a poet's work may tend
towards some moral or actual result," but "that is beside the question" (p. 93n.). The artist need not, in fact, must not, concern
himself with social improvement or moral philosophy; he need be
serious only in one thing, his respect for "the material forms of art,"
since "levity and violence are here prohibited under grave penal-
ties" (p. 198).

Swinburne's aesthetic theory, art for art's sake, was a response to
what was, perhaps, the central problem facing the Victorian artist.
The old order—the belief in a society unified by common beliefs in
religious myths, the order that had originated in Renaissance
humanism and was already crumbling when the first generation of
romantics tried to shore it up by substituting myths of personality
and nature for a dying Christianity—had collided head-on with the
new order, the scientific reductivism of the Utilitarians and industrialists. In Mill's terms, the adherents of Coleridge and Bentham
were irreconcilably at odds. Francis Golffing describes the atmosphere (though of 1880 rather than the 1860s) succinctly:

At this time we find two intellectual elites in sharp confrontation: the
scientific, represented most impressively by T. H. Huxley, and that of the
traditional humanists, whose chief spokesman was Matthew Arnold, insist-

_____

[7]L. M. Findlay, "The Introduction of the Phrase 'Art for Art's Sake' into English," *Notes and Queries*, 20 (1972), 248.

ing vigorously on the redemptive virtues of the Graeco-Judaic-Christian heritage. The two camps were ranged on either side of a fence across which they glared at each other, trying I suppose to stare each other down, for there were really no common terms of discourse by which they could have composed their differences.

Art for art's sake was only one of a wide range of possible responses to the dilemma. Tennyson, as Golffing goes on to say, tried to reconcile the two cultures, "envisaging a social order which would embrace all of mankind, and which would be based on a rational technology and a thoroughly humanized science."[8] Arnold attempted to return art to the supposed objectivity of the classical age, arguing, in total opposition to Swinburne's point of view, that the poet's emphasis should be on the theme of his work, not on felicity of expression.[9] By writing about universal themes, the poet will please all men, not just those in the artistic camp, and will thus unify society through culture. Carlyle argued that art must be true to facts and that it must have a moral, even a religious, purpose and thus unify society in each new age with new myths. For Ruskin, all good art was the product of a society unified by high moral principles, so social morality is a necessary element of art. Even Morris subordinated art to the interests of society, feeling that its highest purpose was to provide amusement for the workers in the perfect socialist state.

Swinburne was unique among Victorian poets in his refusal to attempt a compromise between the two "intellectual elites." He was unique in simply dismissing the Philistines, in addressing art only to the artistic class: "the sacramental elements of art and poetry are in no wise given for the sustenance or the salvation of men in general, but reserved mainly for the sublime profit and intense pleasure of an elect body or church" (p. 36).

[8] "Tennyson's Last Phase: The Poet as Seer," in *Tennyson's Poetry*, ed. Robert W. Hill, Jr. (New York, 1971), pp. 650, 651.

[9] See particularly Arnold's "Preface to Poems" (1853), where he says that the modern poet should learn three things from the ancients: "the all-importance of the choice of a subject; the necessity of accurate construction; and the subordinate character of expression" (in *On the Classical Tradition*, ed. R. H. Super [Ann Arbor, Mich., 1960], p. 12).

As his rather blasphemous language hints, one of the most important effects of Swinburne's rebelliousness against Philistinism and
his concomitant aestheticism was a turn to a shocking neopaganism.
Lionel Stevenson has stated the case eloquently:

The older poets—Tennyson, Browning, Arnold, Clough—tried desperately to reconcile the new dispensation with the former one, but
Swinburne suffered from no such divided loyalty. To him, the essence of
Darwinism was man's identity with the primitive natural forces and instincts. As a basis for their modernized faith, both Tennyson and Browning
emphasized love, but it was strictly *agape*, with scrupulous avoidance of
eros. As an alternative to the defeated stoicism of Empedocles, the melancholy heroism of Omar Khayyam, the tentative groping of *In Memoriam*,
Swinburne hymned unqualified paganism.[10]

In *William Blake* Swinburne picks out for special praise the "hereti-
cal and immoral Albigeois with their exquisite school of heathenish
verse" (pp. 88–89) and the medieval *Court of Love*, then attributed
to Chaucer. He regarded them as symptomatic of a "pagan revival"
(p. 89) and celebrates them as a rebellion against the oppressive
Urizenic morality of the medieval Christian church. In a similar
spirit he praises the poetry of two outlaws from conventional
society, Aphra Behn ("that she-satyr") and François Villon: "François Villon and Aphra Behn, the two most inexpressibly non-
respectable of male and female Bohemians and poets, were alike in
this as well; that the supreme gift of each, in a time sufficiently
barren of lyrical merit, was the gift of writing admirable songs; and
this, after all, has perhaps borne better fruit for us than any gift of
moral excellence" (p. 132*n*.). In praising neopagan, anticonven-
tional poets and poetry, Swinburne is not merely advocating the
separation of art from society, he is striking a blow for liberty and
implying that art should, perhaps, deliberately set out to undermine
repressive social structures and conventions. Art for art's sake, representing his rejection of the Victorian compromise, represented
also his passionate quest for liberty in all matters. Swinburne's doctrine comes less and less to resemble art for art's sake as we nor-
mally think of it.

Swinburne's tendency toward sensationalism was reinforced by

[10] *The Pre-Raphaelite Poets* (New York, 1972), p. 211.

his understanding, faulty though it may have been, of Blake. He saw that Blake exalted the senses only "as parts of the soul" and observed that "this and no prurience of porcine appetite for rotten apples, no vulgarity of porcine adoration for unctuous wash, is what lies at the heart of Blake's sensual doctrine" (p. 212). The same cannot be said for Swinburne's own "sensual doctrine," which had entirely different origins, but in any case, granted a sensual doctrine, the artist has every right to indulge it to the full, since he cannot possibly gauge the "palate of common opinion" (p. 206) and would degrade himself if he tried. The artist must release all his energy in creativity, and not needlessly expend it "to set bounds to the incompetence or devise landmarks for the imbecility of men" (p. 206). Swinburne, understating his case, affirms that "Blake's way was not the worst; to indulge his impulse to the full and write what fell to his hand, making sure at least of his own genius and natural instinct. . . . Passion and humour are mixed in his writing like mist and light, whom the light may scorch or the mist confuse it is not his part to consider" (p. 206). That such freedom of expression was inextricably linked in Swinburne's mind with rebellion against authority is clearly implied at the very beginning of the essay: "Shelley in his time gave enough of perplexity and offence; but even he, mysterious and rebellious as he seemed to most men, was less made up of mist and fire than Blake. He was born and baptized into the church of rebels" (p. 3). The parallel language of the two passages suggests that the rebelliousness Swinburne had in mind was closely connected to Blake's "sensual doctrine" and the sensationalism of his poetry. Not content to defend sensationalism on the grounds of the exuberant energy of the creative imagination, he seems to be defending it as a political act, an act of rebellion against Urizenic oppression. In terms of his own poetic career, all of this suggests that the blasphemy and the overt and often perverse eroticism of *Poems and Ballads* may not have been the result of an aesthetic, but of a political, doctrine. The split between the blasphemy and sensuality of *Poems and Ballads* and the fervent republicanism of *Songs before Sunrise* may not be as great as has commonly been supposed.

Conscious rebellion against the conventional moral order, however, is clearly a moral position, so that Swinburne's rigid separation of art from ideas seems to dissolve. His aesthetic theory, constantly reiterated in the essay, has been that form, not ideas, is all that matters in art and that the artist, therefore, need not be much of a thinker: "Given a certain attainable average of intellect and culture, . . . points of workmanship, by dint of the infinite gifts or the infinite wants they imply, become the swiftest and surest means of testing a verse-writer's perfection of power, and what quality there may be in him to warrant his loftiest claim" (p. 135). Yet one would think a more-than-average intellect would be necessary to perceive the failings of conventional ideas and to rebel against them.

The apparent inconsistencies of Swinburne's aesthetic doctrine are resolved when we fully understand what he means by form. He believed, as we have seen, that technical qualities, such as meter and rhyme, were fundamental, but he also believed that the technical qualities had to be in perfect accord with the subject or theme of the poem. The work of art must have an inner form that somehow projects the essence of the emotional state that its creator felt and wished to communicate. Robert L. Peters, in his excellent study of Swinburne's criticism, has noted that Swinburne referred to this mysterious inner form as "gathering form," comparing his poetry to the sea as its rhythm

pauses and musters and falls, always as a wave does, with the same patience of gathering form and rounded glory of springing curve, and sharp sweet flash of dishevelled and flickering foam as it curls over, showing the sun through its soft heaving side in veins of gold that inscribe and jewels of green that inlay the quivering and sundering skirt or veil of thinner water, throwing upon the tremulous space of narrowing sea in front, like a reflection of lifted and vibrating hair, the windy shadow of its shaken spray. [P. 134]

This passage, as Peters observes, represents Swinburne's critical theory that the form of the poem develops from within and accumulates meaning and significance: "gathering form sheds a collective brilliance upon itself as it proceeds; like the wave curling over, it reveals its accumulating beauty all the while it vibrates toward its total, shimmering consummation in the human mind." [11] The idea of development from within differs only in choice of metaphor from

---

[11] *The Crowns of Apollo* (Detroit, 1965), pp. 137, 138.

the Coleridgean ideal of organic form, an idea with which, in 1869, Swinburne demonstrated his familiarity in a comment on Coleridge's "The Ancient Mariner": "For the execution, I presume no human eye is too dull to see how perfect it is, and how high in kind of perfection. Here is not the speckless and elaborate finish which shows everywhere the fresh rasp of file or chisel on its smooth and spruce excellence; this is faultless after the fashion of a flower on a tree. Thus it has grown: not thus has it been carved."[12] All of this is perfectly consistent with Swinburne's emphasis on the need for untrammeled artistic freedom and creative exuberance. Art, like Hertha, grows and accumulates without hindrance or repression. But the theory of "gathering form," or organic development, poses one obvious question: what is the kernel that undergoes expansion, the seed that grows into the flower or tree of the completed work of art?

The answer provides a striking qualification to Swinburne's aesthetic creed of art for art's sake, for the seed of perfect technical form is the artist's intention. After a long, impressionistic rhapsody on the "incomparable charm of form" (p. 112) of the poems and designs of *Songs of Innocence and Experience*, Swinburne observes that the artistic perfection is "kept fresh by some graver sense of faithful and mysterious love, explained and vivified by a conscience and purpose in the artist's hand and mind" (p. 113). The technical perfection of art reflects the purity of the artistic impulse, as Swinburne makes clear in his description of Blake's poem "Night": "The leap and fall of the verse is so perfect as to make it a fit garment and covering for the profound tenderness of faith and soft strength of innocent impulse embodied in it" (p. 115). The body of the artistic work, the technical form, is the expression of the soul of the work, the emotional impulse that led to its creation.

The perfect harmony of form and content that Swinburne saw as essential to art is generally described in the Blake essay as a "union of sense and spirit" (p. 91*n*.). As we have seen, Swinburne's defense of Blake's sensationalism was based on the argument that the senses are only important as "the chief inlets of soul in this age," and, as

---

[12] "Coleridge," *The Complete Works of Algernon Charles Swinburne*, ed. Edmund Gosse and Thomas James Wise, XV (London, 1926), 145.

Julian Baird has convincingly demonstrated, one of his chief aims in
the essay is to follow Blake in breaking down the traditional
dichotomy between body and soul.[13] Just as the body and soul of
man are a single, indivisible entity, so the soul and body of verse
exist in harmonious unity. Quoting Blake's statement that "allegory
addressed to the intellectual powers, while it is altogether hidden
from the corporeal understanding, is my definition of the most
sublime poetry," Swinburne makes it clear that the form and content of verse are its body and soul, saying of Blake's definition that
"a better perhaps could not be given; as far that is as relates to the
'spirit of sense' which is to be clothed in the beautiful body of
verse." But he makes it equally clear that the artist's first concern is
to make the body beautiful: "when once we have granted the power
of conception, the claims of form are to be first thought of" (p. 35).
Since the body and soul of art are in harmony, if the body is beautiful, the soul must be; so Swinburne can say elsewhere: "Art for art's
sake first of all, and afterwards we may suppose all the rest shall be
added to her" (p. 91). And in a description of the poetry of Coleridge, written in 1867, he again explicitly equates technical form
with the "body" of poetry: "All the elements which compose the
perfect form of English metre, as limbs and veins and features a
beautiful body of man, were more familiar, more subject as it were,
to this great poet than to any other."[14]

Because the soul of poetry is inextricably bound up with authorial intention and because authorial intention is inextricably bound
up with the subject (which Swinburne, misleadingly when discussing Blake, usually refers to as external nature), nature too is brought
into the harmony of art. In a note about the pagan revival he saw
exemplified by the Chaucerian *Court of Love* and the Albigensian
Aucassin et Nicolette, Swinburne brings several of the most important elements of his theory of form into close conjunction:

One may remark also, the minute this pagan revival begins to get
breathing-room, how there breaks at once into flower a most passionate
and tender worship of nature, whether as shown in the bodily beauty of

---

[13] "Swinburne, Sade, and Blake: The Pleasure-Pain Paradox," *Victorian Poetry*, 9
(1971), 49–76.

[14] "Coleridge," p. 146.

man and woman or in the outside loveliness of leaf and grass; both
Chaucer and his anonymous southern colleague being throughout careful
to decorate their work with the most delicate and splendid studies of
colour and form. [P. 89*n*.]

The emotional impulse of the "pagan" artists ("passionate and tender worship of nature") brings together the external beauty of form
of man, nature, and verse. Swinburne is never explicit about the
philosophical basis of his theory of art, but it seems to owe much to
the Coleridgean notion of the creative, esemplastic imagination of
the artist drawing all things into a complex multeity in unity. As
several critics have pointed out, Swinburne's belief in the power of
art to make connections between different realms of being, and
especially between different sensory phenomena, also owes much
to the Baudelairean aesthetic principle of *correspondances*. His wide-
spread use of synesthetic imagery, his use of natural imagery, such
as the sea, to describe the formal qualities of verse, and even his
reliance on impressionist criticism to translate one art into the terms
of another, all indicate how thoroughly Swinburne's language and
thought are influenced by the belief that all things "correspond" on
some level. The connections between the sense and spirit of man
and nature are, moreover, exhibited most clearly in the formal
qualities of art. That is why the pagan artists were so careful to
achieve "the most delicate and splendid studies of colours and
form." Finally, the fact that Swinburne sees this "unison of sense and
spirit" exhibited most clearly in the works of such "pagan" writers as
these medieval poets, Baudelaire (p. 89*n*.), and Blake suggests that
the sensational paganism of *Poems and Ballads* may have had a more
serious philosophical underpinning than has hitherto been supposed.

Once the formal qualities of verse are understood to include the
emotional motivation of the artist, the "conscience and purpose in
the artist's hand and mind," the doctrine of art for art's sake as
Swinburne presented it begins to allow room for moral qualities in
art. Thus even while calling Blake an early exponent of the doctrine, Swinburne can say of him that "no artist of equal power had
ever a keener and deeper regard for the meaning and teaching—
what one may call the moral—of art. He sang and painted as men
write and preach" (p. 5). It is true that the artist must never set to

work with a conscious moral purpose and that beauty of form is all he should strive to achieve, but, as Swinburne explains in describing the superiority of the *Songs of Experience* to the *Songs of Innocence*, the formal beauty of the verse depends on the depth of thought that goes into its creation: "It is natural that this second part, dealing as it does with such things as underlie the outer forms of the first part, should rise higher and dive deeper in point of mere words" (p. 116). Swinburne's critical judgments proceed not from the assumption that an "average of intellect and culture" is all that is necessary to the artist but from the Wordsworthian assumption that the poet is one who has thought long and thought deeply. The seeming contradiction between theory and practice is, I think, only created by Swinburne's tendency to exaggerate for rhetorical effect when making theoretical statements. While it is true that the author must look to perfection of form above all, it is equally true that he will not achieve it without depth of thought. The idea that morality and intellect are a necessary part of form is quite Blakean, in theory as well as in practice. Swinburne's "form" is strikingly similar to Blake's "circumference," "organization," and "outline." The crucial difference, of course, is that, far from including nature within the artistic form, Blake burns it away as a "False Holiness hid within the Center" in order to find "the Sanctuary of Eden . . . in the Camp: in the Outline, / In the Circumference."[15] Despite this obvious difference, for Swinburne, as for Blake, the achieved work of art, the completed "form" or "circumference," represents much more than a pleasing objet d'art; it represents the totality of the artist's vision, the perception, the creation, and even the matter perceived.

   Swinburne's perception of art for art's sake, with all of its qualifications, actually presents a view of art not much less moral than Ruskin's, even though, as Georges Lafourcade has pointed out, Ruskin had

définitivement condamné cette école "esthétique" dont Swinburne se constitua le porte parole: "The theoretic faculty is concerned with the moral

---

[15] *Jerusalem*, Pl. 69, ll. 40–42, *Blake: Complete Writings*, ed. Geoffrey Keynes (Oxford, 1966), p. 708.

perception and appreciation of ideas of beauty. And the error respecting it is the considering and calling it Aesthetic, degrading it to a mere operation of sense, or perhaps worse, of custom, so that the arts which appeal to it sink into a mere amusement, ministers to morbid sensibilities, ticklers and fanners of the soul's sleep" (*Modern Painters*, III, I, 10). Swinburne ne pouvait que se reconnaître dans ces "ministers to morbid sensibilities."[16]

The description does, indeed, bear a superficial resemblance to Swinburne's practices, and though this passage, written in 1856, cannot refer to Swinburne, Ruskin did have reservations about the moral character of his art. Nevertheless, Swinburne, as fully as Ruskin, believed that good art can only be produced by a good man. Blake, he said, was a great artist because in him "above all other men, the moral and imaginative senses were so fused together as to compose the final artistic form" (p. 298), and much of the first section of the book is filled with anecdotes designed to show Blake's superior moral character. In discussing the case of Cromek's and Stothard's swindle of Blake, he asserts (apparently on the basis of his respect for him as an artist) that no one could possibly believe that Blake lied (p. 48*n*.). He places all the blame on Cromek, whose "natural gifts and capacities" were "rapacity and mendacity" (pp. 48–49) and is willing to acquit Stothard, the artist, "as all must gladly do who remember how large a debt is due from all to an artist of such exquisite and pleasurable talent" (pp. 52–53). Even the long digression on Wainewright, the artist "with pen, with palette, or with poison" (p. 68)—which Lafourcade, among others, has taken as an exaltation of the perfect aesthete ("c'est en fait du point de vue de l'art que Swinburne justifie les crimes de Wainewright; l'art remplace donc bien la morale")[17] —is actually ironic and upholds the theory that a bad man can produce only bad art. Since any preference of actions to art is anathema to Swinburne the ironic intention of the "exaltation" of Wainewright is evident: "Those who would depreciate his performance as a simple author must recollect that in accordance with the modern receipt he 'lived his poems;' that the age prefers deeds to songs; that to do great things is better than to

[16] Lafourcade, *La Jeunesse*, Bk. II, p. 336.
[17] Ibid., p. 360.

write; that action is of eternity, fiction of time; and that these poems were doubtless the greater for being 'inarticulate' " (p. 69). The chronically rebellious Swinburne was rarely in agreement with the preferences of the age, and he certainly was not in agreement with any of the preferences stated in this passage. Swinburne's mock praise of Wainewright was intended primarily as an attack on that Victorian philistinism which did prefer deeds to songs, but its underlying assumptions about the moral nature of the artist indicate the extent to which Ruskinian principles affected his practical criticism.

Ruskin's disapproval of the moral character of Swinburne's work, and disagreement with many of his critical judgments, indicates not that they disagreed in theory but only in the practical questions of what constitutes good morality. Ruskin believed in absolute standards of morality and therefore believed that the artist could, and should, teach the truths of that morality in his works. He was essentially conventional in his moral judgments and disapproved of art that was not. Swinburne saw conventional society as immoral and considered attacks on that society highly moral, and he therefore praised such people as Villon, Aphra Behn, Baudelaire, Balzac, and of course Blake. He believed, moreover, that the laying down of absolutes, of morality or anything else, was Urizenic and oppressive, and he therefore opposed didacticism in art. In accordance with his aesthetic principle that the creative imagination, which brings all things into harmony, is the only truth and that any explicit statement of doctrine or dogma undermines man's ability to exercise his imagination, Swinburne believed that art should provoke thought, not dictate opinion. As Jerome McGann has said, all things

are seen to reflect each other, and if they are not the same (as they are not), they are united as different images of the one human reality which dreamed them all into existence, the mind of man. That fundamental reality remains imageless because it is both infinite and specific to every man. Of its character each to himself must be the oracle. Both Shelley and Swinburne approve when Demogorgon refuses to answer Asia's questions directly, thereby forcing her to discover her own truth. For these poets there are no brazen tablets.[18]

[18] *Swinburne: An Experiment in Criticism* (Chicago, 1972), p. 77.

To summarize briefly, Swinburne's doctrinal theory of art, presented in somewhat random and haphazard fashion in *William Blake*, is a modified theory of art for art's sake which states that form is all-important in art but that form itself involves the intellectual, emotional, and moral impulse of the artist. The best art is that which achieves a fusion of the spirit and sense of the artist, the subject, and the work of art itself; as Swinburne's critical judgments imply, this is usually achieved by art that rebels against social conventions. In ascetic, Christian society it is best achieved by a paganism that exalts the senses (a fact to be borne in mind when examining *Poems and Ballads*). Although the artist can have no deliberate moral purpose, art is fundamentally moral because the artist is fundamentally moral. Finally, morality consists essentially of opposing restriction and repression of the imagination and is, for Swinburne, nearly synonymous with a passionate commitment to liberty.

All of this can be gleaned from a careful consideration of statements made by Swinburne about the nature of art and the artist. To the extent that Swinburne used the Blake essay as a platform for the expression of his own views, these are those views. Although most of the passages I have quoted are ostensibly connected with Blake, resulting from interpretations or misinterpretations of his work, none of them resulted from his conscientious grappling with Blake's complex poetry. They were all ideas that Swinburne had from other sources and had imported into the study of Blake. At least as interesting, however, are the ideas not consciously presented by Swinburne but which the reader of his essay can see conditioning his response to Blake. His Blake made in the image of Swinburne is, in Bloomian terms, a strong reading of one poet by another, and as such it is a fascinating document for the study of the influence of Blake on Swinburne, and, incidentally, for the study of influence theory in general. Of course, if we accept Oscar Wilde's judgment of the matter, the study of a man's criticism tells us more about the workings of his mind than would any study of his "creative" work, for the "highest criticism" is the "record of one's own soul": "It is the only civilized form of autobiography, as it deals not with the events, but with the thoughts of one's life; not with life's physical accidents of deed or circumstance, but with the spiritual moods and imagina-

tive passions of the mind."[19] For my purposes, by far the most
interesting interplay between the minds of Blake and Swinburne is
on the subject of myth. As Hugh J. Luke has pointed out, Swinburne was "the first to understand that the Prophetic Books must be
read as myth, not allegory," an understanding that came easily to
him with his predisposition toward seeing the outer form and the
inner meaning of art as a harmonious unity, like the body and soul
of man.[20] Allegory, by its very nature, attempts to separate the
two—poetic form becomes handmaiden to a moral or philosophical
doctrine. Separating form and content in allegory, said Swinburne,
is comparable to making bricks without straw, but Blake's poetry
does not do that: "energies and agencies are not simply cast into the
house of allegoric bondage, and set to make bricks without straw, to
construct symbols without reason; but find themselves baptized
with muddy water and fitful fire, by names inconceivable, into a
church full of storm and vapour; regenerated with a vengeance, but
disembodied and disfigured in their resurrection" (p. 191). The
allegorical house of bondage limits and constrains the exuberant
creativity of the artist, limits the freedom that is central to Swinburne's idea of art for art's sake. Allegory, he says elsewhere in the
essay, is an "exercise of logical patience to which Blake would
hardly have submitted his passionate genius" (p. 178), and later he
contrasts "mere allegory and creative myth" (p. 250). In addition,
and setting aside for the moment Swinburne's objection to Blake's
obscurity—the muddiness of his water and the fitfulness of his
fire—the description of Blake's alternative to allegory tells us a
great deal about Swinburne's conception of myth.

The use of theological language is, of course, an ironic reminder
that the artist's generation of myth is an implicit rejection of the
received myth of Christianity, that mythmaking is an essentially
pagan activity. Allegory is primarily a Christian form, growing out
of the critical exegesis and commentary of the middle ages, and is
intensely moral. Myth is not a critical but a creative form, associated
with ancient primitive cultures, and it is often based on sexual

[19] "The Critic as Artist," in *The Artist as Critic: Critical Writings of Oscar Wilde*, ed. Richard Ellmann (New York, 1968), p. 365.
[20] Introduction, *William Blake: A Critical Essay*, p. xiv.

symbols of creation and generation; by Victorian standards it is rarely moral, except, of course, when allegorized by Christian commentary. Swinburne's use of Christian language to describe the generation of new mythic figures is typical of the tendency shown in his poetry to use the forms of Christianity as mere empty husks that find their meaning in whatever context he uses them. His implication throughout the essay, however, that Blake is a pagan poet is, of course, preposterous, and his failure to comprehend Blake's zealous devotion to Christianity indicates how thoroughly he was capable, through his own prepossessions, of misunderstanding him. Swinburne's own zealous Hellenism blinded him to the glaring fact that though Blake is indeed a mythopoeic poet, he is mythopoeic in the Hebrew tradition—his prophecies are typological responses to the Hebrew prophets of the Bible.

The idea of myth as a regenerating, resurrecting art form is central to another of Swinburne's beliefs about mythopoeic art—the belief that such art truly has life. Once again blasphemously replacing Christianity with art, Swinburne implies that art is the ever-living body and blood of God, which gives life to all who partake of it:

All the more, meantime, because this "bread of sweet thought and wine of delight" is not broken or shed for all, but for a few only—because the sacramental elements of art and poetry are in no wise given for the sustenance or the salvation of men in general, but reserved mainly for the sublime profit and intense pleasure of an elect body or church—all the more on that account should the ministering official be careful that the paten and chalice be found wanting in no one possible grace of work or perfection of material. [P. 36]

It is important to note not only the displacement of Christianity by art and the presence of enduring life in art but also the emphasis Swinburne places on the material form, the workmanship. Elsewhere in the essay he is explicit about the presence of life in the poetry of Blake. Even with all its weaknesses there is always in Blake's poetry "the one invaluable quality of actual life" (p. 5), and later he repeats that "one blessing there assuredly was upon all Blake's work; the infinite blessing of life; the fervour of vital blood" (p. 45).

This life is, in part, the life of the author's subject, the life not only of the author's mind but of what is external to it, and it is always carried in the material form of the verse: "The actual page seems to take life, to assume sound and colour, under the hands that turn it and the lips that read; we feel the falling of dew and have sight of the rising of stars. For the very sound of Blake's verse is no less remote from the sound of common things and days on earth than is the sense or the sentiment of it" (p. 134). Poetry, and therefore the myth it embodies, is alive because by perfectly reflecting the correspondences between the sound of nature and its own form, and the poet's mind and the reader's mind, it brings back to life the original moment of artistic creation. The moment and the original poetic perception are, in fact, regenerated and resurrected every time the poem is read. Swinburne is very clear in saying that mythopoeic poetry, or at least Blake's poetry, carries within itself both the subject and the living individuality of the author: "In all this [Blake's] mythology we may see on one side the reflection and refraction of outer things, on the other side the projection of his own mind, the effusion of his individual nature, throughout the hardest and remotest alien matter" (p. 43). The creative mythopoeic mind fuses "alien matter," poetry, and itself into unity, and yet somehow retains its own individual nature.

The idea of the survival of the intact individual life was to Swinburne as important as it was to Tennyson, and he recurs to it frequently throughout the essay. Even though in point of mere verse, of technical form, it is rather pedestrian, he responds enthusiastically to Blake's "To the Accuser, who is the God of this World," because of what he sees to be its doctrinal content:

Upon the life which is but as a vesture, and as a vesture shall be changed, he who created it has power till the end; appearances and relations he can alter, and turn a virgin to a harlot; but not change one individual life to another, reverse or rescind the laws of personality . . . the underlying individual life is imperishable and intangible. All qualities proper to human nature are inventions of the Accuser; not so the immortal prenatal nature, which is the essence of every man severally from eternity. [P. 27]

That all this is only tangentially related to Blake's poem indicates how heavily the issue lay on Swinburne's mind. He even goes so far as to say, when defending his (and Blake's) central doctrine of the unity of body and soul, that "far from inferring thence that the soul must expire with the body, [Blake] would have maintained that the essence of the body must survive with the essence of the soul: accepting thus . . . in its most absolute and profound sense, the doctrine of the Resurrection of the Flesh" (p. 95). Swinburne, of course, attributes this sentiment not to himself but to Blake, but as it is unsupported by reference to Blake's works, and as it is a mere supposition about what he *would* have said, if asked, it is reasonable to suppose that the thought owes more to Swinburne's grappling with the problem than to Blake's.

Swinburne, the poet of the joys of oblivion, is not, of course, stating a simple-minded belief in bodily resurrection after death; he is stating that the essence of the individual's life is indestructible. At no point in the essay, however, does he explain what this essence is or how it survives, but on the basis of what he says about the perpetual life of art and the fusion of the individual personality of the artist with his work and with the world he perceives, it is possible to conjecture that eternal life is achieved through the preservation of the self in art. This idea, though never stated with the force of dogma, is absolutely fundamental to Swinburne; it underlies all of his references to the body and soul of art, to its sacramental nature and to its life, "the fervour of vital blood."

The belief that art preserves life is closely connected with the rather peculiar variety of pantheism that largely shapes Swinburne's ideas about myth. He repeatedly refers to Blake as a pantheist, a fact which has prompted Ian Fletcher to remark that "failure to grasp that, for Blake, nature and imagination were antithetical, lies at the heart of Swinburne's fruitful misunderstanding of Blake." [21] The remark is, to a considerable extent, true—the idea of Blake as a pantheist in the conventional sense of pantheism is absurd, and Swinburne did fail to appreciate Blake's antithesis between nature and imagination. Considerable qualification is necessary, however, since Swinburne's conception of pantheism was not that nature is divine but that, as in Blake's thought, man is divine. He states this explicitly on several occasions: " 'God is no more than man; *because* man is no less than God:' there is Blake's Pantheistic Iliad in a

[21] Fletcher, p. 49.

nutshell" (p. 166n.). Theism may see God, allegorically, as man, may personify him; pantheism sees God, essentially and inalterably, as man: "But Theism, but the naked distinct figure of God, whether or not he assume the nature of man, so long as this is mere assumption and not the essence of his being—the clothes and not the body, the body and not the soul—this is to him [the pantheist] incredible, the source of all evil and error" (p. 226n.). Allegory, unlike myth, makes a division between man as God and man as a part of nature: "Man can only possess abstract qualities—'allegoric virtues'—by reason of that side of nature which he has *not* in common with God: God, not partaking of the 'generative nature,' cannot partake of qualities which exist only by right of that nature" (p. 155). This passage illustrates not only the fundamental argument against allegory—that it is divisive and degrading whereas art should be unifying and exalting—but also that Swinburne's pantheism does *not*, as has so often been assumed, have reference to any sense of divinity in nature. It also demonstrates that when Swinburne spoke of the eternality of the essence of body and soul, he could not have meant that part of the body which partakes of "vegetative nature."

The two central ideas under discussion—the idea that art perpetuates the life of man and that "God is man, and man God" (p. 155)—are wholly consistent and combine to form a fascinating attitude toward myth. Northrop Frye's description of Blake's mythopoeia could apply equally well to Swinburne:

Everything we call "nature," the physical world around us, is sub-moral, subhuman, sub-imaginative; every act worth performing has as its object the redeeming of this nature into something with a genuinely human, and therefore divine, shape. Hence Blake's poetry is not allegorical but mythopoeic, not obliquely related to a rational understanding of the human situation, the resolution of which is out of human hands, but a product of the creative energy that alone can redeem that situation.[22]

Swinburne sees in art the embodiment of nature and man in harmonious fusion, one interpenetrating the other, and therefore sees art as exalting nature to the level of divine humanity. His aesthetic theory perceives all truly creative art as essentially mythopoeic, as a

[22] "The Road of Excess," in *Myth and Symbol*, ed. Bernice Slote (Lincoln, Neb., 1963), pp. 17–18.

resurrection and redemption of the unified soul and spirit of man and nature.

Insofar as the critical essay on Blake is itself a creative work (as modern schools of criticism, following Wilde, would contend) it exemplifies the very aesthetic theory it obliquely sets forth. The heavy usage of synesthetic imagery that fuses soul and sense and man and nature has already been noted, but in addition the prose style, particularly the extraordinarily long, periodic sentences, should be noted. One example of such a sentence (there is no room for more than one) will serve to illustrate how this type of sentence structure brings disparate elements into harmonious unity. Swinburne describes the similarities between the works of Whitman and Blake:

A sound as of a sweeping wind; a prospect as over dawning continents at the fiery instant of a sudden sunrise; a splendour now of stars and now of storms; an expanse and exultation of wing across strange spaces of air and above shoreless stretches of sea; a resolute and reflective love of liberty in all times and in all things where it should be; a depth of sympathy and a height of scorn which complete and explain each other, as tender and as bitter as Dante's; a power, intense and infallible, of pictorial concentration and absorption, most rare when combined with the sense and the enjoyment of the wildest and the highest things; an exquisite and lyrical excellence of form when the subject is well in keeping with the poet's tone of spirit; a strength and security of touch in small sweet sketches of colour and outline, which brings before the eyes of their student a clear glimpse of the thing designed—some little inlet of sky lighted by moon or star, some dim reach of windy water or gentle growth of meadow-land or wood; these are qualities common to the work of either. [P. 302]

The structure, phrase piled upon phrase and clause upon clause, brings all of nature, excellence of poetic form, and the characters of the poets into at least rhetorical fusion—all, at least, are housed within the same sentence. The doubling of adjectives and nouns—stars and storms, air and sea, resolute and reflective, depth and height, tender and bitter, and so on—increases the sense of getting everything into the sentence. All that is between depth and height, and between resolution and reflection, is implicitly included in the description. Jerome McGann, citing a different passage from the book on Blake, has accurately described Swinburne's "series of im-

pressionistic descriptions" as "the glimpsed fractions of a vast order
of universal relations," and the prose in which these glimpses are
revealed is stylistically designed to imply the continuity between
the glimpses.[23] This prose style, which bears striking resemblance
to Swinburne's poetic style, is perfectly adapted to effect the mul-
tiform unity of inclusion that Swinburne saw as the essence of
creative, or mythopoeic, thought. And it is well that it is, for as he
never tired of saying, the form is the art—and I might add that, for
Swinburne, the form is the myth.

The implication that the essay on Blake is itself mythopoeic in
the same sense that Blake's poetry is mythopoeic is perfectly justified according to the terms of Swinburne's aesthetics. The essay
consists largely of impressionistic criticism, such as the passage cited
above, and the whole purpose of impressionistic criticism is to "re-
generate and resurrect" the original work of art, since the *impression*
properly received from a work of art should, after all, correspond to
the original *expression* of the artist. Since the artistic expression was,
in the first place, bringing man, nature, and verse into living harmony and since the expression is only brought back to life by
making an impression on another mind, Swinburne's creative expression of his critical impression ideally redeems the mind of
Blake. Furthermore, just as Blake's identity, his indestructible individuality, informs his myth by interpenetrating all of the natural
forms which his verse elevates to divinity, so Swinburne's identity,
by virtue of his Bloomian strong reading of Blake, informs Blake's
myth. What we are finally presented with is Swinburne's living myth
of Blake's living myth.

That Swinburne's myth is a metamorphosis of Blake's returns us
to the quotation that began this discussion of Swinburnian myth.
For as well as saying that myth regenerates and resurrects "energies
and agencies," he says that it disembodies and disfigures them.
Frye's description of Blake's mythopoeia, quoted above, refers
explicitly to his transformations of natural forces to human forms,
to the giant figures, such as Albion, of his personal cosmogony, as
does Swinburne's reference to disembodied, disfigured energies
and agencies: "Space fell into sleep, and awoke as Enitharmon:

[23] McGann, p. 17.

Time suffered eclipse, and came forth as Los" (p. 191). Frye's description, which I think is probably accurate, places Blake's creation of human forms in the Christian tradition—the analogue to the creative poet is the Christian God: "Blake was the first and most radical of the Romantics who identified the creative imagination of the poet with the creative power of God."[24] And Blake's creation, like the Christian God's, is the construction of an eternal city, a cosmos fallen into disunity by the fall and gradually being pulled back into unity by the "providential" creative imagination of the poet. Blake's giant forms, eternal and unchanging in their essential natures, represent various complex facets of the still more complex Eternal Man, and the job of the poet's synthetic imagination is to "organize" them within the "circumference" of his vision and his art. Swinburne's description of these forms, another misreading conditioned by his paganism, implies, however, an almost Ovidian idea of metamorphosis. The analogy to Ovid becomes clear when Swinburne describes the myth in *Milton*: "There is much more of the same mythic sort concerning the duration of time, the offices of the nerves (*e.g.*, in the optic nerve sleep was *transformed* to death by Satan the father of sin and death, even as we have seen sensual death *re-transformed* by Mercy into sleep), and such-like huge matters" (p. 273, emphasis mine).

This characterization of the giant forms is especially informative because it lies at the root of Swinburne's most fundamental misunderstanding of Blake, and it demonstrates some of his strongest intellectual tendencies—tendencies strong enough to lead an acute critical intellect far astray. He refers to Blake's use of giant mythic figures as a "curious habit of direct mythical metaphor or figure peculiar to Blake," but his parenthetic description of that habit indicates that it is not at all peculiar to Blake, for it perfectly describes Swinburne's own techniques in such poems as "Dolores" and "Faustine": "his custom of getting whole classes of men or opinions embodied, for purposes of swift irregular attack, in some one representative individual" (p. 101). In Swinburne's poetry the "representative individual" represents the animating principle, the underlying spirit in its successive incarnations in the generations of men—

[24] Frye, "The Road of Excess," p. 17.

Faustine represents the principle of the "fatal woman" in all its incarnations throughout history.[25] The shape of the principle changes, but not the principle itself; as Swinburne said of the spirit of Blake's figures, it is "capable of change but not of death" (p. 197). But what is true of Swinburne's myth is not true, as he supposed, of Blake's. Albion, Los, and Urizen, even Bacon, Locke, and Newton, are not used to *represent* historical principles—they *are* eternal states and incapable of change. As Blake said, "In Eternity one Thing never Changes into another Thing."[26] Despite all his arguments against it, Swinburne divides body and soul, incarnation and essence, in a way Blake never did, and in his particular, rather than general, comments in the essay he sees Blake as doing the same. The mythic principle of metamorphosis of forms is central in Swinburne, and he fails to see that the principle is nonexistent in Blake—nothing falls into sleep and awakes as something else; all the giant forms, embodiments of the fallen parts of the Eternal Man in the world of generation, exist eternally in the world of vision.

Swinburne fails to see that Blake's mythic view of man's history is entirely different from his own because his predisposition is toward a pagan idea of repeated cycles of history. He cannot adjust to Blake's working in the Hebrew tradition with an apocalyptic concept of history. Swinburne's myth of history, reiterated throughout his poetry but perhaps stated most clearly in the "Hymn to Proserpine," is that the old gods die and give place to new, that though progress may be made in any one cycle of history, the general pattern is not progress but simply change. And it is this myth that he imposes on Blake, reading "The Book of Thel," for example, as a statement that "each thing is redeemed from perpetual death by perpetual change" (p. 202). This is not the gospel of the imaginative Christian, Blake, who sees only two significant changes in human history, the fall into generation and the sudden apocalyptic redemption of the imagination; it is the gospel of the pagan Swinburne, who sees history only as a series of metamorphoses, of mutations.

[25] See Mario Praz, *The Romantic Agony*, trans. Angus Davidson (Oxford, 1951), pp. 228–30.
[26] "A Vision of the Last Judgment," *Complete Writings*, p. 607.

Nothing could be more fitting than that Swinburne's reading of Blake presents us with a mutated version of the original. Blake has undergone a metamorphosis, has fallen asleep and rewakened as Swinburnian Blake. Obviously it was not Swinburne's intention to misread Blake, but it is ironic, and was inevitable, that in so doing he should provide a perfect illustration of the principles of his myth. By living again in the mind of Swinburne, Blake is "regenerated with a vengeance, but disembodied and disfigured in [his] resurrection."

Swinburne was a fervent admirer of Blake and saw him—sometimes correctly and sometimes not—as a champion of the causes he himself believed in. As a result I have, in this chapter, dealt entirely with Swinburne's praise of Blake and the significance of its validity or invalidity. His one fundamental dispute with Blake, however, points to the entire course of Swinburne's development—the course I shall be following in succeeding chapters. He objected to Blake's obscurity (which is interesting, since Blake may be the only major poet in the language more obscure than Swinburne) because he saw it as resulting to a large extent from the "names inconceivable" of his mythic protagonists. This "monstrous nomenclature, this jargon of miscreated things in chaos" (p. 42), seemed to him arbitrary and needlessly confusing. As we shall see, the course of Swinburne's development was largely a movement away from such nomenclature. From the beginning, as in "Faustine" or the poems to Lucrezia Borgia, his own mythic figures were given not arbitrary names but historical names. From these he returned, in *Atalanta in Calydon*, to the original Greek myth, making the names still less arbitrary by choosing ancient figures. The figures continued, however, to represent both themselves and some eternal principle, thus coming dangerously close, Swinburne may have felt, to mere allegorical representations. In *Erechtheus* the figures, once again with their original Greek names, become so thoroughly identified with the elemental forces underlying them that it is difficult, if not impossible, to separate them. And finally, in the late nature poetry, Swinburne avoids names altogether, making the elemental forces themselves the protagonists of his myth. Ironically, as Swinburne moves further and further away from the "monstrous nomenclature" he saw as plaguing Blake, his poetry becomes more and more obscure. Also ironically, it becomes ever closer in spirit to the poetry of Blake and, as we shall see, becomes more genuinely and emphatically mythopoeic.

Poems and Ballads
Swinburne's
CHAPTER 2   "Centre of Indifference"

HE BROKE IN on that rather agreeably tedious Victorian tea-party with the effect of some pagan creature, at once impish and divine, leaping on the sleek lawn, to stamp its goat-foot in challenge, to deride with its screech of laughter the admirable decorum of the conversation. The disorder that followed remains indescribable."[1] T. Earle Welby's description of the publication of *Poems and Ballads* in August of 1866 colorfully but accurately describes the effect produced by the sensational verses of England's own "libidinous laureate of a pack of satyrs."[2] Thomas Hardy later described the volume as "a garland of red roses . . . fallen about the hood of some smug nun,"[3] and an abundance of further commentary upon the reaction of the shocked Victorians has not been wanting. The event is so amusing a part of literary history, in fact, that *Poems and Ballads* has been slighted while attention has been focused on the symptoms of Victorian culture shock and on Swinburne's motivations in producing it. In spite of his defense of the poems as dramatic monologues intended to explore certain stages in the growth of the mind, Swinburne's critics have persistently charged him with producing poetry designed merely to shock. Robert Buchanan, reviewing the volume in the *Athenaeum*, was the first of a long line of

[1] T. Earle Welby, *A Study of Swinburne* (1926; rpt. New York, 1969), p. 14.

[2] John Morley, unsigned rev., *Saturday Review*, 4 Aug. 1866; rpt. in Clyde K. Hyder, ed., *Swinburne: The Critical Heritage* (New York, 1970), p. 29.

[3] "A Singer Asleep," *The Complete Poems of Thomas Hardy: New Wessex Edition*, ed. James Gibson (London, 1976), p. 265.

critics to accuse him of being "deliberately and impertinently insin-
cere as an artist" and of abandoning the high moral purpose of art,
not for art for art's sake, but for dirt for dirt's sake—uncleanness
"for the mere sake of uncleanness."[4] Other critics, who are con-
vinced of the poet's sincerity, have lamented the degradation of his
mind. In both cases, the poems tend to be ignored or, at best,
treated as symptoms.

The best of Swinburne's critics have always recognized (one
might almost say reveled in) the absurdity of the uproar. Welby, for
example, has noted that the conjunction of explicit violence and
explicit passion has always been allowed in literature and is as old as
Catullus' *"odi et amo."*[5] And though Swinburne would never have
defended himself on the grounds of realism, there can be no doubt
that his violent and sensual poems treat the theme of passionate
love realistically. Geoffrey Tillotson has observed that "the account
of passion, even if of abnormal passion, is an account of a reality. It
does not insult the power of the passion, as the speaker of 'Locksley
Hall' insulted it when in a famous line he made the fancies of a
young man turn to thoughts of love lightly. The epithet that Swinburne awards to 'kisses' is 'heavy.'"[6] Just as Baudelaire's exquisite
sense of sin and guilt proves the possibility of good and as his own
debasement exalts the virtues of others, so in a curious way Swinburne's lascivious riot in perverse sexuality proves and exalts the

[4]Rpt. in Hyder, ed., *Swinburne*, p. 31. For a discussion of the contemporary
attacks on *Poems and Ballads*, see ibid., pp. xviii-xxv, and also Hyder's *Swinburne's
Literary Career and Fame* (Durham, N.C., 1933), pp. 34–72. Later critics have
attempted to praise or merely justify the book by placing it in the tradition of
French aestheticism or by citing the influence of Blake and Whitman (see especially
Georges Lafourcade, *La Jeunesse de Swinburne* [Oxford, 1928], Bk. II, pp. 425–72)
or by invoking the freedom of the artist and the experiential truth of the verses (see
Welby, pp. 33–90) or even, with some condescension, by discussing the Byronic
tendencies of the Victorian age and the puerilities of Swinburne's youth (see
Samuel Chew, *Swinburne* [Boston, 1929], pp. 77–95). The prevailing critical ap-
proach to *Poems and Ballads* has only recently changed from justification to exposition, notably in the work of Cecil Y. Lang, Jerome McGann, and Julian Baird and
David A. Cook, cited in the notes.

[5]Welby, p. 68.

[6]"Swinburne," *Mid-Victorian Studies* (New York, 1965), p. 214.

power of the emotional as opposed to the rational side of man's nature. The analogy to Baudelaire may be made on firmer ground than the paradoxical realism of the two poets, however, for Swinburne saw Baudelaire as justifying the doctrine of art for art's sake—that art can make even the most debased subject beautiful—and probably saw himself as doing the same thing. Baudelaire had made a putrescent corpse beautiful in "Une Charogne"—Swinburne would make necrophilia beautiful in "The Leper." The best way to prove a point is to demonstrate it in the hardest case possible.

But Swinburne based his main defense of the poems neither on their realism nor on the aesthetic doctrine of the freedom of the artist but on the claim that they were dramatic monologues. His defense has never been taken as seriously as it deserves. That the poems are indeed dramatic is beyond question (though one wonders about Buchanan's apparent criterion of sincerely dramatic poetry), for as Cecil Y. Lang has said, even in Swinburne's most patently autobiographical poetry, such as "The Triumph of Time" or "A Leave-Taking," "he is always seen behind the esthetic mask that makes it impossible for us to disengage literal from symbolic truth." [7] This is not to say that the perverse sexuality of his various speakers was not very much a part of Swinburne's emotional makeup—as, say, Bishop Blougram's casuistry was not a part of Browning's—but only that it was being aesthetically distanced. Moreover, Swinburne's decision to distance himself from the themes of his work has an important bearing on how we are to understand his poetry.

However much the perverse eroticism may have been intended to shock, and however fundamental it may be in Swinburne's psyche, its use in the dramatic monologue serves an independent artistic function. Robert Langbaum has demonstrated that the dramatic monologue functions by creating a tension between sympathy and judgment. In Browning this is achieved by the presentation of an engaging character who adopts an extraordinary moral position; in Tennyson the "pathology of the emotions" takes the

---

[7] "Swinburne's Lost Love," *PMLA*, 74 (1959), 124.

place of the extraordinary moral position. Swinburne's speakers are
characterized by both eccentric morality and pathological emotions—what they may seem to lack is a pole for sympathy.[8] The real
objection to the erotic poems is that the speakers lack the independent vitality and humanity of Browning's characters—they all seem
to speak with one voice, and that voice seems to be Swinburne's.
Poems and Ballads, taken as a whole, belongs to the genre of monodrama, which is concerned, as A. Dwight Culler has recently shown,
not with the psychology of the speaker, the subtle movements of
the mind from one thought to the next, but with a sequential ex-
hibition of the passions themselves without concern as to how they
come into being.[9] Each poem in the volume exhibits one particular
impassioned outlook. Swinburne did not attempt to flesh out the
characters in his lyrics. His purpose was not to generate sympathy
for the individual eccentric, like Browning's Duke of Ferrara, but to
see the world from a new and fresh perspective. The adoption of a
naive character in a strikingly unusual situation allows the poet to
see his theme with an unjaundiced eye. Just as Blake chose, for a
time, to see with the eyes of a child in *Songs of Innocence*, as
Wordsworth chose to see through the eyes of idiots, beggars, and
peasants, and as Byron saw life as a sated reveler, so Swinburne
chose to see with the eyes of pagans and passion-crazed lovers. The
speakers, then, are not developed, rounded dramatic characters at
all; each is a sort of Everyman, reacting to, rather than shaping, the
terms of his existence. Far from merely representing Swinburne's
peculiar brand of perversity, they are *types* of nineteenth-century
Western man and, as we shall see, can be used to explore not only
the responses of an individual to the determining forces of his
civilization but also the responses of the civilization itself to its own
cultural, moral, and philosophic premises. Consequently *Poems and
Ballads* is not merely an exploration of the diseased psyche of the
individual—it is an exploration of the diseased psyche of Western
civilization.

[8] *The Poetry of Experience* (New York, 1963), pp. 92–93.
[9] "Monodrama and the Dramatic Monologue," *PMLA*, 90 (1975), 366–85.

I

The central theme of *Poems and Ballads* is love, and the moral position, constantly reiterated, is that love made life more beautiful in the days before a restrictive, oppressive morality set in. The "Hymn to Proserpine," a dramatic monologue that explores the theme by contrasting the beauty of paganism with the drab grayness of Christianity, is particularly effective because put in the mouth of a pagan poet in the era of Julian the Apostate, the last of the pagan emperors of Rome. Christianity seen with the eyes of a lusty pagan is a far different affair from the Christianity of a prudent Victorian man of business. "Anactoria," a dramatic monologue spoken by Sappho, explores the metamorphic connections between eroticism and creativity and is particulalry effective because voiced by a sexually perverse poet of acknowledged greatness.

Both the "Hymn to Proserpine" and "Anactoria" are, however loosely, based on history, but the best example of Swinburne's use of the dramatic monologue, "The Leper," presents a purely fictional character in a highly unusual situation. The sense of historical perspective was so important to him, however, that he actually created a historical setting. Using his immense talent for literary imitation, he himself wrote the legend of the leper in fake medieval French, attributing it to the *Grandes Chroniques de France, 1505.* The story is appallingly repugnant; a lowly clerk, who has voyeuristically observed the loves of a beautiful but lascivious noblewoman, seizes his opportunity when leprosy renders the lady ugly and detestable and when all her loves have abandoned her. With a necrophiliac passion he revels in the decomposition of her features:

> Love bites and stings me through, to see
>   Her keen face made of sunken bones.
> Her worn-off eyelids madden me,
>   That were shot through with purple once.[10]

---

[10] *The Poems of Algernon Charles Swinburne,* 6 Vols. (London, 1904), I, 133. All subsequent references to Swinburne's poetry are cited in the text by volume and page numbers of this edition.

The situation is repulsive, but serious points are being made. Briefly, the poem is concerned with the injustice of God. In a world ruled by a just God, such a situation could not occur. Sensuous beauty would never be punished in such a way. Like the medieval poetry it imitates, "The Leper" takes place within the omnipresent frame of Christianity, but it is nevertheless pagan in its constant and quite deliberate elevation of sensuality over God's law:

> Sometimes when service made me glad
>   The sharp tears leapt between my lids,
> Falling on her, such joy I had
>   To do the service God forbids.
>
> [I, 132]

The mischievously ambiguous placement of "Falling on her" compels doubt as to what the service is, but the point is that the central question raised by the poem, the question explicitly asked in the last stanza, is whether there is justice in the Christian scheme:

> I am grown blind with all these things:
>   It may be now she hath in sight
> Some better knowledge; still there clings
>   The old question. Will not God do right?
>
> [I, 134]

Earthly sexuality is degraded to the utmost in this poem, not simply because Swinburne enjoys degradation, but because it is an emblem of the degradation of Christian society. A political point is being made as well as a religious one, for the disease reduces the noblewoman to a status lower than the clerk's. This leveling of rank demonstrates a central truth of republicanism: under the skin (literally—and wittily—in this case) we are all equal.

The poem can only work if there is some pole for sympathy— otherwise our moral judgment cannot be overcome—and sympathy for the speaker, the clerk, does result from a consideration of his circumstances. He loved the beautiful lady when she was unattainable, but, unlike those noblemen who merely lusted for her in her beauty, he continued to love her after disease had made her repulsive. Even though the penalty was leprosy, the love was too strong to be cast aside. Both the strength of his passion and the fact that he was a commoner who was only allowed access to debased sexuality make the clerk a sympathetic figure and make the poem successful as a dramatic monologue. Still, the end and aim of the poem was not to develop a character, as Browning would do, and, least of all, to play a variation on the theme of "all for love," but to articulate the urgencies of Swinburne's moral being: the injustice of the Christian scheme and a hierarchical society, the degradation of the senses in a morally ascetic body politic, the conjunction of love and death, the immense power of love.

Swinburne's much-abused defense of his poems is disingenuous only if we assume that he meant Browningesque in calling them dramatic. His language describing this "lyrical monodrama of passion" is more suggestive of the Tennyson of *Maud* than of Browning, but even Tennyson is far more concerned than Swinburne with exploring the workings of the mind.[11] Whatever may be implied by calling lyrics dramatic in the age of Browning and Tennyson, Swinburne merely meant that the poems were to be understood as utterances by speakers not himself, that the myriad speakers provide myriad perspectives. The actual "lyrical monodrama" selected for special defense, the trilogy consisting of "Dolores," "The Garden of Proserpine," and "Hesperia," in many respects epitomizes the central ideas in the volume. The three poems, Swinburne asserts, show a mind in the process of development from a lust induced by weariness of life, to a stage of longing for death and oblivion, and finally to a stage of constant striving for love rather than lust. Browning or Tennyson, perhaps, would have put it all into one poem. Swinburne sees three distinct attitudes toward life and love and dramatizes each separately. He doesn't show us character in action or the idiosyncracy of the individual mind because he sees the three stages as characteristic not only of the maturation of the individual but also of the maturation of Western civilization.

---

[11] "Notes on Poems and Reviews," *The Complete Works of Algernon Charles Swinburne*, ed. Edmund Gosse and Thomas James Wise, XVI (New York, 1926), 361.

II

In "Notes on Poems and Reviews" Swinburne described the first
phase, the "Dolores" phase, as "that transient state of spirit through
which a man may be supposed to pass, foiled in love and weary of
loving, but not yet in sight of rest; seeking refuge in those 'violent
delights' which 'have violent ends,' in fierce and frank sensualities
which at least profess to be no more than they are."[12] The verses
describing this state, "Dolores," "Faustine," and others, have always
formed the nucleus of poems that Swinburne's detractors have seen
as evidence of his licentiousness and immorality. While the "fierce
and frank sensualities" celebrated in these poems may "profess to be
no more than they are," the actual poems are far more than they
seem.

"Dolores" is genuinely blasphemous, erotic, perverse. Dolores is
a satanically inverted Virgin Mary, the poem a parody of Christian
litanies to the Virgin:

> O garment not golden but gilded,
>   O garden where all men may dwell,
> O tower not of ivory, but builded
>   By hands that reach heaven from hell;
> O mystical rose of the mire,
>   O house not of gold but of gain,
> O house of unquenchable fire,
>   Our Lady of Pain:

>   [I, 166–67]

The subtitle, "Notre-Dame des Sept Douleurs," and the very form
of the poem emphasize the obvious—that Swinburne associates the
"Dolores" phase of consciousness, the phase of lust and fierce, frank
sensualities, with inverted Christianity. Perhaps the most memorable of many passages in which Swinburne posits passionate, painful love as the mirror image of Christian asceticism is a simile from
"Hesperia:" "As the cross that a wild nun clasps till the edge of it
bruises her bosom,/ So love wounds as we grasp it, and blackens
and burns as a flame" (I, 190).[13] What is new is not the association

[12] Ibid., p. 360.
[13] See also Swinburne's letter of 14 Jan. 1876 to Edmund Gosse in which he
rages against Cardinal Newman's "finding 'amorousness' and 'religion' 'such ir-

of Christian asceticism and perverse sexuality—an association that is, of course, common in Blake—but the extremes to which Swinburne took the idea. Dolores, like Proserpine in the "Hymn to Proserpine," and like Venus in "Laus Veneris," is a pagan alternative to the virgin mother of God, and she substitutes lasciviousness and cruelty for chastity and mercy. If this weren't blasphemous enough, the Eucharistic images of bread and wine are employed in a black mass of sensuality, and vice is explicitly exalted over virtue.

According to Georges Lafourcade, Swinburne's inversion of Christianity, his substitution of sadism for mercy as the cosmic law, demonstrates his belief in the philosophy of the marquis de Sade. He asserts that Swinburne saw cruelty as the law of nature and argued backward to discover the cruelty of the creator: "si le Mal (souffrance et mort) est le grand principe auquel se conforme le monde, le Créateur de ce monde participera lui aussi de ce principe: Dieu sera mauvais et par essence cruel."[14] Another argument in defense of Swinburne's satanic inversion has been that, like Baudelaire and Mallarmé, his recognition of sin and evil implies the existence of virtue, since the terms are relative. If there has been a fall, there must be, or at least must have been, an ideal. The argument that inverted Christianity is still Christianity is invincible (Saint Peter was crucified upside down, after all), but unfortunately it does not hold as a defense for Swinburne. Both this and Lafourcade's Sadic rationale assume that the blasphemous pagan sensuality of Dolores is put forth by Swinburne as in itself a defensible position. The assumption is directly contrary to Swinburne's own statement that the poem is dramatic and represents an unredeemed

---

reconcilable elements'": "has he never heard of the last goddess of his church, Marie Alacoque, the type and incarnation of *furor uterinus?* It may be convenient, but it is at least cool, for a priest of that faith to forget that his church has always naturally and necessarily been the mother of 'pale religious lechery' (as Blake with such grand scorn labels the special quality of celibate sanctity 'that wishes but acts not'), of holy priapism and virginal nymphomania. Not to speak of the filthy visions of the rampant and rabid nun who founded 'the worship of the Sacred Heart' (she called it heart—in the phallic processions they called it a more—and less—proper name), he might have found passages from St. Theresa which certainly justify from a carnal point of view her surname of the Christian Sappho" (*The Swinburne Letters*, ed. Cecil Y. Lang, III [New Haven, 1960], 116–17).

[14] Lafourcade, *La Jeunesse*, Bk. II, p. 443.

attitude. Swinburne, no doubt, thoroughly enjoyed indulging in the blasphemous sensationalism of the poem, but his enjoyment does not indicate that he found it ethically defensible as doctrine, and in fact both his "Notes on Poems and Reviews" and all his subsequent works indicate that he did not. As I suggested in the last chapter, the inversion of religion in *Poems and Ballads* (1866) is not a mere inversion of moral good and evil, partly because Christianity did not represent a moral norm for Swinburne and partly because those poems that most clearly invert it are not put forth as moral statements but as characterizations of an unredeemed stage of development.

The main theme of the poems of the "Dolores" phase of consciousness is that the senses must be exalted. The celebration of fierce and frank sensuality is a celebration of the body to the exclusion of the soul. "Dolores" is a purely fleshly poem about lust which has nothing to do with the heart or the soul: "Ah beautiful passionate body/ That never has ached with a heart!" (I, 169). In the subtitle the word *douleurs* refers to the spiritual, emotional suffering of the Blessed Virgin, but as the word takes on meaning in the context of the poem, it refers to the pain inflicted by Dolores, "Our Lady of Pain." It is typical of Swinburne to make a major point with a pun, but the point is nevertheless serious. The passive suffering of the soul is replaced by the active infliction of pain to the flesh. The masochism of Christian asceticism is replaced by the sadism of pagan sensuality.

Julian Baird has convincingly argued that Swinburne saw in Sadic philosophy only another form of the Christian asceticism that degrades the body to a lower level than the soul. A letter from Swinburne to Monckton Milnes, quoted by Baird, demonstrates unequivocally that he considered sadism as merely inverted Christianity, and no better than what it seeks to replace: "We took you [Sade] for a sort of burlesque Prometheus; you are only a very serious Simeon Stylites—*in an inverted posture.* You worship the phallus as those first ascetics worshipped the cross; you seek your heaven by the same road as they sought theirs." [15] The alternative to

---

[15] *Letters*, I (1959), 57 (emphasis mine). Quoted in Julian Baird, "Swinburne, Sade, and Blake: The Pleasure-Pain Paradox," *Victorian Poetry*, 9 (1971), 52.

both asceticism and sadism, Baird continues, is that ideal extolled in *William Blake*, the absolute unity of soul and spirit. He explicates the first three poems in *Poems and Ballads* ("A Ballad of Life, " "A Ballad of Death," and "Laus Veneris") and demonstrates that for Swinburne conventional morality destroys the unity of soul and sense by chastening the flesh. Baird is, on the whole, correct, but he fails to recognize that the deficiencies of sadism as an ethic are not quite identical with the inadequacies of asceticism. Sadistic sensuality, by exalting the flesh at the expense of the soul (the pain inflicted by Dolores is not, after all, undesired) acts as a counterweight to asceticism, which exalts the soul at the expense of the flesh. Sadism then, is not an ideal, but the most effective reaction is, as Swinburne knew, overreaction—a pendulum comes to rest in the center only after repeated oscillations.

The eroticism of "Dolores" is particularly degrading because it consists entirely of lust. Swinburne described how the spirit in this stage of its development "plays for awhile with its pleasures and pains, mixes and distorts them with a sense half-humorous and half-mournful . . . sports with sorrow and jests against itself."[16] The spirit is, as it were, an apathetic observer of the revels of the body. It is, in effect, on vacation from the ardors of spiritual life and has, for the time, given up the fight. Swinburne noted in "Hesperia" that "desire is a respite from love, and the flesh not the heart is her fuel" (I, 190). This is precisely what he dramatizes in "Dolores," where the speaker seeks gratification in lust to avoid the pains of love:

> On thy mouth though the kisses are bloody,
>   Though they sting till it shudder and smart,
> More kind than the love we adore is,
>   They hurt not the heart or the brain. . . .

[I, 169]

Lust is a vacation from love, an avoidance of commitment in life:

> For the crown of our life as it closes
>   Is darkness, the fruit thereof dust;
> No thorns go as deep as a rose's,
>   And love is more cruel than lust.

[16]"Notes on Poems and Reviews," pp. 360–61.

> Time turns the old days to derision,
>   Our loves into corpses or wives;
> And marriage and death and division
>   Make barren our lives.

[I, 171]

Dolores serves the same function as any common prostitute, relief of the flesh without commitment of the heart. The flesh, like the heart, has its reasons, which reason does not know.

The degradation of sensual gratification is, as Baird has said, symptomatic of an age in which religious and moral repression has destroyed the harmony of soul and sense. Soul and sense, heart and flesh, have been separated, and the gratification of the flesh has become a soulless, mechanical affair—Faustine is a "love-machine"—a symptom of the soulless, mechanical England of the Industrial Revolution.[17] Not Lawrence himself is more explicit or more emphatic on the subject.

The suggestion that sex has been degraded in the modern age implies that it had been something different, and better, in past ages. In Swinburne's poetry, the symbol of the gradual degradation of sex is the archetypal whore—giantesses of lust and perverse licentiousness like Dolores, Faustine, Phaedra, Aholibah, Lucrezia Borgia in "A Ballad of Life" and "A Ballad of Death," Venus in "Laus Veneris," and twenty-two queens of pleasure in "The Masque of Queen Bersabe." The image is so natural to Swinburne that even in "Ave atque Vale," his elegy for Baudelaire, the particular poem he chooses to commemorate is "La Géante." These giant forms, reminiscent of the giants of Blake's prophetic books, are embodiments of the principle of lust and the power it bestows on women to dominate men. They are, as Mario Praz says, embodiments of the type of the "fatal woman," a type he shows to be almost omnipresent in both English and continental romanticism. But however prevalent the type may have been in other writers, Swinburne's use of it in *Poems and Ballads* is original and personal, and a study of it is particularly helpful in understanding both his perception of the "Dolores" phase of consciousness and his use, in 1866, of myth.

[17] Ken Russell, in his perverse film on Rossetti, actually provided Swinburne with a machine to make love to.

The most salient fact to be noted is that while the figures addressed or discussed in the poems are individuals, they are representatives of a type. The poems that deal with them are dramatic, but they deal not with dramatic conflict and tension or with the mind and motivations of the speaker so much as with the thematic concerns embodied in the eternal female. The dramatic format allows Swinburne to see this figure from myriad perspectives, but the figure itself is always essentially the same. The universality of the theme—the existence of the type in all places and at all times—indicates that the "Dolores" phase is a stage not merely in the evolution of the individual mind but in the historical development of the race.

"Faustine," addressed to a woman whose face reminded Swinburne of the lascivious Roman empress,[18] provides the clearest example of the historically ubiquitous figure who "could do all things but be good / Or chaste," (I, 117) the spirit of the ancient Roman reincarnate in a modern woman:

> As if your fed sarcophagus
>   Spared flesh and skin,
> You come back face to face with us,
>   The same Faustine.
>
> [I, 118]

But though she has the same features and the same lust for destruction, she is not "The same Faustine," for as we have seen, she is spoiled by the age, "This ghastly, thin-faced time of ours" (I, 121). The giant figure, which is reminiscent of Blake's mythic incarnations of essential forces, is unlike Blake's in this, for the historical process of the archetype is not the Hebraic progress to an apocalyptic goal but the Hellenic and Roman idea of cyclical alternation in generations. Faustine is transformed in a process that clearly is not typological but metamorphic:

> Then after change of soaring feather
>   And winnowing fin,
> You woke in weeks of feverish weather,
>   A new Faustine.
>
> [I, 120]

[18] "Notes on Poems and Reviews," p. 365.

The same idea is expressed in "Dolores," where the giantess's "skin changes country and colour" (I, 176):

> But the worm shall revive thee with kisses;
>> Thou shalt change and transmute as a god,
> As the rod to a serpent that hisses,
>> As the serpent again to a rod.
>
> [I, 179]

The simile of the rod metamorphosing to a serpent and back again to a rod indicates that there is no historical development whatever in those changes—they are simply changes. The idea of constant flux without progress is absolutely central in Swinburne, and it is reiterated in the poems of the "Dolores" stage (the idea of stages in a historical development does not, as we shall see, imply historical progress), which deal with the eternal feminine principle.

The Victorian incarnation of the type is thoroughly debased. Sin has lost its glory: "Weak sins yet alive are as virtue/ To the strength of the sins of that day" ("Dolores," I, 177). The principle may never change, but the shape it takes varies with the age, and the nineteenth century is a particularly vile age. Praz and others who have understood Swinburne to be celebrating the principle have failed to recognize that while he is emotionally committed to the "mystical Cotytto," he is intellectually using the degraded form she has taken as an emblem of the moral depths to which Victorian society has fallen. Though the argument that the existence of sin proves the existence of heaven is invalid for Swinburne, the argument that the intensity of possible sin is related to the intensity of possible virtue is as true for him as it was for Dostoevski (Father Zossima kneels to Dmitri Karamazov, not to Alyosha or Ivan). The ability to sin intensely implies the ability to live intensely, and this has been lost:

> Though we match not the dead men that bore us,
>> At a song, at a kiss, at a crime—
> Though the heathen outface and outlive us,
>> And our loves and our longings are twain—
>
> ["Dolores," I, 180]

Our lives and our longings are "twain" because our Christian code of ethics insists upon the subjugation of the flesh, but our longings

insist on the identity of flesh and spirit. As a result, man has become
a creature of divided aims who can act, literally, only half-heartedly.
The intense evil of Browning's Guido is the obverse of the intense
good of Pompilia, and the lesson learned by Caponsacchi is that a
man must choose his course and act with his whole being, even in
the face of convention and ecclesiastical law; in Tennyson's *Idylls* the
kingdom collapses because soul and sense are divided in the persons of Arthur and Guinevere. Swinburne was unique in presenting
the matter in a seemingly amoral manner—praising the intensity of
the experience without regard to conventional virtue and vice, and
in this respect he followed Blake and foreshadowed Pater's "Conclusion" to *The Renaissance.* Unlike Pater's aestheticism, however,
Swinburne's apparent amorality has a sharp, if unconventional,
moral edge in its implicit attack on the Christian asceticism that has
robbed man of half his being.

His metaphoric use of lust as a desire for more than merely
fleshly fulfillment, consistent throughout *Poems and Ballads*, represents his version of a central tenet of romanticism, that life must be
a continual, unsatisfied longing. Phaedra's lust, for example, is, as
she describes it, a Promethean urge:

> Man, what have I to do with shame or thee?
> I am not of one counsel with the gods.
> I am their kin, I have strange blood in me,
> I am not of their likeness nor of thine:
> My veins are mixed, and therefore am I mad,
> Yea therefore chafe and turn on mine own flesh,
> Half of a woman made with half a god.

[I, 133]

The first line of this quotation recalls Blake's rejection of his vege-
table existence ("Then what have I to do with thee?") in "To Tirzah," a poem Swinburne interpreted to mean that "those who live in
subjection to the senses would in their turn bring the senses into
subjection; unable to see beyond the body, they find it worthwhile
to refuse the body its right to freedom" (p. 125).[19] Thus Phaedra's

---

[19] The line also, of course, recalls Blake's source, Christ's rejection of merely
mortal ties in his sharp response to his mother: "Woman, what have I to do with
thee?" (John 2:4).

sinful lust seems to be connected with a rejection of the body, a
rejection that lies at the root of the degradation of man. The rest of
the passage, however, echoes not Blake but Byron and suggests the
sleepless, unsatisfied urge of the romantic. The essence of Byronic
romanticism is summed up in a few lines of Byron's "Prometheus":

> Thou art a symbol and a sign
>   To Mortals of their fate and force;
> Like thee, Man is in part divine,
>   A troubled stream from a pure source;
> And Man in portions can foresee
> His own funereal destiny;
> His wretchedness, and his resistance,
> And his sad unallied existence:
> To which his spirit may oppose
> Itself—and equal to all woes,
>   And a firm will, and a deep sense,
> Which even in torture can descry
>   Its own concenter'd recompense,
> Triumphant where it dares defy,
> And making Death a Victory.[20]

Phaedra, like Prometheus and like Byronic man, is "in part divine,"
and her illicit lust is a Byronic craving, impossible to satiate and
leading only to ultimate death, but affirmed in the face of its impossibility. Swinburne is not, however, condoning this lust, because the
rebellion of the manlike part against the godlike part is a rebellion
of the body against the soul. Once again Christian asceticism is
inverted, but once again the inversion works against the ideal condition of a unified body and soul.

As David A. Cook has shown, the attempt to resolve the dilemma of man's mixed endowment of spirit and sense by sexual
fulfillment is necessarily futile. The lust of Phaedra and, as Cook
suggests, of Sappho in "Anactoria" is a perfect metaphor for the
tormenting desire of romantic man, for it is the rebellion of the
manlike against the godlike. The speakers, says Cook, "owe their
unmitigated torment not to faithless lovers but to the implacably

---

[20] "Prometheus," ll. 45–59, in *Byron: Poetical Works*, ed. Frederick Page, corrected by John Jump (Oxford, 1970), p. 98.

cruel creator of love himself, not to the finite objects of their desire but to the archetypal condition of desiring."[21] Sappho's sadism, and the sadism of all the "fatal women" in Swinburne's poetry, aims at breaking down the barriers of the flesh in order to achieve mergence of spirits; as an attack on the flesh it is an attack on the ideal harmony of soul and sense. Licentious and perverse forms of sexuality are, paradoxically, on the side of the angels—the angels, at least, of orthodox Christianity. At various points in "Anactoria" Sappho expresses the desire to eat her lover, to make Anactoria one with her, and, similarly, Ian Fletcher has noted that in "The Leper," the "subdued metaphor throughout is 'the body of love': communion. The speaker searching still for total communion emphasizes happily: he is necrophiliac, sacrilegious, vampiristic. The girl has been reduced to a *thing*."[22] And the same is true for the sexuality of the "Dolores" phase throughout the volume. Lust is a desire to eliminate the soul, to cast it aside and thus be relieved of the hardship of existence as a "troubled stream from a pure source."

Lust, in Swinburne, serves the same purpose as the craving for oblivion in Tennyson; the speaker of "Dolores" or "Faustine" is seeking to lose himself in sensuality in the same way the lotos-eaters seek to lose themselves in the drug or as Tithonus wishes to lose himself in death. Fully understood, Swinburne's description of hedonistic lust is, in fact, a death wish, for if the desire is fulfilled, the strife of desire ended, it is accomplished only because the soul has been destroyed. The only way in which sexual desire can be quelled in life is by complete mergence of the lovers, and this is achieved only in "Hermaphroditus." But the resulting satiety, though beautiful, is beautiful as objects are beautiful. Hermaphroditus is a "*thing* of barren hours" (I, 89, my emphasis); it is a sterile object, "The double blossom of two fruitless flowers" (I, 89) in which all productive striving has been stilled:

> Sex to sweet sex with lips and limbs is wed,
> Turning the fruitful feud of hers and his
> To the waste wedlock of a sterile kiss.

> [I, 88]

[21] "The Content and Meaning of Swinburne's 'Anactoria,'" *Victorian Poetry*, 9 (1971), 80.

[22] *Swinburne* (London, 1973), p. 18.

Sappho's desire in "Anactoria" to reduce her lover to the level of an object to be consumed ("And in my flesh thy very flesh entombed!" [I, 67]) is ultimately a desire to end the strife of her own spirit, and her suicide, her entombment in "Thick darkness and the insuperable sea" (I, 73), serves the same purpose.

The conjunction of pain and sex throughout *Poems and Ballads* is only a step away from the conjunction of death and sex, which is almost as prevalent. The use of sadism as a symbol of the destructive power of lust is compelling, but the use of necrophilia in "The Leper," "Faustine," and "Dolores" is overpowering. The equation of death and sex is commonplace—the word *death* being commonly used to denote orgasm in the Renaissance—but had never before been carried to the extreme to which Swinburne takes it. Death not only metaphorically but literally replaces sexual fulfillment in poem after poem, as in "Rondel" ("Kissing her hair I sat against her feet"):

> Sleep were no sweeter than her face to me,
> Sleep of cold sea-bloom under the cold sea;
> What pain could get between my face and hers?
> What new sweet thing would love not relish worse?
> Unless, perhaps, white death had kissed me there,
>   Kissing her hair?
>
> > [I, 139]

Even in such patently autobiographic poems as "The Triumph of Time" and "Les Noyades" the speaker expresses a desire for death and oblivious mergence with the sea. In both poems the ideal condition, the condition to which the speaker aspires, is, simultaneously, recognition by the object of his love and death. Emotional attraction, however, does not necessarily lead to intellectual commitment, and as his devotion to the principle of unbridled energy in writers such as Blake and the overall scheme of *Poems and Ballads* indicate, Swinburne is not to be understood as advocating a surrender to oblivion. The tension between the temptation to annihilation and the commitment to never-ending strife runs throughout the volume, but as in Tennyson's "The Two Voices," the commitment to life will eventually triumph.

The pain and longing for oblivion that accompany sexual love in the "Dolores" phase as well as the metaphors of fire and destruction that are constantly used to describe it indicate that the degraded eroticism in question is essentially nihilistic. The ethical position which Swinburne is reacting against had dictated Western morality ever since the time of Socrates and is based on a Socratic distinction between essence and appearance, soul and body. This philosophy elevates mind over body and, as Gilles Deleuze, discussing the philosophy of Nietzsche, has said, it sets up thought as the judge and controller of action: "il fait de la vie quelque chose qui doit être jugé, mesuré, limité, et de la pensée, une mesure, une limite, qui s'exerce au nom de valeurs supérieures—le Divin, le Vrai, le Beau, le Bien."[23] Since the values to which the soul has recourse are necessarily established, received values, this is an essentially submissive rather than creative philosophy, life-defeating rather than life-enhancing. The philosophy that separates thought from life is itself nihilistic, and the degraded sexuality of sadism and the equation of sex with death are wholly of a piece with it. Swinburne's graphic portrayal of perverse eroticism is not presented as an alternative to Victorian prudery and complacency as has too often been supposed, but as a ghastly parody of it. His sensationalistic verses are a description of a nihilistic philosophy in its last stages before reaching its goal of oblivion. Moreover, as Deleuze has said, the destruction of a nihilistic philosophy is brought about not by rebellious blows from without but by its own inner development, by the eventual production of a man who detests the body so much he wishes to destroy it, by "l'homme qui veut périr." At this point, when man wishes for nothing but oblivion, says Deleuze, the time for a change has come: "Et á ce point d'achèvement du nihilisme (Minuit), tout est prêt—prêt pour une transmutation."[24]

III

Deleuze's description of "Minuit," the moment when a nihilistic philosophy reaches its last stage in the desire for oblivion, the moment before the dawn of a new day of creative philosophy, exactly

[23] *Nietzsche* (Paris, 1971), p. 17.
[24] Ibid., p. 28.

corresponds to Swinburne's description of the moment of transition between the first and second part of his "lyrical monodrama." Of this phase he said: "it is not without design that I have slipped in, between the first and second part, the verses called 'The Garden of Proserpine,' expressive, as I meant they should be, of that brief total pause of passion and of thought, when the spirit, without fear or hope of good things or evil, hungers and thirsts only after the perfect sleep."[25] "The Garden of Proserpine" supports the claims made for it as an integral part of a monodrama. The speaker refers to the intense joys and sorrows described in "Dolores" and expresses his emotional exhaustion:

> I am tired of tears and laughter,
>   And men that laugh and weep,
> Of what may come hereafter
>   For men that sow to reap:
> I am weary of days and hours,
> Blown buds of barren flowers,
> Desires and dreams and powers
>   And everything but sleep.
>
> [I, 183]

At this stage man can be sure of nothing in life, not even "sorrow / And joy was never sure" (I, 185). The only certainty is that life ends in death and oblivion, that

> no life lives for ever;
> That dead men rise up never;
> That even the weariest river
>   Winds somewhere safe to sea.
>
> [I, 186]

At this point, recognizing fully that life is a "sad, unallied existence" without significance, the speaker is truly "l'homme qui veut périr," desiring "Only the sleep eternal / In an eternal night" (I, 186).

This death-wish pause in Swinburne's lyrical monodrama is precisely analogous to a stage that recurs repeatedly in the spiritual autobiographies of other romantic and Victorian writers. It corresponds to the "centre of indifference" through which Carlyle's

---

[25] "Notes on Poems and Reviews," p. 362.

Teufelsdröckh had to pass to get from the "Everlasting Nay" (corresponding to Swinburne's "Dolores" phase) to the "Everlasting Yea." It represents that period in a man's development when, after a reasoned battle against convention, he gives up the strife of conscience, like Wordsworth, who

> lost
> All feeling of conviction, and, in fine,
> Sick, wearied out with contrarieties,
> Yielded up moral questions in despair.[26]

The death wish is that stage of development which eighteenth-century rationality had bequeathed to mankind, that stage where reason has emptied life of meaning and even made of Faustine a "love-machine / With clockwork joints" (I, 121). Byron had rebelled against the lifelessness of rationality with satire, the other romantics with an affirmation of the imagination, but spectrous reason came back to haunt the Victorians. Tennyson fought his strong yearning for oblivion only by a willed commitment to Victorian orthodoxy; Arnold flirted with the temptation in *Empedocles on Etna* but turned to fight it with a religion of culture. Even Mill, the most direct heir of eighteenth-century utilitarianism, found that a philosophy which allows room only for reason leads to a nihilistic destruction and a yearning for void. Realizing that the achievement of all his utilitarian goals would not bring about the supposed aim of life, happiness, he reached nihilistic rock bottom: "I seemed to have nothing left to live for."[27] Mill recovered from his nervous breakdown, his journey into the "centre of indifference," partly, he tells us, by reading Wordsworth, who, as Arnold and other Victorians insisted, is the greatest healer among poets. The message he found in Wordsworth was the message we have seen in Swinburne: emotional breakdown occurs when soul and sense, thought and life, are divided and thought is set up as a judge over life and the feelings, when by the aid of a reason which murders to dissect, man destroys his soul. Wordsworth described the process cogently:

---

[26] *The Prelude* (1850), XI.302–5, ed. Ernest de Selincourt (Oxford, 1926), p. 411.

[27] John Stuart Mill, *Autobiography* (1873; rpt. New York, 1924), p. 94.

> I warred against myself—
> A bigot to a new idolatry—
> Like a cowled monk who hath forsworn the world,
> Zealously laboured to cut off my heart
> From all the sources of her former strength;
> And as, by simple waving of a wand,
> The wizard instantaneously dissolves
> Palace or grove, even so could I unsoul
> As readily by syllogistic words
> Those mysteries of being which have made,
> And shall continue evermore to make
> Of the whole human race one brotherhood.[28]

And so Mill, like many of his contemporaries, passed through the "centre of indifference," emerging with an appreciation of the necessity of acknowledging both the spirit and flesh, thought and feelings. The crises of so many individual Victorians, of course, are representative of the crisis of an age. The point of "Minuit," which had been anticipated by Blake with his idea of the "consolidation of error, " has been reached—the mistaken premises of society have been carried to their conclusions, and the conclusions are so fundamentally inadequate, so easily recognizable as in error, that the premises themselves must be scrapped and a new beginning made.

Swinburne's recognition of the problem is characteristic of his age, but he is unique insofar as the first stage, in which moral questions are yielded up in despair, is not characterized by a slavish devotion to rationality but by devotion to sensual gratification. Since, however, lust breaks down the unity of body and soul in the same way as eighteenth-century rationalism and since it is, in fact, a metaphor of that nihilistic philosophy, the paradigm remains the same. The battle of soul and sense ends. In the case of Swinburne's contemporaries the victory goes to the soul, in his own case, to the flesh. The result is the same—a longing for death, a journey into the "centre of indifference."

The closest Swinburne ever came to writing a spiritual autobiography on the nineteenth-century model was "The Triumph of

---

[28] *The Prelude* (1850), XII.76–87, p. 427.

Time," a poem about the one great emotional crisis of his life. The poem tells of the disappointment of a great love, a love which, unlike lust, seeking to unify bodies while sundering souls, would have as its end the perfect union of souls:

> We had grown as gods, as the gods in heaven,
> Souls fair to look upon, goodly to greet,
> One splendid spirit, your soul and mine.
>
> . . . . .
>
> Twain halves of a perfect heart, made fast
> Soul to soul while the years fell past.
>
> [I, 40]

The love that is lost is a love like that of Heathcliff and Cathy, or Wagner's Tristan and Isolde, or Swinburne's own Tristram and Iseult, for that matter, or Shelley's ideal in "Epipsychidion," or Donne's in "The Ecstasy"—it is the total mergence of souls. The ideal is, of course, impossible to achieve in life, for it depends on the obliteration of the body in much the same way as does the perverted lust of sadism. This was the lesson of "Anactoria" and of "The Leper," and it is the reason why perfect bliss is found in "Les Noyades" and *Tristram of Lyonesse* only when the bodies of the lovers are dissolved in the sea. It is the reason why Shelley panted, sank, trembled, and expired at the end of "Epipsychidion," and why Donne rakishly concluded "The Ecstasy" with the comment that "pure lover's souls" must

> descend
> T' affections and to faculties
> Which sense may reach and apprehend.[29]

In "The Triumph of Time" the recognition of the futility of this ideal of love leads to a wish to embrace the all-dissolving sea—a "perfect lover" (I, 49) because it allows complete mergence, complete dissolution of the body:

> I will go down to her, I and none other,
> Close with her, kiss her and mix her with me. . . .

[29] "The Ecstasy," *The Poetical Works of John Donne*, ed. F. J. Child (Boston, 1855), p. 300.

. . . . .
This woven raiment of nights and days,
   Were it once cast off and unwound from me,
Naked and glad would I walk in thy ways,
   Alive and aware of thy ways and thee. . . .

                                                                [I, 48, 49]

The ideal love is wholly and appallingly nihilistic: "I wish we were dead together today" (I, 43) is the soul-cry of the desperate lover.

The poem is unquestionably autobiographic, and there can be no doubt that Swinburne sincerely felt the impulse to oblivion that runs through it like a dark thread. On the other hand, there is little doubt that the impulse is being studied with a degree of intellectual and aesthetic detachment. Swinburne is, on the whole, an impersonal poet, not one to unlock his heart with a sonnet-key. The generalizations about the destructive power of a love that separates soul from sense were, perhaps, a result of the biographical fact that Swinburne had committed his heart to a woman who had committed her flesh to another man: "you are twain, you are cloven apart, / Flesh of his flesh, but heart of my heart" (I, 42). The simple biographical fact that this division of sense from spirit made Swinburne long for death may be at the root of all his poetry about the pain of man's mixed nature, or, as has been suggested, his experience with Mary Gordon may have simply followed the pattern of his poetry. In either case, "The Triumph of Time" traces the pattern perfectly—the spiritual struggle resulting from the division of man against himself and corresponding to the division of man from woman becomes too great an agony to bear, and the speaker yearns for self-destruction. Robert A. Greenberg has said, correctly, that "Les Noyades," a poem celebrating the blessing of oblivion, follows "The Triumph of Time" for the same reasons that "The Garden of Proserpine" follows "Dolores,"[30] and he quotes a letter from Swinburne to Rossetti in support of his argument: "I should not like to bracket 'Dolores' and the two following as you propose. I ought (if I did) to couple with them in front harness the 'Triumph of Time' etc., as they express the state of feeling the reaction from which is

[30] "Gosse's Swinburne, 'The Triumph of Time,' and the Context of 'Les Noyades,'" *Victorian Poetry*, 9 (1971), 109.

expressed in 'Dolores.'"[31] Greenberg is correct, but only up to a point, since "The Triumph of Time" includes within itself the stage represented by "The Garden of Proserpine."

The point is that these themes run throughout the 1866 volume and that in the clearly autobiographic poetry they are identical with those of the dramatic poetry. The oblivion toward which a nihilistic philosophy tends is brought about from within, by its own inner workings, so it is important that Swinburne is not only dramatizing "l'homme qui veut périr," but *is* "l'homme qui veut périr." His ability to distance himself from his own pathology enables him to come to an understanding of it, and in so doing, to come to an understanding of the pathology of his age. In this he is wholly unlike Wordsworth, Tennyson, Mill, Carlyle, and others who saw the problem of man's divided nature by seeing it in themselves. They saw the problem during an emotional crisis, when their lives were at a "centre of indifference," and in different ways they struggled to escape the dread vision of nothingness. Swinburne alone lingered at the void to explore the pathology that urged him toward it, and his conclusion was not that the "centre of indifference" was something to be shunned but that all of Western society should be pushed toward it and into the void. Swinburne's belief superficially resembles Blake's notion of vortices—the belief that complete contraction into the sensual self, the consolidation of error, brings man to and through a "vortex" from which he emerges resurrected from the bondage of the senses and free to perceive the infinite. The crucial difference, of course, is that for Swinburne man is a genuinely limited, finite creature who must recognize that nothing lies beyond life but death and emptiness. The "Garden of Proserpine" stage of development dramatizes the condition of man when he has reached this point, when he has realized that "no life lives for ever" and that "dead men rise up never." Only at this point is he freed from "too much love of living."

The most important reason why man must recognize—even welcome—death is that only then can he welcome life. Swinburne attacks Christianity because it is an ascetic code of ethics that denies life on earth for the deluded hope of life in heaven. In the same

[31] *Letters*, I, 197.

way, the perverted, sadistic love of Sappho for Anactoria is destructive because it holds out a false and impossible ideal of love; even Swinburne's own love, dramatized in "The Triumph of Time," is based on a false ideal. Delusive beliefs which set themselves up as consolations for man's sad, unallied existence are, ironically, the sources of his greatest pain. Man's experience cannot live up to his expectations, so his life is a constant frustration; he cannot live up to his thought and so feels constantly degraded.

Recognition of oblivion as the end of life, moreover, puts an end to the nihilistic model of the soul as exalted above the body. This is, as we have seen, an essentially submissive pattern of thought, and Swinburne, a born rebel, could not tolerate submission in any form. Because the contemplative thinker who accepts this model follows the precepts of earlier generations and accepts the handed-down values of elders, he is essentially a bearer of other men's ideas. As Deleuze says, "Rien n'est plus opposé au créateur que le porteur," [32] and nothing was more important to Swinburne than the ability to create. True creativity must always begin with chaos; the contemplative rearrangement of received ideas is not creation. To accept the myths of another age—Christianity, for example—would be to deny modern man's ability to create his own. Swinburne must have been genuinely pleased with the comments in John Morley's unsigned review for the *Saturday Review* about the complete lack of contemplative thought in *Poems and Ballads*, for contemplation is not in essence creative.[33] Jean-Paul Sartre's gloss on Baudelaire will also serve as a gloss on Swinburne: "Il admet 'trois êtres respectables: le prêtre, le guerrier et le poète. Savoir, tuer et créer.' On remarquera que destruction et création font ici un couple: dans les deux cas il y a production d'événements absolus; dans les deux un homme est à lui tout seul responsable d'un changement radical dans l'univers. A ce couple s'oppose le savoir qui nous ramène à la vie contemplative."[34] Swinburne would not have admitted the respectability of the priest (though he would certainly respect any other vessel for the retention of knowledge), but he would have been in complete accord on all other points. Nihilism becomes

[32] Deleuze, p. 16.
[33] Rpt. in Hyder, ed., *Swinburne*, p. 29.
[34] *Baudelaire* (Paris, 1947), p. 141.

creative only at that point where it comes full circle (moving from the exclusion of the senses, as in Christian asceticism, to the exclusion of the soul, as in Swinburnian eroticism) and destroys itself. And not only is the recognition of man's finitude a creative act in itself, it is also a basis for further creative acts. When nothing can be accepted as given, every man must create his own truths.

IV

"Hesperia," the magnificent but grossly neglected poem of the dramatic troika Swinburne discussed in "Notes on Poems and Reviews," clarifies these issues. "The next act in this lyrical monodrama of passion," Swinburne said, "represents a new stage and scene": "The worship of desire has ceased; the mad commotion of sense has stormed itself out; the spirit, clear of the old regret that drove it upon such violent ways for a respite, healed of the fever that wasted it in the search for relief among fierce fancies and tempestuous pleasures, dreams now of truth discovered and repose attained." [35] The poem, like this description, reviews the stages through which the speaker has passed. In a prolonged apostrophe to Dolores, "Our Lady of Pain," he recalls the period in which "desire is a respite from love" (I, 190), the phase dramatized in "The Triumph of Time," when idealistic love was agony. Dolores is followed by the second giantess of the trilogy, Proserpine: "Let her lips not again lay hold on my soul, nor her poisonous kisses, / To consume it alive and divide from thy bosom, Our Lady of Sleep" (I, 191). And finally he returns to the third and last of the giantesses, Hesperia herself, "the tenderest type of woman or of dream, born in the westward 'islands of the blest,'" described in the poem as the "daughter of sunset and slumber" (I, 191). [36]

Hesperia is clearly a symbol of hope, but how she fulfills this function is not so clear. Somehow the speaker is redeemed; his heart, which had been ravaged and finally laid to sleep in the earlier poems, is resurrected in its love for Hesperia. In the end the two

[35] "Notes on Poems and Reviews," p. 361.
[36] Ibid.

ride off on the twin steeds, Fear and Love, both stronger than death. Swinburne's hope, born of desperation, is strikingly similar to Shelley's forlorn affirmation in the conclusion of the "Lines Written among the Euganean Hills," where the only basis for the utopian vision is a heartbroken "Other flowering isles *must be* / In the sea of Life and Agony."[37] For Swinburne, as for Shelley, affirmation is a product of the undaunted human will; it is a willed refusal to submit to life and agony. The speaker's heart, not surprisingly, is resurrected in a chastened form: "Closed up from the air and the sun, but alive, as a ghost rearisen, / Pale as the love that revives as a ghost rearisen in me" (I, 189). Hesperia, as a type, represents the land of the dead and of memories, and the ghost rearisen in the speaker's heart seems to consist of the memory of a calm and happy past. The resurrected soul is, as in Wordsworth, a heightened awareness of the continuity of the self. The wind, most romantic of emblems of resurrection, inspires the speaker with "memories beloved from a boy" (I, 187). Moreover, the landscapes of the mind, "the meadows of memory, the highlands of hope" (I, 192), imply a confidence in the ability of the mind to create its own eternity, encompassing all of the past in memory and all of the future in hope. Further, the flight of the lovers on the swift steeds at the end, this last ride together, ineluctably summons Browning and suggests the same kind of existential joy in the moment. As in "The Last Ride Together" the intensity of the experience, its special poignance, is born of the lover's unblinking awareness that the end is near: "ah love, shall we win at the last?"(I, 192).

Hesperia does not, however, represent a Wordsworthian vision. Named for the home of the dead and described as the "daughter of sunset and slumber," she is Swinburne's version of the faith that looks through death, but that faith is not Wordsworthian pantheism. As the existential discovery of eternity in the moment and of intensity in life implies, the faith involves a denial, not an affirmation, of consolatory divinities, either transcendent or immanent.

---

[37] "Lines Written among the Euganean Hills," ll. 335–36 (emphasis mine), in *Shelley: Poetical Works*, ed. Thomas Hutchinson, corrected by G. M. Matthews (Oxford, 1970), p. 558.

The nature of the faith that consoles Swinburne can be understood by reference to the wind that inspires the speaker at the beginning of the poem. The wind does not merely bring him memories of his own past, but brings memories of the past of the race:

> a wind sets in with the autumn that blows from the region of stories,
> Blows with a perfume of songs and of memories beloved from a boy,
> Blows from the capes of the past oversea to the bays of the present. . . .
>
> [I, 187]

The lines suggest that the giantess Hesperia represents the entire historical and legendary past and that a devotion to her is a devotion to the stories, the songs, and the memories that carry the past into the present; it is a devotion to art. There is, moreover, just a hint that the soul of man consists of his internalization of these memories of the past, for it is only by union with Hesperia that the soul is brought back to life. This reading is strengthened by the fact that the second line of the poem, "Full of the sunset, and sad, if at all, with the fulness of joy," is a clear recollection of the idea of being "Sad with the whole of pleasure" which pervades those sonnets of Rossetti dealing with the harmonious interpenetration of soul with sense.[38]

The salvation of the soul by art emerges more clearly in other works. The paired poems imitating classical meters, "Hendecasyllabics" and "Sapphics," deal with the same themes as the three-act lyrical monodrama. "Hendecasyllabics," a poem of apocalypse, echoes the language of the book of Revelation:

> I heard as it were a noise of waters
> Moving tremulous under feet of angels
> Multitudinous, out of all the heavens. . . .
>
> [I, 216]

The vision is not of regeneration, however, but of the bland emptiness of sea and water. Recalling Shelley's description of the dead Keats in "Adonais," the poem concludes with a vision of unredeemable death:

[38] "For a Venetian Pastoral," *The Works of Dante Gabriel Rossetti*, ed. William M. Rossetti (London, 1911), p. 188.

the winter begins, the weeping winter,
All whose flowers are tears, and round his temples
Iron blossom of frost is bound for ever.

[I, 217]

After the recognition of the void in "Hendecasyllabics," "Sapphics" proposes the same small hope that "Hesperia" had proposed after "The Garden of Proserpine." "Hesperia" offered a gentler love than the passion of the "Dolores" phase; it offered, in fact, compassion, and by contrasting it with the ephemerality of love, implied that pity is immortal: "Pity, not love, that is born of the breath and decays with the blood" (I, 189). Hesperia is both the land of the dead and a daughter of Venus (I, 187) and is clearly associated with song and story. The giantess of "Sapphics" is, fittingly, Sappho, who is associated with Aphrodite and, by virtue of her suicidal leap into the oblivious sea, death. In both poems, then, the hope is associated with a figure who represents a strange mixture of life, death, and song. In "Sapphics," moreover, as in "Hesperia," the song that redeems is not the original song of "exceeding passion" (I, 220) but the song of infinite pity, the song of love seen through a filter of the certainty of death. The last three stanzas of "Sapphics" describe the death of passion and, as in "Hesperia," "the love that revives as a ghost rearisen":

All withdrew long since, and the land was barren,
Full of fruitless women and music only.
Now, perchance, when the winds are assuaged at sunset,
    Lulled at the dewfall,

By the gray sea-side, unassuaged, unheard of,
Unbeloved, unseen in the ebb of twilight,
Ghosts of outcast women return lamenting,
    Purged not in Lethe,

Clothed about with flame and with tears, and singing
Songs that move the heart of the shaken heaven,
Songs that break the heart of the earth with pity,
    Hearing, to hear them.

[I, 221]

The only absolute available to man is that unredeemable death is his eternal portion. The desolating vision of "Hendecasyllabics" represents a kind of paradoxical affirmation of the one fixity in a relative world. But in accepting this absolute the poet has a firm, if limited, basis on which to build. The same basic pattern recurs persistently: "Anactoria" is, essentially, about passionate love that leads to a quest for oblivion but also to an immortality of song; "The Triumph of Time" follows the same course, ending with both the description of the singer, Jauffré Rudel, and with the finished poem as evidence that the poet's own passion, followed by a longing for death, finally resulted in the production of a song of compassion.

The essential ideas underlying the dramatic pattern can now be briefly summarized. The first stage, that of passion—whether the ideal passion of "The Triumph of Time" or the perverse lust of "Dolores"—shows man tormented by his divided nature, by the incompatibility of soul and sense. The second represents man exhausted by passion and willing to still the battle within himself by destroying both body and soul. At this point he comes to the crucial recognition that body and soul are equal, at least insofar as both are perishable. In the final stage, the first is seen muted by the second, and it is here that art, carrying passion through death, redeems the soul. This phase provides at least a meager consolation for existence, the consolation that something of a man lives on in the record of his passion commemorated in song.

All of this is consistent with Swinburne's exposition of the morality of his lyrical monodrama—all of it, that is, except the most important point. The pattern applies both to the individual man and to all of society, and Swinburne leads his readers to believe that it represents a progressive movement from wild hedonism to serene contemplation. For the individual, this is true—passionate youth gives way to a sober recognition of mortal limitations and finally to a calm, reflective old age: years bring the philosophic mind. Nothing could be more unsuitable, however, as a pattern of history. The cycle moves from passion through recognition and finally to aesthetic detachment, but if there is to be more art, there must be a return to passion—the cycle must begin again. But the past, memorialized and retained in art, provides an ever-expanding base and allows ever-increasing passion and art. Mankind is continually building, as in Blake, a New Jerusalem, a celestial city of art. Swinburne is wholly disingenuous in implying that the stage of pagan pleasures, of "fierce and frank sensualities," is an unfortunate and regrettable fact of life. Rather it is absolutely necessary, since if it were not for Sappho's fierce pain and pleasure there would be no Sapphic poetry. Nothing of Sappho would survive her plunge into the sea, and, in addition, no song of Sappho's would float in the wind to redeem the spirit of the poet of "Hesperia" or "Sapphics."

The central historical doctrine of *Poems and Ballads* is that of continual change without progress. The spirit of mankind passes through various stages, but not toward some far-off divine event. As the "Hymn to Proserpine" emphasizes, man's gods change and die; paganism gives way to Christianity in the speech of the fourth-century Roman poet and Christianity gives way to paganism in Swinburne's dramatic monologue of the nineteenth century. The symbol of continual change without progression, in "The Hymn to Proserpine" as everywhere in Swinburne, is the sea:

All delicate days and pleasant, all spirits and sorrows are cast
Far out with the foam of the present that sweeps to the surf of the past;
Where beyond the extreme sea-wall, and between the remote sea-gates,
Waste water washes, and tall ships founder, and deep death waits:
Where, mighty with deepening sides, clad about with the seas as with
          wings,
And impelled of invisible tides, and fulfilled of unspeakable things,
White-eyed and poisonous-finned, shark-toothed and serpentine-curled,
Rolls, under the whitening wind of the future, the wave of the world.
                                                              [I, 77]

Like Proteus, its god, the sea constantly changes shape as waves rise and fall, but it never changes in its essence. For Swinburne the fact that changes on the sea of life are only superficial was irrelevant— the important point was that each wave, once past, never returns, that death is oblivion. Like Tennyson, or like Beddoes, who saw death as a joyous return to the universal All, he was capable of seeing death as a welcome event (as in "The Garden of Proserpine"), but his main concern was not how man should die but how he should live in the face of death. His answer, in spite of the disingenuousness of the "Notes on Poems and Reviews," appears to be that man's mortality should compel him to live and love with the greatest possible intensity and that his consolation should be found in the art that results from intense pain and pleasure. He believed, with Blake, that a man who fails to live in life will certainly fail to live thereafter, that a man who lives fully and creatively will at least live on in his work. His energy will survive him, as Sappho's did, to be passed on to inspire succeeding generations.

The elegy on Baudelaire, "Ave atque Vale," written in 1867, just after the publication of *Poems and Ballads*, shows the point at which Swinburne's thought had arrived by the time the volume was completed, and is the culmination of his early thought on the subject of art's consolation for mortality. The greatest consolation for Baudelaire is that the life of passion and pain, "Fierce loves, and lovely leaf-buds poisonous" (III, 53), is over, and he has found the peace of oblivion:

> Content thee, howso'er, whose days are done;
> > There lies not any troublous thing before,
> > Nor sight nor sound to war against thee more,
> > For whom all winds are quet as the sun,
> > All waters as the shore.
>
> [III, 60]

The consolation for those who survive him, however, is that because he lived life intensely, Baudelaire produced works of art that pass on to us the sound of his sad soul:

> > this the sound of thy sad soul,
> > The shadow of thy swift spirit, this shut scroll
> I lay my hand on, and not death estranges
> > My spirit from communion of thy song—
> > These memories and these melodies that throng
> Veiled porches of a Muse funereal—
> > These I salute, these touch, these clasp and fold
> > As though a hand were in my hand to hold,
> Or through mine ears a mourning musical
> > Of many mourners rolled.
>
> [III, 56]

The passion, the suffering, of Baudelaire, tamed of its fierceness and transmuted to compassionate mourning, reaches across the grave, out of oblivion, to comfort the mourner. Death is defeated, to a limited extent at least, not by repression of the body by the soul, as the prevailing ascetic morality insists, but by energetic life and creation. The void is filled by art, and human life is given significance. As the metaphorical clasping of hands suggests, moreover, the loneliness and solitude of the individual man are overcome by communion in art, and, as the very idea of communion implies, art has become a sort of secular religion.

These lines from "Ave atque Vale," the very summit of Swinburne's poetic achievement, are also the culmination of all the thought that went into *Poems and Ballads*. The central concern of that volume had been the problem of how to cope with the agony of life and the inevitability of death. The idea, tentatively and obscurely set forth in such poems as "Hesperia," "Sapphics," and "Anactoria," that art can provide needed comfort for man and break through his solipsistic isolation, finally finds full expression in "Ave atque Vale," a poem that sets forth for the first time a comprehensive myth of poetry as salvation.

V

The truth of poetry, however, as Swinburne would be the first to insist, is not in its ideas, but its form, and *Poems and Ballads* is not a philosophical tract. Discussion of form is, nevertheless, simplified when the ideas are first understood, for in this volume Swinburne strives to meet his own critical standard that form and content should be fused in perfect harmony, that one should be a perfect reflection of the other.

In the universe of *Poems and Ballads* change and flux hide but do not conceal the gaping void in which man seeks meaning just as the waves of the sea only superficially hide its eternal depths; change is the only constant, certainty of oblivion the only truth. Swinburne insists, repeatedly, that before art can be created, man, subjecting himself to the painful flux of life, must acknowledge his mortal limits. The aim of poetry is to create truth in order to fill the void of meaninglessness and to bridge the emptiness between life and death. The truth created must be based on direct experience; it must reject all handed-down values unless they are proved upon the pulses, for the acceptance of traditional values is submission, not creation. Because true creativity begins without inherited assumptions, because it evolves meaning from a direct confrontation of life facing life, without intermediaries of conscience or moral purpose, it is essentially mythopoeic. The real meaning of the phrase "art for art's sake," as the essay on Blake gradually makes clear, is that poetic form and content must be in complete harmony, both with themselves and with the external world; and it is, therefore, basically a plea for a mythopoeic creation that grows organically and inevitably out of a direct confrontation of man with his surroundings, out of a complete merger of the self in the flux of experiential reality—an experiential reality, of course, that includes the continual reexperiencing and recreation of the creative Apollonian song of man.

Swinburne's poetry, in a number of ways, is particularly well adapted to its mythopoeic function. The most notable quality of his verse, its remarkable euphony, expresses in form what Swinburne was attempting to express in content, for music, as he said in a memorable passage in "The Triumph of Time," has the power of bringing all things into unity. Lamenting the broken love affair that has divided his heart from his flesh, he says:

> I shall hate sweet music my whole life long.
>
> The pulse of war and passion of wonder
>   The heavens that murmur, the sounds that shine,
> The stars that sing and the loves that thunder,
>   The music burning at heart like wine,
> An armed archangel whose hands raise up
> All senses mixed in the spirit's cup
> Till flesh and spirit are molten in sunder—
>   These things are over, and no more mine.

[I, 51–52]

Swinburne, though for very different reasons from Pater's, saw all art aspiring to the condition of music—his highest term of critical approbation is *harmony*—and, as this passage indicates, he saw the essence of all things characterized by the sounds they make. Throughout his career his poetry expresses the Paterian idea of the supremacy of music among the arts and merges it with his own idea

of music as the soul of art. Perhaps the clearest expression of the
idea is found in the late poem "Plus Ultra":

> From depth and height by measurers left immense,
> Through sound and shape and colour, comes the unsure
> Vague utterance, fitful with supreme suspense.
>
> All that may pass, and all that must endure,
> Song speaks not, painting shows not: more intense
> And keen than these, art wakes with music's lure
>   Soul within sense.

            [V, 140]

He refers to poetry almost invariably as song, and in "Ave atque
Vale" it is the *sound* of Baudelaire's sad soul that he perceives across
the abyss. When the distinctive sounds of all things are merged in
the harmonious fusion of music, soul and sense are reunited and the
full life of the artist merges with the full life beyond him. The prime
condition for mythopoeic poetry is met.

    In spite of the euphony of his verse and in spite of his vast respect
for music in principle, Swinburne was the most unmusical of poets.
He had little or no musical training and was, according to Edmund
Gosse, "remarkably devoid of 'ear.'"[39] Francis Jacques Sypher, Jr.,
however, has shown that Swinburne had a keen appreciation of the
music of Wagner,[40] and though it is unlikely that Wagner's music
could have had much influence on Swinburne's prosody by 1866, an
interesting similarity between the music of the composer and the
prosody of the poet may be noted. Even the most unmusical of
listeners would be aware of Wagner's remarkably long, unbroken
passages held together by the subtle and continual metamorphoses
of the central themes, or leitmotifs. The syntax of Swinburne's
poetry follows the same pattern and is well described by Robert A.
Greenberg: "Swinburne's typical mode in the poems that make up
the 1866 volume is to establish a governing context for each of his
poems, and then, the context in control, to press it, tonally and

---

[39] Quoted by Francis Jacques Sypher, Jr., in "Swinburne and Wagner," *Victorian Poetry*, 9 (1971), 167.
[40] Ibid., pp. 165–83.

thematically, to its outer limits."[41] The stanzaic forms and rhythms never change within the poem, but persistently (some might say monotonously—of Swinburne as of Wagner) expand until everything that can be said has been said. "Dolores," for example, consists of fifty-five rhythmically identical stanzas, all embellishing an essentially simple description of the archetypal whore. A more profound similarity may be noted, however, in Swinburne's long, almost interminable, sentences, such as the closing sentence of "Hesperia":

> They [Swift horses of fear or of love] are swifter than dreams, they are
>> stronger than death; there is none that hath ridden,
> None that shall ride in the dim strange ways of his life as we ride;
> By the meadows of memory, the highlands of hope, and the shore that is
>> hidden,
> Where life breaks loud and unseen, a sonorous invisible tide;
> By the sands where sorrow has trodden, the salt pools bitter and sterile,
>> By the thundering reef and the low sea-wall and the channel of years,
> Our wild steeds press on the night, strain hard through pleasure and peril,
>> Labour and listen and pant not or pause for the peril that nears;
> And the sound of them trampling the way cleaves night as an arrow
>> asunder,
>> And slow by the sand-hill and swift by the down with its glimpses of
>> grass,
> Sudden and steady the music, as eight hoofs trample and thunder,
>> Rings in the ear of the low blind wind of the night as we pass;
> Shrill shrieks in our faces the blind bland air that was mute as a maiden,
>> Stung into storm by the speed of our passage, and deaf where we past;
> And our spirits too burn as we bound, thine holy but mine heavy-laden,
>> As we burn with the fire of our flight; ah love, shall we win at the last?
>>   [I, 192]

The sentence goes on and on, held together by the persistent, rushing meter as by a leitmotif and achieving its meaning not by thematic progression but by inclusion. Swinburne could have ended the sentence after any semicolon, but chose instead to fill the interstices between independent clauses with subordinate clauses that modify either the preceding or succeeding main clause equally well. The result is a blurring of grammatical divisions as the sentence

---

[41] Greenberg, p. 100.

piles on series of parallel phrases, gradually accumulating and expanding until it seems to encompass all of nature (meadows, highlands, shores, reefs), all of time (the past in memory, the future in hope), all of human emotion (fear, love, hope, sorrow), the illusion of dreams and the reality of death. Josephine Miles has observed that expanding syntactical structures reflect a perception of reality as consisting of indissoluble interconnections, noting that writers "from De Quincey to Carlyle to Macaulay to Darwin, Ruskin, Arnold, Pater and then to Julian Huxley, with the support of poets like Keats, Tennyson, Swinburne, Whitman" all use such structures to describe what she calls "Victorian reality."[42] Swinburne employs such structures to an extent that leaves even those other Victorian masters of volubility behind, but for him (as for De Quincey and perhaps Carlyle) the syntax reflects not a perceived reality but a created reality. It is significant that the best example of his use of this type of syntax in *Poems and Ballads* is from "Hesperia," a poem that sets out to fill the void seen in "The Garden of Proserpine," for his replacement of grammatical divisions with connections, his housing of disparate elements of reality within the conceptual framework of a single sentence, represents the ability of the artist to create harmony from chaos. The disparate elements are fused in harmonious unity by the elaborate rhetorical structure and by the poetic form. The characteristically Swinburnian glut of alliteration, assonance, consonance, and vowel play enhances the effect by fusing the words together by sound, and even his habitual pairings of nouns and phrases (such as "dreams" and "death," "meadows of memory," and "highlands of hope," and "slow by the sand-hill and swift by the down") contribute to the sense of all-inclusiveness. In a description of the prose of Thomas De Quincey, J. Hillis Miller has described a similar syntactic strategy in a way that is strikingly relevant to an understanding of Swinburne:

If De Quincey's aim is to fill the largest possible mental space, then it follows that he should seek the most widely separated opposites which he can still manage to keep in pregnant tension. Poetry it is, or poetic prose, which creates the most expanded continuum by oscillating between the most widely distant polar antagonists. De Quincey's descriptions of poetry

---

[42] Josephine Miles, *Poetry and Change* (Berkeley and Los Angeles, 1974), p. 126.

often contain the idea of an equilibrium of opposing forces combined with the notion that language can, like opium dreams, be a "cloud-scaling swing" which will traverse and fill up the whole distance between the lowest deep and the highest height.[43]

Swinburne's pairings, frequently of opposites, do exactly that, filling mental space and obliterating the abyss of meaninglessness which a simpler, less creative perception would leave uncovered. When he pairs dreams and death, for example, Swinburne not only brings illusion and stark reality into at least grammatical relationship, but by implication he also includes all the gradations of consciousness between the extremes. Greenberg observes that the "integrative quality" of Swinburne's verse, "the sense of space occupied and explored," is one of his norms of excellence.[44] I would add that it becomes an increasingly more important aesthetic standard as Swinburne saw the necessity of filling the cosmic void left by the absence of a guiding purpose in the universe. The elaborate syntactic form of "Hesperia" provides only a feeble hint of the remarkable lengths to which Swinburne would go later in his career, as in the astonishing forty-four line sentences that begin the "Prelude" and the final book of *Tristram of Lyonesse* or, as we shall see, in the astonishingly expansive and accumulative diction of such poems as "On the Cliffs."

Swinburne's more than liberal use of synesthetic imagery adds to the effect of the elaborate syntax and euphony of his verse, as a line describing the charms of Hesperia illustrates: "Thy silence as music, thy voice as an odour that fades in a flame" (I, 188). This synesthetic tour de force brings the senses of hearing, smell, sight, and even touch into a harmony of apprehension. The paradox that all of these senses are focused on nothing at all, on mere silence, is particularly interesting, for it reveals the extent to which Swinburne's mythopoeic poetry is built on void. At the heart of the unity is nothing at all; only the imagery, the art, exists meaningfully. Hesperia, the gentler love that completes Swinburne's trilogy of giantesses, follows the realization of nothingness in "The Garden of

[43] *The Disappearance of God: Five Nineteenth-Century Writers* (Cambridge, Mass., 1963), p. 45.
[44] Greenberg, p. 100.

Proserpine." Hesperia is created out of direct experience of life,
even though that experience is of oblivion. The synesthesia, the
musicality of the verse, and even the remarkable, if much chastised,
monotony of the cadences and rhymes in his poetry all indicate an
integrated apprehension that perceives the unified substratum of
existence, but that substratum is an impenetrable eternity. Swinburne's favorite metaphor for poetic form, as it is his favorite
metaphor for earthly life, is the sea. He describes human life as the
waves, individual human existence as a foam-flower, and acknowledges that these are merely superficialities when compared to the
eternal depths. As mortal life covers the oblivious, eternal sea,
Swinburne's imagery covers the void of meaninglessness. In the
face of a great emptiness, Swinburne constructs connections, ways
to unify the experience of life. His strategy for dealing with the void
is precisely analogous to Melville's in *Moby-Dick*, of which Robert
Martin Adams has brilliantly written that

if it is a triumph at all, *Moby Dick* has to be the triumph of an illusion and
suggestion in which the reader cooperates a little more than passively. Its
distinctive effects are hypnotic and incantatory—it flourishes before us
words like "profound," "mysterious," and "unbounded," which denote little
but gesture largely. And on the plane of verbal pantomime *Moby Dick* may
be a momentous experience. . . . For the antagonism between the eagerly
grasping mind and elusive reality is fundamental to all other antagonisms in
the book; so that it is the book's ultimate failure after exhaustive efforts to
express its theme which is presumed to constitute best evidence of its
success in handling it.[45]

The attempt to unify the senses with synesthetic imagery has its
obverse in Swinburne's poetry in his use of a Baudelairean scheme
of correspondences among external things. Just as one sense may
shade off into another, so the object of perception may suddenly be
transmuted. The synesthetic imagery itself transforms color to
sound, sound to smell, and so on, but Swinburne's transformations
are contextual as well as imagistic. In "Felise," to take the simplest
case, the description of a lover's eyes demonstrates how perception
of external reality constantly metamorphoses that reality:

[45] *Nil: Episodes in the Literary Conquest of Void during the Nineteenth Century*
(New York, 1966), p. 146.

> O fervent eyelids letting through
> Those eyes the greenest of things blue,
> The bluest of things grey. . . .
>
> [I, 206]

On a larger scale, all his giantesses are metamorphoses of something else. The embodiment of a universal ideal in a single figure is a metamorphosis of the abstract into the concrete. As Susanne K. Langer has said, in a remark that applies perfectly to Swinburne's mythopoeia: "The 'making' of mythology by creative bards is only a metamorphosis of world-old and universal ideas."[46] Proserpine, for example, is a metamorphic embodiment of the certainty and finality of death. All metaphor, of course, involves metamorphosis in this very broad sense, but what is unique in Swinburne's personifications is that they themselves constantly change their shape. Faustine, as we have seen, changes in every successive incarnation; Dolores's "skin changes country and colour" (I, 176); and Swinburne's description of Hesperia shifts from the description of a wind to that of a bird, a dream, and finally a woman.

Meredith's famous comment that Swinburne's early work "lacks an internal centre" is therefore, in a sense, true—at least for such poems as "Hesperia."[47] Those poems that follow the recognition of void center on nothing at all. Swinburne's poetic strategy in such poems is entirely devoted to filling that void or, to use his own metaphor, to covering the still depths of oblivion with meaningful, moving life. His mythopoeic technique, the personification of abstract ideas in archetypal but constantly metamorphosing figures, is a determined strategy to create meaning. The recognition that no higher reality exists than the body of man makes Swinburne's choice of personification as a mythopoeic technique almost inevitable. One element of mythmaking is the elevation of nature to the status of a divinity, and this is exactly what Swinburne is doing when he personifies death and oblivion in the person of Proserpine, or sadistic lust in the person of Dolores. The most striking fact about

[46] Quoted by Sister M. Bernetta Quinn, in *The Metamorphic Tradition in Modern Poetry* (New Brunswick, N.J., 1955), p. 8.

[47] George Meredith, from a letter to a friend in 1861, rpt. in Hyder, ed., *Swinburne*, p. 124.

the world, as he saw it, was its continual change, and the constant metamorphoses of his giant personifications reflect that truth.

The deeper truth, that no meaning exists in life beyond change, that no transcendent god is directing these metamorphoses, that no principle of direction is shaping them into a pattern of significance, is reflected in the constant tendency of Swinburne's verse to skirt nullity. Significantly, those poems of Swinburne that are intended to give hope, such as "Hesperia," are those poems in which a concrete figure is hardest to pin down. Hesperia's constant changes of shape correspond to the view that there is no absolute to give consolation but only the creation of a hope from the emptiness, from the wind, a bird, a dream. The real meaning of "Hesperia" is its form, not its content, for it is the form of the poem, its subtle transformations of nothing at all into a principle of love, that represents the real consolation for Swinburne. There is no god but man—the idea recurs constantly throughout Swinburne's poetry—and man would be no god without the godlike power of creation from the void.

Poems and Ballads is not characterized by "Hesperia." Though that poem foreshadows Swinburne's later work in many ways, it is not typical of the volume published in 1866. The majority of the poems are concerned not with how to deal with life once the bitter truth is known but with the necessity of coming to the bitter truth. Those poems dealing with the first stage of development, "Dolores," "Faustine," and so on, do not begin with an assumption of life's meaninglessness, of the oblivion beyond the grave. They are poems of rebellion against the existing order, but they are within the tradition that separates body and soul, and they begin with inherited materials. The speaker of "Dolores" is, in Deleuze's terms, a "porteur," one who bears the weight of his ancestor's ideas, and his headlong rush toward self-destruction only serves to show how firmly entrenched he is in the last ages of a nihilistic mode of thought. For this reason the poems of the "Dolores" phase and even of the "Proserpine" phase are not so essentially creative, or mythopoeic, as "Hesperia." Dolores is not a creation from the void but an inversion of the Virgin; Faustine is based on a historical reality, and Proserpine is borrowed from Greek myth with only slight changes. These poems using giant figures borrowed from other myths and other cultures, are, to a considerable extent, mythological rather than mythopoeic. To the extent that they borrow from received mythology and legend they are comparative rather than creative; and to the extent that they operate within the received framework of Western thought they fall short of the aesthetic goal Swinburne had established in his *William Blake*: the harmonious fusion of soul and sense, form and content, man and his world. These poems are brilliantly successful on other grounds, but it is only in poems like "Hesperia," "The Triumph of Time," "Anactoria," and "Hermaphroditus," poems which both acknowledge and defeat the emptiness of life caused by the absence of a transcendent god, that Swinburne fully meets the requirements of his rigorous artistic standards.

In a sense *Poems and Ballads* may be read as an autobiographical record of Swinburne's own passage through the "Dolores" and "Proserpine" stages and of his emergence on the other side in "Hesperia." Because most of the volume is concerned with the recognition of oblivion, of man's limits and isolation, it may be considered Swinburne's "centre of indifference." In the next chapter we shall see how *Atalanta in Calydon*, written in the same period as *Poems and Ballads*, presents much the same problems, and how *Erechtheus*, written after passing through the void, achieves the aesthetic, formal goals foreshadowed in "Hesperia."

The Greek Plays
Atalanta in Calydon
and *Erechtheus*

SWINBURNE'S TWO GREEK tragedies, *Atalanta in Calydon* and *Erechtheus*, were published at the beginning and end of the most turbulent decade of his life. Between the publication of *Atalanta* in February 1865 and *Erechtheus* in January 1876 Swinburne went through repeated phases of alcoholic collapse and recovery, astonished literary London with his antics, generated vastly exaggerated tales of his debauchery, and, most importantly, shifted his perspective dramatically from the art for art's sake of *William Blake: A Critical Essay* and *Poems and Ballads* to the republican ardor of *Songs before Sunrise* and *Songs of Two Nations*. The divergence of theme and style in the two plays reflects the substantial changes wrought on Swinburne by this eventful decade, as critics have always recognized. T. Earle Welby, with his usual vigor, has pointed out the fundamental difference: "The two plays on the Greek model have much less in common than their structure suggests. . . . *Atalanta* is the work of an inspired boy: *Erechtheus*, with as real though less readily recognizable an inspiration, is the work of a man."[1] William R. Rutland agreed, adding that, of the two tragedies, "the first is a ruined spring; and the second high summer in full serenity."[2] Swinburne was, of course, a full twenty-eight years old when *Atalanta in Calydon* was published, yet while the implicit denigration of the earlier play in these critical judgments cannot be accepted, the suggestion that Swinburne is a far more mature poet in *Erechtheus* cannot be denied. The process of matur-

[1] *A Study of Swinburne* (1926; rpt. New York, 1969), p. 156.
[2] *Swinburne: A Nineteenth Century Hellene* (Oxford, 1931), p. 191.

ing, however, was more complex than Welby and Rutland realized and, as we shall see, follows the pattern of growth prefigured in *Poems and Ballads*.

Before taking up the differences between the two plays, however, it is worth while to examine briefly the similarities implied by the choice of form. The extent to which the tragedies follow Greek form and structure and adhere to the Greek spirit has been hotly debated ever since their initial publication. Douglas Bush, always on the attack where Swinburne is concerned, states categorically that "no modern English poet has been more saturated in Greek drama and poetry than Swinburne, and none has been more essentially un-Greek in spirit, form, and style," while Samuel Chew, less emphatically, observes that although *Erechtheus* is very classical indeed, the "exuberance of its form and the angry fatalism of its contents" render *Atalanta* "un-Greek." C. M. Bowra takes the position that though "the form of *Atalanta* is not always or strictly Greek, its subject and spirit are." Harold Nicolson and Rutland, on the other hand, have both broken *Atalanta* down into its component parts to show that it is essentially, if not scrupulously, faithful to the Greek models in form, but both agree that it is unfaithful, to its credit, in content.[3] In short, a great deal of ink has been expended on the question. The important point is not how scrupulously Swinburne followed his models structurally but why he followed them at all, why he thought them fit vehicles for the poetic urges he wished to articulate.

He must, unquestionably, have considered the themes of *Atalanta in Calydon* and *Erechtheus* to be essentially Greek, for his strong belief in the necessary harmony of form and content in art would have dissuaded him from a merely arbitrary adoption of the form. By 1865 he had already established himself as a master of literary imitation—he had adopted the form of Elizabethan tragedy to write *The Queen Mother*, *Rosamond*, and *Chastelard*, had imitated the border ballads in poems like "The King's Daughter" and "The

[3] Bush, *Mythology and the Romantic Tradition in English Poetry* (Cambridge, Mass., 1937), p. 328; Chew, *Swinburne* (Boston, 1929), p. 61; Bowra, *The Romantic Imagination* (Cambridge, Mass., 1949), p. 225; Nicolson, *Swinburne* (New York, 1926), pp. 73–92; Rutland, pp. 114–21.

Bloody Son," had imitated medieval French in the prose argument of "The Leper" and medieval sentiments in the poem itself, and had adopted Greek metric forms in "Sapphics" and "Hendecasyllabics." In every case the form and content of the poems were in perfect harmony. "Hendecasyllabics," for example, adopts the meter of classical elegy to mourn the mortal condition of man, "Sapphics" the meter of Sappho herself to capture the song of Sappho heard on the wind. All of Swinburne's imitations, in fact, rise above the level of mere pastiche without being false to the form. The poetry of Aeschylus, Sophocles, and even Euripides (whom Swinburne loathed but was indebted to) is passed on to future generations in the same way as Sappho's, and Swinburne catches and memorializes the memory of the ages by recreating forms fit to hold it. That the exact sentiments of the Greek tragedians could, or should, be captured cannot be expected, for Swinburne's intention is to recreate them as they make themselves felt by modern consciousness, by his own consciousness. Just as his reading of Blake is conditioned by all that he has thought, read, and experienced, by all that he *is,* so his reading of Aeschylus presents not the Greek Aeschylus but Swinburnian Aeschylus. The result is not the pastiche of Arnold's *Merope*, Greek tragedy exhumed, but a new, reinvigorated drama, Greek tragedy revivified.

The choice of form is significant in other ways as well. Greek tragedy is, to point out the obvious, pagan. No myth comparable to the dogmatic Christianity of later ages governs man's perceptions of the natural world; rather, he is left on his own to create meaning and consolation within a world of primal, seemingly indifferent forces. The Greek tragedian, having no faith in an afterlife that justifies human suffering, was forced to deal with the problem of mortality in precisely the way Swinburne was forced to deal with it after perceiving the void. Further, to the extent that the Greek tragedians used received myths to structure the universe of their plays, they used myths made by an earlier generation of poets—epic poets like Homer and Hesiod. This generation of epic poets was to the tragedians of Periclean Athens what the tragedians were to Swinburne; in both cases the structure of the universe is not provided by a transcendent God but by man.

Atalanta in Calydon, though published earlier, was written during the composition of *Poems and Ballads* and *William Blake* and gives utterance to the same themes. Swinburne was midway between the "Dolores" and the "Garden of Proserpine" phase at this time, seeing the emptiness at the end of life and raging against it. The outlook of the play therefore resembles that of the much despised Euripides, who sentimentalized man and attacked the gods in order to heighten the sense of man's tragic fate. It is significant, however, that Meleager's final cry, "the night gathers me, / And in the night shall no man gather fruit" (IV, 363), alludes to John 9:4 ("the night cometh, when no man can work"), for in so doing it echoes Teufelsdröckh's final cry in "The Everlasting Yea": "Work while it is called Today, for the Night cometh, wherein no man can work."[4] In Swinburne, as in Carlyle, the allusion marks the end of a period of despair and the beginning of a period of work and hope. *Erechtheus*, written shortly after *Songs before Sunrise*, shows Swinburne at the "Hesperia" phase of consciousness, having passed through the void and begun to create meaning on the other side. The outlook of this play resembles that of Aeschylus in its willingness to see significance in human actions and to build toward a City of Man. A more detailed account of each play will show how the themes, structures, and art embody Swinburne's developing mythopoeia and also how the poetry of his republican period conforms to the pattern of his development.

I

The story of Meleager and the burning brand was a perfect choice for Swinburne's first tragedy. It was one of the most popular tales among classical artists and was therefore demonstrably appealing to the Greek spirit. Since few of the ancient works dealing with the story survive in more than fragmentary form, the subject would be fresh to modern readers, and since none of the dramatic versions

[4] Thomas Carlyle, *Sartor Resartus* II.ix, ed. Charles Frederick Harrold (New York, 1937), p. 197.

survive, Swinburne would not be inviting inevitable, if odious, comparison.[5] Most importantly, the material of the Meleager myth was ideal as a vehicle for expressing the concerns actuating Swinburne in the early 1860s. The story tells of inflamed passions divided against moral will, of the body divided against the soul, of how, literally, the fierce flame burns on until, ineluctably, nothing is left but ashes and blank death.

The central theme of *Atalanta in Calydon* is the central theme of "Dolores": "Our lives and our longings are twain" (I, 180); the central truth of the Greek universe, expressed by the chorus, is the gods' dictum that "Joy is not, but love of joy shall be" (IV, 315). Man's fate is succinctly described in the famous second chorus: "In his heart is a blind desire, / In his eyes foreknowledge of death" (IV, 285). The drama is an enactment of the fatal truth of this generalization. Meleager, the tragic hero, longs for the unattainable ideal, for Atalanta, and thereby tears himself from Althaea, from the rule of natural bonds. Love, in *Atalanta*, as in *Poems and Ballads*, is a symbol of the desire which separates body and soul; the chorus describes the result of love as "soul's division" (IV, 280) and as "division of soul and disease" (IV, 301) extending from the individual to society, as "The dividing of friend against friend, / The severing of brother and brother" (IV, 303). The clearest expression of the theme, however, comes not from the chorus but from Althaea:

> The gods have wrought life, and desire of life,
> Heart's love and heart's division; but for all
> There shines one sun and one wind blows till night.
> And when night comes the wind sinks and the sun,
> And there is no light after, and no storm,
> But sleep and much forgetfulness of things.
>
> [IV, 282]

Althaea sees the dangers of love clearly, but sees also, to her comfort, that the end of all is oblivion, the sweet sleep of the garden of

---

[5] An account of the ancient popularity of the theme can be found in Rutland, pp. 93–112. Rutland notes that both Sophocles and Euripides wrote plays entitled *Meleager* and that there is some evidence that Aeschylus may have dealt with the legend. Swinburne was indebted to a number of ancient writers, but primarily to Ovid, who recounts it in *Metamorphoses* VII.273–544.

Proserpine. It is Althaea, also, who most clearly recognizes that the tragedy of division is not limited to the individual or to society but extends to the very cosmos. For her the gods themselves are images of division. In one of the most enlightening comments in the play, she describes the war of Meleager and the Calydonians against the tribes stirred up against them by Artemis in terms of cosmic battle:

> for ye twain stood
> God against god, Ares and Artemis,
> And thou the mightier
>
> [IV, 293]

Althaea's perceptions of the divided cosmos are completely justified by the ensuing course of events—she is, in fact, almost omniscient in her grasp of the issues.

Her omniscience is not surprising, for she controls the central events of the play. But Althaea's role in the play is far more complex than this suggestion implies; she is, in fact, the very heart of the play. As William R. Rutland has observed: "there is only one character in it who is more than the merest outline. This is Althaea. In one sense she is the whole of the play, for she dominates it almost until the end. She brings about the tragedy; and the choruses are, as it were, prompted by her utterances."[6] To understand the primary theme of *Atalanta in Calydon*, the division of son from mother, we must first understand the complex characterization of Althaea.

Critics have always understood that the central act—almost the only act—of the play is the breaking of the maternal bond, but the play has never been fully understood because the nature of the bond has never been wholly apprehended. Althaea, making one of Swinburne's dominant points, informs Meleager that the love between them, between mother and son, is the strongest tie known to man; though nothing can be counted on in life, if anything of man endures, this love will:

> there is nothing stabile in the world
> But the gods break it; yet not less, fair son,
> If but one thing be stronger, if one endure,
> Surely the bitter and the rooted love

⁶Rutland, p. 178.

> That burns between us, going from me to thee,
> Shall more endure than all things.
>
> [IV, 298]

Althaea expresses the Swinburnian conviction that nothing is certain but change, and with unconscious irony she refers to the primary metaphor of the play, the burning brand, to remind us how little even the maternal bond can be counted upon. As if this were not sufficient, Swinburne emphasizes the futility of human calculations with Meleager's chillingly ominous reply:

> For what thou art I know thee, and this thy breast
> And thy fair eyes I worship, and am bound
> Toward thee in spirit and love thee in all my soul.
> For there is nothing terribler to men
> Than the sweet face of mothers, and the might.
>
> [IV, 298–99]

Every reference to the strength of the attachment between mother and son, in fact, is fraught with ironic implications that it is not strong enough. Repeatedly the characters and chorus refer to it with the communion imagery which, in *Poems and Ballads*, consistently implies frustrated attempts to achieve unity. The chorus, for example, reminds Althaea that

> the son lies close about thine heart,
> Full of thy milk, warm from thy womb, and drains
> Life and the blood of life and all thy fruit,
> Eats thee and drinks thee as who breaks bread and eats,
> Treads wine and drinks, thyself, a sect of thee;
> And if he feed not, shall not thy flesh faint?
> Or drink not, are not thy lips dead for thirst?
>
> [IV, 335]

The chorus refers to a period when the union between mother and son is complete, when the infant, suckling at the breast, is literally a part, a "sect," of the mother.[7] What they do not recognize, however,

---

[7] See John O. Jordan, "The Sweet Face of Mothers: Psychological Patterns in *Atalanta in Calydon*," *Victorian Poetry*, 11 (1973), 101–14. Jordan notes the significance of this passage and this word and rightly observes that it is part of a pattern of imagery in the play that stresses the importance of a return to primal

is that this Wordsworthian unity has ended, that Meleager has his own separate individuality—they ignore, in short, the cause of the tragedy.

The chorus is nevertheless correct, in an interesting way, in seeing Meleager as a part of Althaea, for from a certain perspective, he is. A man's life takes on meaning, individuality, because of its continuity—this is the consolation of Proustian and Wordsworthian memory and, as we have seen, part of Swinburne's consolation in "Hesperia." Meleager's individuality, in a sense Meleager himself, is contained within the remarkable memory of Althaea. Althaea is not only, as Rutland suggests, the whole of the play to the extent that she instigates the action and inspires the chorus, but also, because of her memory and her dreams, she is, in an idealistic sense, the whole universe of the play. Her memory, as Welby and Rutland have recognized, is her most striking characteristic;[8] she is constantly recalling past days—her own earlier life, her brothers as children, and all of Meleager's life. At one point she reminds Meleager that his whole life, all that he is, is preserved within her mind:

> what lies light on many and they forget,
> Small things and transitory as a wind o' the sea,
> I forget never; I have seen thee all thine years
> A man in arms, strong and a joy to men
> Seeing thine head glitter and thine hand burn its way
> Through a heavy and iron furrow of sundering spears;
> But always also a flower of three suns old,
> The small one thing that lying drew down my life
> To lie with thee and feed thee; a child and weak,
> Mine, a delight to no man, sweet to me.
>
> [IV, 297]

Insofar as Swinburne is sentimentalizing, his Greek model is Euripides, but Althaea's "remarkable tenderness of memory" is not merely Euripidean sentimentality, as Welby suggests, it is the single factor giving a sense of continuity to the lives of the characters.[9]

---

unity. Jordan, however, sees the central concern of the play as the Freudian, Oedipal conflicts of various characters rather than a more general concern with the role of man in nature.

[8] Welby, p. 159; Rutland, pp. 181–82.

[9] Welby, p. 159.

Althaea's memory serves an Aeschylean as well as a Euripidean function, for it makes connections with the past and with the vast body of Greek legend. Her recollections of her sister, Leda, and of Leda's children, Helen and Clytaemnestra, remind us of the tragic lot of all men, just as Aeschylus' chorus constantly reminds us of the past and the elsewhere. It is largely through Althaea that Swinburne is able to make *Atalanta in Calydon* a cosmic tragedy, like Aeschylus' *Agamemnon*, rather than a domestic tragedy, like Euripides' *Hippolytus*. And it is her memory that precipitates the tragedy, forcing her to choose duty over love—to avenge her brothers by slaying her son. At the bottom of the primitive Greek conception of the universe is the sense of kinship, of the unbreakable blood ties of family relationship; in *Atalanta in Calydon* the intensity of Greek family feeling is recreated by Swinburne in the memory of Althaea. Her poignant memories of her sister and father, and particularly of her childhood spent with her brothers, provide the context in which the slaying of Meleager is possible, for the affections of her childhood vividly impinge upon her perceptions of the present. She sees Toxeus and Plexippus not only as they now are, "violent-souled" and "over-swift with hand and tongue" (IV, 288), but in all their continuity, from childhood to manhood. Like Meleager's, their individuality lives within her, is part of her essential being, and, as she tells the chorus, the murderer of these men murders a part of her:

> these my brethren born
> Ye have no part in, these ye know not of
> As I that was their sister, a sacrifice
> Slain in their slaying. I would I had died for these;
> For this man dead walked with me, child by child,
> And made a weak staff for my feebler feet
> With his own tender wrist and hand, and held
> And led me softly. . . .
>
> [IV, 331–32]

The reminiscence goes on, verging at times on bathos, its Euripidean sentimentality providing, perhaps, the only blot on a magnificent play, but the exploitation of feeling is necessary if Swinburne is to make Althaea's actions comprehensible to a modern audience. Not only does she lament the loss of her brothers in terms of memory, but the dread of memory, as Rutland has pointed out, immediately follows.[10]

> How shall I bear my dreams of them, to hear
> False voices, feel the kisses of false mouths
> And footless sound of perished feet, and then
> Wake and hear only it may be their own hounds
> Whine masterless in miserable sleep,
> And see their boar-spears and their beds and seats
> And all the gear and housings of their lives
> And not the men?
>
> [IV, 333]

Althaea's memory not only evokes for the reader the ways of primitive Greece, the ties of kinship as a social code; it forces her to live by the primitive code, the code of Nemesis and blood justice. She knows that if she sins against duty by failing to avenge her brothers, her memory will torment her like the very Furies.

Althaea unquestionably stands for the old order—a fact that has led to the most common reading of *Atalanta in Calydon*, which sees the fundamental division between Althaea and Meleager as a split between the old and new orders. In this view Althaea represents submission to the will of the gods, stoic acceptance of fate, and unquestioning obedience to law, while Meleager stands for a new order, an order that "sees life as something not merely to be endured but to 'lighten and lift up higher.'"[11] This reading is justified, to an extent, by Althaea's choice of duty over love, which establishes her as an advocate of the old ways—the ways of *Agamemnon* and *The Libation Bearers* rather than of *The Eumenides*. Her gods are the Furies of blood justice rather than the Athenian gods of wisdom, and her rejection of prayer to the gods ("I marvel what men do with prayers" [IV, 275]) and of love ("a thwart sea-wind full of rain and foam" [IV, 278]) reflects her belief in a soulless universe ruled only by fate and the laws of retribution. This interpretation is correct only in a limited way, however, for it fails to acknowledge the magnitude of Althaea's presence, fails to see that she does not

---

[10] Rutland, pp. 181–82.

[11] Thomas L. Wymer, "Swinburne's Tragic Vision in *Atalanta in Calydon*," *Victorian Poetry*, 9 (1971), 5.

merely advocate a certain social order but actually embodies a cosmic order. Her memory encompasses the lives of most of the major characters, and, as Rutland has said, she causes all of the most important events in the play. In addition, she is a dreamer, and her dreams are truth. She is a prophet who speaks from within the laws of nature:

> for wise men as for fools
> Love is one thing, an evil thing, and turns
> Choice words and wisdom into fire and air.
> And in the end shall no joy come, but grief,
> Sharp words and soul's division and fresh tears
> Flower-wise upon the old root of tears brought forth,
> Fruit-wise upon the old flower of tears sprung up,
> Pitiful sighs, and much regrafted pain.
> These things are in my presage, and myself
> Am part of them and know not; but in dreams
> The gods are heavy on me.
>
> [IV, 280]

These lines show us not only that Althaea's mind holds the future as well as the past, encompassing all of time, but also that she sees all things coming to an end with the inevitability of organic growth. The metaphoric use of flowers and fruit is, as we shall see, of primary importance in the play; for now it is sufficient to note that Althaea's vision is in complete harmony with the cycles of nature. Further, she does not merely speak for and in the terms of the laws of nature, but herself acts as a law of nature. Althaea states her own function later in the play:

> Fate's are we,
> Yet fate is ours a breathing-space; yea, mine,
> Fate is made mine for ever; he is my son,
> My bedfellow, my brother. You strong gods,
> Give place unto me; I am as any of you,
> To give life and to take life. Thou, old earth,
> That hast made man and unmade; thou whose mouth
> Looks red from the eaten fruits of thine own womb;
> Behold me with what lips upon what food
> I feed and fill my body; even with flesh
> Made of my body.
>
> [IV, 343]

Althaea defines herself in terms of the earth and of fate, which is, clearly, no more than natural law. The gods themselves must give place, for they have only the power of nature, and, in fact, as the lines imply, they do not exist outside of nature. The equation of Althaea and the earth, implicit throughout the play in such passages as this, becomes explicit at the end, when the dying Meleager bids her farewell, describing her as

> The source and end, the sower and the scythe,
> The rain that ripens and the drought that slays,
> The sand that swallows and the spring that feeds,
> To make me and unmake me—thou, I say,
> Althaea, since my father's ploughshare, drawn
> Through fatal seedland of a female field,
> Furrowed thy body, whence a wheaten ear
> Strong from the sun and fragrant from the rains
> I sprang and cleft the closure of thy womb,
> Mother. . . .
>
> [IV, 360]

As an archetypal earthmother, Althaea encompasses—at least in dramatic terms—reality; she is the source and end of Meleager, the source and end of the play.

I have dwelt upon the importance of Althaea because only when we fully appreciate what she stands for can we understand the significance of Meleager's love for Atalanta. Before the advent of Atalanta in Calydon, Meleager was in harmony with Althaea and with the cycles of nature. But Atalanta does not belong within those cycles. Oeneus describes her in terms that establish her as the polar opposite of Althaea; she is a "Virgin, not like the natural flower of things / That grows and bears and brings forth fruit and dies" (IV, 296). Even Plexippus, in ominous words, recognizes that she does not fit into the natural order of things, claiming that when a woman will go armed among men

> Then shall the heifer and her mate lock horns,
> And the bride overbear the groom, and men
> Gods; for no less division sunders these;
> Since all things made are seasonable in time,
> But if one alter unseasonable are all.
>
> [IV, 307]

Atalanta, the armed virgin, will never bear fruit, will never come to season, because she is separated from the life of nature. She herself says that she will always be "Far off from flowers of any bed or man," and, in a long series of images of winter, she implies her own unseasonableness:

> me the snows
> That face the first o' the morning, and cold hills
> Full of the land-wind and sea-travelling storms
> And many a wandering wing of noisy nights
> That know the thunder and hear the thickening wolves—
> Me the utmost pine and footless frost of woods
> That talk with many winds and gods, the hours
> Re-arisen, and white divisions of the dawn,
> Springs thousand-tongued with the intermitting reed
> And streams that murmur of the mother snow—
> Me these allure, and know me; but no man
> Knows, and my goddess only.
>
> [IV, 308–9]

As Atalanta implies, she is not to be identified with the natural world of men but with the ideal world of the gods. She is a votary of Artemis, was sent by Artemis (as Althaea recognizes) as a plague to Calydon, and is, in fact, almost indistinguishable from Artemis. According to Rutland, in fact, in early versions of the legend "it is probable that originally Atalanta was simply Artemis under another name." [12] When Meleager falls in love with her, he falls in love not with a natural woman but with a goddess, "holiest Atalanta" (IV, 305), a "light lit at the hands of the gods" (IV, 306). Any reference made by Melager to torches must be rather ominous; this one is especially so. His love for Atalanta is impossible to fulfill—like the love of "The Triumph of Time" or Sappho's love for Anactoria— because it seeks a transcendent rather than an earthly goal. Meleager's love for Atalanta is precisely analogous to that of the poet of Shelley's "Alastor" for a vision of the ideal; it is a denial of nature, a denial of the universe of Althaea. In the terms of *Poems and Ballads* and of *William Blake* his love is a denial of the body which seeks to exalt the soul, a denial symbolized by Atalanta's

---

[12] Rutland, p. 100.

ascetic virginity, her inability to bear fruit—her sterility. Meleager, worshiping an ideal, is not, as Wymer and others have maintained, advocating a new, creative kind of law—rather, he is advocating a form of theism. He does not, as has too often been suggested, lust after Atalanta, but worships her with a chaste love; he does not, like the worshiper of Dolores, exalt the body at the expense of the soul, but, like the Christian ascetic, exalts the soul at the expense of the body. The result, as we have seen, is the same in either case.

The hunting of the boar is, as Richard Mathews has said, emblematic of the denial of the world of generation that Atalanta and Meleager's love for her represent. Mathews rightly notes that

the boar is obviously masculine, and it becomes the focus of the opposition of male and female principles. There is something self-destructive in the hunt, for men are, in a sense, like Attis, killing their own symbol. Atalanta and Artemis are the true victors; only Atalanta, who first wounds the boar, is able to laugh at its carcass. For the men in the play, the hunt is intensely serious. Hyleus is killed on the tusk of the boar; Peleus shoots his own comrade; Ancaeus is destroyed by the charge of the wounded boar; Meleager kills Toxeus and Plexippus in a fight over the carcass; and Meleager himself is finally destroyed as a direct consequence of the hunt. The killing of the boar becomes a kind of self-emasculation on the part of the male hunters.[13]

As Mathews goes on to note, the play sets forth not only the negation of the male principle but of the female principle as well. It demonstrates, in fact, the negation of the world of generation, the world of the corporeal body.

The separation of Meleager from Althaea, then, must be understood as that of the spirit from the body, and this is precisely how the chorus describes his death:

How art thou rent from us,
    Thou that wert whole,
As with severing of eyelids and eyes, as with sundering of body and soul.
                                                                  [IV, 353]

Althaea herself sees that the division of sense and spirit is more than the tragedy of an individual, for she recognizes that in killing

[13] "Heart's Love and Heart's Division: The Quest for Unity in *Atalanta in Calydon*," *Victorian Poetry*, 9 (1971), 39–40.

Meleager she slays her "own soul" (IV, 339). This division of soul
from body is not just a division of mother from son; insofar as
Althaea represents the whole of the cosmos, it is a cosmic tragedy
comparable to the sundering of Blake's Eternal Man. And just as
Blake's Albion falls into division when the moral sense, represented
by Urizen, establishes itself as a false god, so Althaea falls into
division when her moral sense, represented by the delusory gods of
dreams, seizes control over her natural instincts:

Althaea: My dreams are fallen upon me; burn thou [Meleager] too.
Chorus: Not without God are visions born and die.
Althaea: The gods are many about me; I am one.
Chorus: She groans as men wrestling with heavier gods.
Althaea: They rend me, they divide me, they destroy.

[IV, 329]

All of this, of course, is brought about by love, which represents
man's desire to transcend his mortal state. As in *Poems and Ballads*,
man's failure to recognize his mortal limits, his insistence on a
dichotomy of body and soul, destroys him.

But Swinburne's most important points are made not just in the
dramatic action but in the images. *Atalanta in Calydon* is a lyrical
drama in which lyrical imagery is at least as important as dramatic
action. In this respect—despite critical judgments that the profusion of metaphor is unclassical[14]—Swinburne's dramatic form is
Aeschylean. Just as Aeschylus uses the central metaphor of the net,
embellished with such subsidiary metaphors as the curb, bit, yoke,
and snare, to portray the inevitability of fate in *Agamemnon*,[15] Swinburne uses that of the brand, embellished with such subsidiary
metaphors as branches, flowers, fruit, and the flame of passion, to
render the inevitable result of Meleager's revolt against the natural
order. The same early critic who found the profusion of images
unclassical found fault with the technique, claiming that

[14] Unsigned rev., in *Saturday Review*, 1865; rpt. in Clyde K. Hyder, ed., *Swinburne: The Critical Heritage* (New York, 1970), p. 13.
[15] See Richmond Lattimore's introduction to his translation of the *Oresteia*, in
Aeschylus I, ed. David Grene and Richmond Lattimore (New York, 1970), pp.
1–37.

the stock of things in the world which can be made to yield similes is, after all, not inexhaustible, and if every line is to contain a new figure, it needs a wonderfully acute and fertile mind to prevent the same or similar ones from recurring. Thus, through the poem we have a sense of flowers, stars, sea foam, wine, thunder, and fire, which grows at last a little fatiguing, and blunts the force of each particular image.[16]

In fact the repetition of key images is the glory of the play, for the repetitions are handled with such skill that the myriad images merge in an "intense diffusion" (in Shelley's phrase) so that, in the end, each implies the other. Richard Mathews has said that "if there is unity in *Atalanta*, it is a unity of form, a lyric unity which frames diversity within the creative and imaginative language of the poet."[17] Indeed, all nature is fused into a whole by Swinburne's esemplastic, lyrical imagination. Like Althaea, Swinburne speaks from within the very heart of nature.

The brand, the central symbol, metaphorically represents Meleager; it is "his twin-born fate" (IV, 290), born with him to die with him. All of the most important images in the play are present in Althaea's description of the twin birth of Meleager and the brand:

> I dreamed that out of this my womb had sprung
> Fire and a firebrand; this was ere my son,
> Meleager, a goodly flower in fields of fight,
> Felt the light touch him coming forth, and wailed
> Childlike. . . .
>
> [IV, 280–81]

Althaea's prophetic dream implicitly compares Meleager's birth not only to the brand but also to the growth of a flower and to the dawn of a new day. This last image—part of the play's network of references to the cycles of nature—invokes the beginning of the diurnal cycle and consequently implies its end. The inevitable completion of natural cycles is suggested from the beginning. The opening chorus sings of the return of spring:

[16] Rpt. in Hyder, ed., *Swinburne*, p. 13.
[17] Mathews, p. 46.

> frosts are slain and flowers begotten,
> And in green underwood and cover
> Blossom by blossom the spring begins.
>
> [IV, 274]

And Althaea answers with the assurance that regeneration is only a
prelude to another death:

> Night, a black hound, follows the white fawn day,
> Swifter than dreams the white flown feet of sleep;
> Will ye pray back the night with any prayers?
> And though the spring put back a little while
> Winter, and the snows that plague all men for sin,
> And the iron time of cursing, yet I know
> Spring shall be ruined with the rain, and storm
> Eat up like fire the ashen autumn days.
>
> [IV, 275]

Every reference to day or night, spring or winter, carries with it the
suggestion of continuing change and inevitable death. The appearance of Atalanta with her hounds, for example, suggests the return
of spring, celebrated by the chorus in terms of Artemis as the time
"When the hounds of spring are on winter's traces, / The mother of
months in meadow or plain" (IV, 273). The later association of
Atalanta with images of winter, however, equally implies the completion of the cycle in death.

Althaea's reference to Meleager as a "goodly flower" fits the pattern of this seasonal imagery and also opens into another network
of imagery, that of organic growth from seed to flower, flower to
fruit, fruit to destruction. The images of natural growth, as the
chorus makes clear, bear the same implications as those of natural
cycles:

> we wax old,
> All we wax old and wither like a leaf.
> We are outcast, strayed between bright sun and moon;
> Our light and darkness are as leaves of flowers,
> Black flowers and white, that perish; and the noon
> As midnight, and the night as daylight hours.
> A little fruit a little while is ours,
> And the worm finds it soon.
>
> [IV, 312–13]

Growth, in this world, is only progress toward destruction, so every reference to organic life is a reminder of death. Helen and Clytaemnestra are ominously described as "in their bloomless bud / And full of unblown life" (IV, 287). Everywhere in the play the ironic implication of fruition is the real point of the metaphor.

Althaea's prophetic dream of Meleager's death prefigures the fulfillment of her dream of his birth and also suggests how that fulfillment comes about:

> again
> I dreamt, and saw the black brand burst on fire
> As a branch bursts in flower, and saw the flame
> Fade flower-wise, and Death came and with dry lips
> Blew the charred ash into my breast; and Love
> Trampled the ember and crushed it with swift feet.
>
> [IV, 282]

The lines not only complete the image of fruition and death but also equate flame with the principle of growth and, interestingly, with love. The connection is made more clearly in the choral hymn to Aphrodite, who, it is said, was born an "evil blossom" and grew to be "bitter of fruit" (IV, 299), and, completing the metaphoric connection between love, organic growth, flame, and man's life, the chorus describes Love as a "fleshly blossom, a flame" (IV, 300). Love, the yearning for an ideal, is the flame that brings man's life to fruition in death. The branch that represents Meleager, then, represents the utter futility of human life—it must inevitably end in death, and the deluded attempts to find transcendence in an ideal only accelerate the process of burning out.

Meleager's defection from his mother, Althaea, can be finally understood as a defection from his mother, earth. He must ultimately die in any case, but his implicit denial of the natural cycles of life hastens the process. His devotion to Atalanta, in effect a "vision of winter in spring," represents a fall from harmony with nature, and, as in all myths of the fall, man brings nature down with him. Althaea, representing unfallen nature, is Meleager's source and end, and she is inextricably bound to him. The bond of motherhood, which Althaea said would endure if nothing of man did, is consummated in flame, for, after setting fire to the brand, Althaea burns along with Meleager; "behold," she says,

> I am kindled with the flames that fade in him,
> I am swollen with subsiding of his veins,
> I am flooded with his ebbing; my lit eyes
> Flame with the falling fire that leaves his lids
> Bloodless; my cheek is luminous with blood
> Because his face is ashen.
>
> [IV, 346]

Althaea is divided against herself just as Meleager was, and as she recognizes, her essential nature is changed utterly:

> all my life turns round on me;
> I am severed from myself, my name is gone,
> My name that was a healing, it is changed,
> My name is a consuming. From this time,
> Though mine eyes reach to the end of all these things
> My lips shall not unfasten till I die.
>
> [IV, 347]

Atalanta in Calydon presents a myth of the fall of man and nature, a fall symbolized by the mute presence of Althaea, the silent, passive symbol of nature, throughout the last quarter of the play. When man seeks higher gods, when Meleager seeks Atalanta, he turns his back on the true source of his being and destroys even the small comfort that may be gained from acceptance of life as it is.

The essential ideas of the play are, as has so often been noted, all present in the famous antitheistic chorus, "Who hath given man speech," that chorus which describes man's dilemma in terms of the "Dolores" phase of consciousness: "Joy is not, but love of joy shall be." It is worth quoting this chorus at some length because it has always been misunderstood, with the result that the play is not appreciated for what it is. Mostly on the basis of this chorus, *Atalanta in Calydon* has almost invariably been interpreted as "a tremendous denunciation of the all-powerful malignant providence that is responsible" for man's sufferings.[18] The actual lines, however, do not support this interpretation:

> now *we know not of them* [the Gods]; *but one saith*
> The gods are gracious, praising God; *and one,*
> *When hast thou seen? or hast thou felt his breath*

[18] Rutland, p. 124.

> Touch, nor consume thine eyelids as the sun,
> Nor fill thee to the lips with fiery death?
> *None hath beheld him, none*
> *Seen* above other gods and shapes of things,
> Swift without feet and flying without wings,
> Intolerable, not clad with death or life,
>   Insatiable, not known of night or day,
> The lord of love and loathing and of strife
>   Who gives a star and takes a sun away;
> Who shapes the soul, and makes her a barren wife
>   To the earthly body and grievous growth of clay;
> Who turns the large limbs to a little flame
>   And binds the great sea with a little sand;
> Who makes desire, and slays desire with shame;
>   Who shakes the heaven as ashes in his hand;
> Who, seeing the light and shadow for the same,
>   Bids day waste night as fire devours a brand,
> Smites without sword, and scourges without rod;
>   The supreme evil, God.
>
> Yea, with thine hate, O God, thou hast covered us,
>   *One saith. . . .*
>
> [IV, 314, emphasis mine]

Certainly the gods are being denounced for all of the grievous
injuries which man must suffer—the division of body and soul, the
inevitability of death. But it requires an uncommonly careless reading to neglect the lines italicized and conclude that the chorus,
speaking for Swinburne, is denouncing God. Yet on the basis of
such a reading even such an astute critic as Rutland, immediately
after citing a letter in which Swinburne declared that his religious
feeling consisted solely of a "turbid Nihilism," could interpret the
chorus as proof of the author's inverted theology: "When he wrote
Atalanta he believed passionately in a god (the slight verbal confusion of god and gods with fate is immaterial); without a god he could
not be; but the god he believed in was not good but evil."[19] Rutland
is clearly a little embarrassed by his interpretation, and well he
might be, for the chorus is obviously voicing nothing more than

[19] Ibid., p. 132.

agnosticism. The antitheism is not an attack on God, who may or may not exist, but an attack on theism, on religions that hold out a false ideal. The first "one" who "saith" represents conventional theology, the second represents Sadic inverted theology, and there is no more justification for the one than the other. The point of this chorus is the point of *Atalanta in Calydon* and of all of Swinburne's writing which we have so far examined: those who live their lives in accordance with an unsubstantiated faith, whether in good or evil, destroy themselves by dividing body and soul. The only truth man can know is the truth of nature, of Althaea, and he must, perforce, accept it.

This reading of the play is in some respects very close to that put forth by C. M. Bowra in *The Romantic Imagination*, for he too sees Meleager's love for Atalanta as a crime against the natural order, and yet Thomas L. Wymer is undoubtedly correct in refuting Bowra: "to suppose that Swinburne, the admirer of Blake, Sade, and Mazzini, could have written a serious play extolling, as Bowra says, 'the harmonious frame in which man can best live,' constructed of 'established habit and respected rules,' is little short of absurd."[20] Swinburne is not extolling "the harmonious frame in which man can best live"; he is lamenting the cosmic law in which man *must* live. Swinburne's vision in *Atalanta in Calydon* is almost intolerably bleak. He sees nothing but change and death at best, and destructive love at worst. Man cannot win, he can only try not to exacerbate his agony with false hopes.

This bleak vision is precisely what Swinburne had expressed in the "Dolores" and "Garden of Proserpine" poems of *Poems and Ballads*, but the play also provides some slight intimation of the consolation of "Hesperia." Richard Mathews, seeing that "*Atalanta* ends in disintegration," goes so far as to say that the play even denies the hope of artistic redemption: "Even the redemption of artistic vision is denied, impossible within the limits of an art which is but a part of the same universal laws operative in all creation."[21] Yet the very form of the play, a recreation of Greek tragedy, clearly implies the hope of "Sapphics"—that continual recreation in art

[20] Wymer, p. 8.
[21] Mathews, p. 45.

does redeem something of man. The love of Meleager for Atalanta, and even more "the bitter and the rooted love / That burns between" Althaea and Meleager, does endure, preserved and revivified by art. The play ends not with the divisions of the "Dolores" phase, but with the unity of death, acceptance of "The Garden of Proserpine." Meleager, dying, accepts his life and his death for what they are:

> this death was mixed with all my life,
> Mine end with my beginning: and this law,
> This only, slays me, and not my mother at all.
>
> [IV, 361]

And in the end, though he still longs for Atalanta, he worships Althaea, the principle of generation:

> Mother, I dying with unforgetful tongue
> Hail thee as holy and worship thee as just
> Who art unjust and unholy.
>
> [IV, 360]

She is neither just nor holy, but she is what is. Meleager, in the culmination of the metaphors of fruition, realizes that after this life there is no other: "the night gathers me, / And in the night shall no man gather fruit" (IV, 363). The only redemption Meleager can hope for is preservation in the generational memory of the race, and so he asks forgiveness of Althaea ("Ye know my soul albeit I sinned" [IV, 362]) and begs that she will remember him:

> Mother, thou sole and only, thou not these,
> Keep me in mind a little when I die
> Because I was thy first-born; let thy soul
> Pity me, pity even me gone hence and dead,
>
>   . . . . .
>   do thou
> Forget not, nor think shame; I was thy son.
>
> [IV, 361]

As in "Hesperia" and "Sapphics," the strong and bitter love must be transmuted to gentler compassion in order to find endurance in the memory of man. And, like the passion of Sappho, the song of Meleager's love is carried down the winds of memory and picked up in the song of Swinburne.

Swinburne's mythic technique in *Atalanta in Calydon* is identical with that in *Poems and Ballads*. The burden of the symbolic meaning is carried by giant forms of mythic women, Atalanta and Althaea, and the technique is essentially mythological rather than mythopoeic. The myth he presents is really an antimyth, for both the dramatic action and the lyrical imagery combine to argue the point that no transcendent values exist, that "no life lives for ever," and that the inevitable end of all man's strivings is oblivion. The whole play is designed to demonstrate its motto, a fragment from the lost *Meleager* of Euripides, which reads, in part, "each man, dying, is earth and shadow; the nothing sinks into nothingness." *Atalanta in Calydon* is perhaps the bleakest piece Swinburne ever wrote; its bleakness is forcibly stated in the second dedicatory poem to Landor: "Ah, fugitive is dust, fugitive is life. Which of these transient things is the lesser? Not dust but life."[22]

The only consolation in *Atalanta in Calydon* is that it was written in a form to reecho Greek tragedy and that it was written so well. The quality that saves the play from utter pessimism is the fusion of all of the images of natural cycles—flowers, fruit, flame, the hunt—into a perfect unity. C. M. Bowra has suggested that the pessimism is not oppressive because the remarkable music lifts us above it: "the special sweetness which lurks in all truly tragic poetry . . . is here separated from the fuller emotions which create it. It is too sweet to be distressing, and yet is none the less poetry."[23] While Bowra overstates the dichotomy of music and meaning in Swinburne's poetry, his comments point in a fruitful direction. Swinburne's imagery goes right to the heart of nature, captures the rhythms of the natural world, and speaks with prophetic voice from that world. To the extent that *Atalanta in Calydon* is mythopoeic, it is so because the imagery proceeds from a poetic perception of the actual life in nature. In a Nietzschean sense, the music and the imagery of the play are Dionysian, and the beauty and exuberance of the Dionysian world provide a context in which the Apollonian world of dramatic events becomes tolerable. The perfect fusion of the imagery, the constant sense that every image in every line im-

---

[22] Translated by Rutland, p. 394.
[23] Bowra, p. 247.

plies all of the other chains of imagery and, in fact, all of the play's meaning provides that intensity which Keats saw as the essential quality of tragic art: "the excellence of every Art is its intensity, capable of making all disagreeables evaporate, from their being in close relationship with Beauty & Truth—Examine King Lear & you will find this examplified throughout."[24] And, indeed, *King Lear* is precisely the Shakespearean play with which one would compare *Atalanta in Calydon*, for in that play too the bleak existential despair of man in a godless universe is only made beautiful by the playwright's intense perception of the natural world—of heath, storm, and cliffs. Like *King Lear*, *Atalanta in Calydon* is high art, built around a perception of man's insignificance in nature, but ennobling by its beauty his tragic sufferings.

II

William Blake, *Poems and Ballads*, and *Atalanta in Calydon* show Swinburne working his way from the "Everlasting Nay" into the "Centre of Indifference" and finally, very tentatively, peering out toward an affirmation, an "Everlasting Yea." By October 1866, hard at work on his first republican poem, "A Song of Italy," he had found, or refound, as he put it, "something to love and believe in," the goddess Liberty. He breezily repudiated his earlier aesthetic doctrines in a letter to William Rossetti—"It was only Gabriel and his followers in art (l'art pour l'art) who for a time frightened me from speaking out"[25]—and dedicated himself passionately to the cause, prostrating himself before the great republican leader, Mazzini, and producing two volumes of poetry, *Songs of Two Nations* and *Songs before Sunrise*. Before proceeding to an examination of *Erechtheus*, it is necessary briefly to examine the poetry of this period, for, as Welby has said, "we cannot, when we desire to apprehend the political, or, as I almost prefer to call it, the religious, thought of Swinburne fully, concentrate on *Erechtheus* and wave aside the *Songs before Sunrise*. But *Erechtheus* represents, not only with a uniform majesty of temper, but also with a lucidity far from

[24] *The Letters of John Keats*, ed. Hyder Edward Rollins (Cambridge, Mass., 1958), I, 192.

[25] *The Swinburne Letters*, ed. Cecil Y. Lang, I (New Haven, 1959), 195–96.

usual with Swinburne, the ideal towards which his imagination was
moving when he composed *Songs before Sunrise*."[26] In fact, the ideas
qua ideas are expressed more lucidly in *Songs before Sunrise*, a volume
widely praised as Swinburne's most philosophic work and, oddly
enough, as his greatest lyrical achievement as well. Edmund Gosse
speaks for a generation of critics: "His intellect was at its zenith; he
was capable, as rarely before and still more rarely afterwards, of
clothing his thought with the most sumptuous and most radiant
veils of imagination . . . we are surprised to discover the most rap-
turous of troubadors transformed into one of the great poetic intel-
ligences of the modern world."[27] Yet it is precisely because the
republican poetry shows Swinburne at his most philosophical that it
shows him at his least lyrical, for he is most lyrical when he is most
mythopoeic, and mythopoeia and philosophy are completely antithetical. Because the ideas of this period are stated so clearly—
philosophically—in the two volumes of songs, it is convenient to
glance at them here before proceeding to Swinburne's return to
mythopoeia in *Erechtheus*.

Swinburne describes his conversion in the opening section of "A
Song of Italy." Looking outward from the spiritual abyss of *Poems
and Ballads*, looking "From the clear gulf of night," he saw two
giantesses "And knew the first of these / Was Freedom, and the
second Italy" (II, 262). His symbol is still the giant woman, but she
is no longer a mythic figure, for now idea and image are divided—
the woman is not herself an archetypal force, like Dolores or Faustine, but merely the symbol of an external body of ideas. The mode
is allegorical, not mythopoeic. The philosophical idea, however, is
all the more clear. The black night of the soul is ended, a new hope
seized.

The renewal of faith in the possibility of a new dawn for mankind
becomes, as the title suggests, the central theme of *Songs before
Sunrise*, a volume that celebrates man's ability to change the course
of change and build toward a better daybreak in spite of "death's
dateless night." The penultimate stanza of the "Prelude" voices the
essential philosophy of the volume:

[26]Welby, pp. 113–14.
[27]*The Life of Algernon Charles Swinburne* (New York, 1917), p. 177.

A little time we gain from time
To set our seasons in some chime,
    For harsh or sweet or loud or low,
    With seasons played out long ago
And souls that in their time and prime
    Took part with summer or with snow,
Lived abject lives out or sublime,
    And had their chance of seed to sow
For service or disservice done
To those days dead and this their son.

             [II, 9]

Man's time on earth is short. When his season is out, he dies, but the course of every life affects the course of all those that follow—something of man lives beyond the grave. Swinburne has added nothing new to the vision of the world set forth in *Atalanta in Calydon*, but he has shifted his perspective—the importance of the generational memory of Meleager's life and death now takes center stage. The something that lives on, however, is not strictly limited to memory, nor is it related particularly to art, as in "Ave atque Vale," "Anactoria," and "Hesperia," but, as he says in the final stanza of "Prelude," to

        such good works or such ill
As loose the bonds or make them strong
Wherein all manhood suffers wrong.

             [II, 9]

Man's life has a moral purpose—he cannot simply live intensely, but must live intensely and for good. Swinburne, having passed through nihilism and the void, has not passed beyond good and evil.

Not only did Swinburne now conceive of a moral purpose in life, he also saw a moral purpose in death. He claimed that he was willing to die for the cause (though he was unlikely to have opportunity),[28] and in poem after poem of *Songs before Sunrise* he praised the willingness to die for an ideal, as in "Super Flumina Babylonis":

---

[28] In a letter to his mother, Swinburne wrote of his first meeting with Mazzini: "I know, now I have seen him, what I guessed before, why, whenever he has said to anyone, 'Go and be killed because I tell you,' they have gone and been killed because he told them. Who wouldn't, I should like to know?" (*Letters*, I, 237).

Unto each man his handiwork, unto each his crown,
    The just Fate gives;
Whoso takes the world's life on him and his own lays down,
    He, dying so, lives.

[II, 38]

He seems almost to be advocating an asceticism and martyrdom reminiscent of Christianity. In "Blessed among Women," in fact, he goes so far as to substitute Signora Cairoli, the bereaved mother of two soldiers martyred on the altar of Italian republicanism, for the Virgin Mary—and he does it without a trace of irony. Signora Cairoli is the republican version of Althaea, but her sons do not die, like Meleager, because they must, but because they will, because they wish to serve mankind. The willingness to die that Swinburne praises is not, however, a return to Christian asceticism. In "Before a Crucifix," in fact, Christ's martyrdom is condemned because it led not to freedom but to oppression. The man who dies for freedom is no ascetic; he is the man who "takes the world's life on him," and therefore the man who lives most fully.

In the somewhat elusive phrase "the world's life" lies the philosophical core of Swinburne's republicanism and, in fact, of all his later work. The phrase can best be elucidated by an examination of "Hertha," the poem Swinburne described in 1875 as the best he had ever written. "Of all I have done I rate *Hertha* the highest as a single piece, finding in it the most of lyric force and music combined with the most of condensed and clarified thought. I think there really is a good deal compressed and concentrated into that poem." [29] Hertha, another of Swinburne's giantesses, closely resembles Althaea in certain important respects. Like Althaea, she is described in terms of organic growth, and also like Althaea, though more explicitly, she is the source and end of all life: "The search, and the sought, and the seeker, the soul and the body that is" (II, 74). Althaea, however, is only "the body that is," the temporal, corporeal manifestation of nature; Hertha is the eternal soul of nature as well:

---

[29] *Letters*, III (1960), 15.

I am that which began;
> Out of me the years roll;
Out of me God and man;
> I am equal and whole;
God changes, and man, and the form of them bodily; I am the soul.
[II, 73]

To borrow Swinburne's favorite metaphor, she is the deep eternal sea as well as the waves on the surface. Hertha is, in fact, "the world's life," and it is to her that Swinburne asks us to surrender our lives:

The free life of thy living,
> Be the gift of it free;
Not as servant to lord, nor as master to slave, shalt thou give thee to me.
[II, 76]

In calling for submission to the life force, Swinburne is simply calling for submission to the laws of nature; he is asking man to recognize that he is, bodily, a part of the surface change in nature. He is, in a sense, inviting Meleager to submit to Althaea, but he is doing more, for Hertha is greater than Althaea.

Althaea represented cyclical nature; Hertha is the soul of that nature. She is not, however, an immanent, pantheistic deity—at least not in any conventional sense—for she consists of "Man, pulse of my centre, and fruit of my body, and seed of my soul" (II, 81). The organic metaphor is precise: living man, the temporal, ever-changing body, is the fruit, and man dying, like fruit, provides the seed for new growth of the universal soul. His deeds live after him, producing new fruit in the actions of other men, in later days. In *Atalanta in Calydon* fruit grew, rotted, and died; in "Hertha" it produces new fruit. Though man cannot hope for personal immortality, he will at least live on in "the world's life":

The tree many-rooted
> That swells to the sky
With frondage red-fruited,
> The life-tree am I;
In the buds of your lives is the sap of my leaves: ye shall live and not die.
[II, 77]

Whether for good or evil, every man is a part of Hertha, but now, very clearly, man's life has a moral purpose. Hertha does not represent the progress of mankind toward an eternal republic, as has too often been supposed, but simply change:

Though sore be my burden
        And more than ye know,
And my growth have no guerdon
        But only to grow,
Yet I fail not of growing for lightnings above me or deathworms below.

[II, 79]

In order for the change to be progress, man must live freely, for in living freely he lives intensely, unbowed by the weight of authority:

A creed is a rod
        And a crown is of night;
But this thing is God,
        To be man with thy might,
To grow straight in the strength of thy spirit, and live out thy life as the
        light.

[II, 76]

The moral impact of Swinburne's "mystic atheistic democratic anthropologic poem called 'Hertha'" is that man must submit himself to the eternal spirit of man.[30] Paradoxically, his submission, far from being asceticism, is a casting off of the bonds of political and religious repression.

It is because the eternal spirit of nature and the eternal spirit of man are one, are Hertha, that, as Philip Henderson has said, "for Swinburne, the idea of liberty was ever associated with the great forces of nature, the seas, the stars, the irresistible flood of great rivers, recalling Byron, Shelley, Dante, Victor Hugo and Landor."[31] This association, passionately felt by Swinburne, provides the inspiration for the best parts of the poetry of his republican period. In "On the Downs," for example, one of the few poems of this period which attempts a lyric fusion of form and content, the inspiration for a song of liberty comes from a perception of unchanging, elemental nature:

[30] *Letters*, II (1959), 45.
[31] *Swinburne: The Portrait of a Poet* (London, 1974), p. 27.

A multitudinous monotone
Of dust and flower and seed and stone,
    In the deep sea-rock's mid-sea sloth,
In the live water's trembling zone. . . .

[II, 204]

The stanza describing the poet's actual inspiration reads like a gloss on the genesis of *Songs before Sunrise* from the growth of Hertha in nature and in Swinburne's mind:

For all things come by fate to flower
At their unconquerable hour,
    And time brings truth, and truth makes free,
And freedom fills time's veins with power,
    As, brooding on that sea,
        My thought filled me.

[II, 205]

In a remarkable passage in the "Prelude" Swinburne makes the connection between elemental nature, freedom, and personal strength even clearer:

For what has he whose will sees clear
To do with doubt and faith and fear,
    Swift hopes and slow despondencies?
    His heart is equal with the sea's
And with the sea-wind's, and his ear
    Is level to the speech of these,
And his soul communes and takes cheer
    With the actual earth's equalities,
Air, light, and night, hills, winds and streams,
And seeks not strength from strengthless dreams.

[II, 4]

The passage philosophically describes the strength to be gained from abandoning conceptualized dogma and seeking communion with the life of man in nature.

Though mythopoeic poetry results from a perception of life in nature, Swinburne's republican poetry is not, for the most part, mythopoeic. Hertha is a giantess, but she is an allegorical, not a mythic, giantess. She stands for certain conceptualized ideas rather than embodying a living perception. Though the poem may not strike us as particularly "condensed and clarified thought," it certainly strikes us as thought rather than myth. Even while discussing the unity of man and nature, of man and man, and of body and soul, Swinburne divides them by separating form and content in his poems. He resorts to the allegory he had condemned in his essay on Blake, and at times even sinks to the worst kind of eighteenth-century personification, as in the first stanza of "Prelude":

> Between the green bud and the red
> Youth sat and sang by Time, and shed
>   From eyes and tresses flowers and tears,
>   From heart and spirit hopes and fears,
> Upon the hollow stream whose bed
>   Is channeled by the foamless years;
> And with the white the gold-haired head
>   Mixed running locks, and in Time's ears
> Youth's dreams hung singing, and Time's truth
> Was half not harsh in the ears of Youth.
>
>   [II, 3]

The contrivance of weaving the green, red, and white of the Italian flag—a contrivance that damages poem after poem in the volume, including "On the Downs"—only adds to the sense of self-conscious artifice. "We hate," as Keats said, "poetry that has a palpable design upon us,"[32] and we hate it not because of the design, but because it is generally not well done. Swinburne's republican poetry, with few exceptions, fits the pattern.

The ideas Swinburne was philosophically expounding, however, would become the raw materials of a truly lyric, mythopoeic poetry once, no longer mere intellectual counters, they became assimilated into his entire being. This assimilation was completed by the time he wrote *Erechtheus*, a play that creates a myth to embody the ideals of Swinburne's republicanism.

III

Athens, the first republic, the seat of Greek arts and wisdom, and the home of Aeschylus, was for Swinburne the perfect type of the

---

[32] *Letters of Keats*, I, 224.

eternal City of Man. It was almost inevitable that he should choose the legend of its salvation as the subject of a major poetic endeavor. The establishment by Athena and Apollo of a new order in Athens, the subject of *Erechtheus*, had been the subject of Aeschylus' *Oresteia*, a work which Swinburne revered as his Bible and which, according to Edmund Gosse, he knew by heart. *Erechtheus* is, as Jerome McGann has observed, Swinburne's "own version of the grand theme of the *Oresteia*," the submission of the individual will to universal law.[33] Universal law does not, however, mean to Swinburne what it meant to Aeschylus, and *Erechtheus* can be understood as a misreading or reinterpretation of the *Oresteia* in the same way the essay on Blake was a misreading of its subject.

In every respect the legend of Erechtheus was a perfect vehicle for the beliefs of Swinburne's republican period. The story itself, or at least that part that constitutes the plot of Swinburne's play, is simple: Athens is at war with Thrace and can only be saved, according to the oracle, by the sacrifice of King Erechtheus' daughter, Chthonia. Chthonia goes willingly to her death and the Athenian army, despite the death of Erechtheus, defeats the invading force. By virtue of the Aeschylean chorus, which continually alludes to the events of the past, however, Swinburne is also able to use the legend of the founding of Athens and all of the stories relating to the house of Erechtheus—particularly the rape of Oreithyia by Boreas and the killing of Procris by Cephalus.

At the center of *Erechtheus*, nevertheless, is the sacrifice of Chthonia for the sake of Athens. Once the oracle has declared the sacrifice necessary, no one—not Chthonia herself, nor Praxithea, her mother, nor Erechtheus—hesitates for a moment. Their willing submission provides, as Welby, Rutland, and Samuel Chew have all observed, a perfect illustration of the virtues of citizenship. But the play is more than a civics lesson, because Athens is more than a city. Chthonia's death is a death into life: she will live on in the spirit of Athens, just as every man who dies lives on as a part of Hertha. Praxithea tells Chthonia that

---

[33] Gosse, p. 110; McGann, *Swinburne: An Experiment in Criticism* (Chicago, 1972), pp. 125–26.

> thou, dead, shalt live
> Till Athens live not; for the days and nights
> Given of thy bare brief dark dividual life,
> Shall she give thee half all her agelong own
> And all its glory.
>
> [IV, 392]

Athens can never die because it *is* Hertha. Both, for Swinburne, represent the eternal soul of man, the accumulation of the acts and deeds of every man in his "bare brief dark dividual life." Chthonia, dying, "takes the world's life" on herself, and she "dying so, lives."

This much, however, could have been said, and was said, in *Songs before Sunrise*. The deeper meaning of *Erechtheus* must be understood from its form, not its plot. Jerome McGann and Ross C. Murfin have both noted that the extremely simple plot of the play functions not as an end in itself but as the basis for a metaphoric tour de force, in which all the actions and characters correspond with and imply actions and characters on other levels of reality. Both Murfin and McGann cite Rutland's confession of inability to distinguish the armies of Thrace from the waves of the sea and observe that Swinburne was deliberately using a system of correspondences—an echo system McGann calls it—so that everything in the play eventually suggests everything else.[34] One passage, a description of the Thracian warhorses, will serve to illustrate the technique:

As the swing of the sea churned yellow that sways with the wind as it swells
Is the lift and relapse of the wave of the chargers that clash with their bells;
And the clang of the sharp shrill brass through the burst of the wave as it
    shocks
Rings clean as the clear wind's cry through the roar of the surge on the
    rocks;
And the heads of the steeds in their headgear of war, and their corseleted
    breasts,
Gleam broad as the brows of the billows that brighten the storm with their
    crests,
Gleam dread as their bosoms that heave to the shipwrecking wind as they
    rise,
Filled full of the terror and thunder of water, that slays as it dies.

[IV, 430]

[34] Ross C. Murfin, "Athens Unbound: A Study of Swinburne's *Erechtheus*," *Victorian Poetry*, 12 (1974), 205–17; McGann, pp. 118–20.

The inclusive grammar of this remarkable sentence is reminiscent of "Hesperia," as is the slightly blurred focus. In both cases the shadowy outlines are symptomatic of Swinburne's mythopoeic metamorphoses—the army of Eumolpus actually becomes the sea, and the sea becomes an army; Eumolpus becomes his father, Poseidon, as Poseidon becomes Eumolpus. Because he perceives the life in nature, and perceives it in human form, the actual forces of nature become literally "con-fused" with the forces of man. The conflation of the life in man with the life in nature is the basis of the mythopoeic experience. Here it is carried to its extreme. In addition, the effects of what McGann called Swinburne's echo system and what I called, in discussing *Atalanta*, his perfect fusion of all metaphors, can be seen in the last line of the quotation. The water, already a simile for the sound of horses, is described in terms of the breaking of a wave, which "slays as it dies," but with an added suggestion of the confrontation of the two mortal kings, Eumolpus and Erechtheus, for Eumolpus dies as Erechtheus is slain. Erechtheus, however, is slain not by Eumolpus, but by the thunderbolt of Zeus, who is, of course, suggested by the word "thunder." Thus by virtue of his magisterial economy of metaphor, Swinburne is able to suggest, within this single image, Poseidon, Zeus, Eumolpus, Erechtheus, the armies of Thrace, and the actual climax of the battle.

I have used this example of Swinburne's poetic technique both because it demonstrates his return to a mythopoeic poetry of metamorphoses and because it has become something of a locus classicus among Swinburne scholars. It would be impracticable to do justice here to the immense amount of metaphoric correspondences in the play, but the scope of Swinburne's effort may be briefly suggested. Most obviously, the division between Athens and Thrace, between Erechtheus and Eumolpus, suggests a division between Erechtheus' mother, earth, and Eumolpus' father, the sea. Whenever man, god, or element is named, the name suggests the other two on his side of the conflict. Within the house of Erechtheus, moreover, two daughters, Oreithyia and Procris, have already been sacrificed, and they become metaphors of the two wars already waged on Athens, by the Thriasians and Carians, and wars and children both become images of the ravages of time. All three are described in terms of the sea, as the chorus cries out to Zeus,

"Let a third wave smite not us, father, / Long since sore smitten of twain" (IV, 378). The third wave, the one which Chthonia's sacrifice must guard against, traditionally suggests death but is particularly suggestive when used by Swinburne who, in "The Triumph of Time," had lamented man's condition:

> It is not much that a man can save
> On the sands of life, in the straits of time,
> Who swims in sight of the great third wave
> That never a swimmer shall cross or climb.
>
> [I, 42]

Chthonia's death, evidently, will be an attempt to cross or climb that great third wave, death. This third wave of the all-devouring sea, moreover, is suggestive throughout the play of the waters of apocalypse, Swinburne's images frequently echoing the language of the book of Revelation: "A noise is arisen against us of waters, / A sound as of battle come up from the sea" (IV, 376). The stakes are clearly enormous—Chthonia's death must obviate the apocalyptic end of man.

All of this suggests that the essential division of forces in the poem is that between cyclical life and eternality, and, indeed, the metaphoric interconnections form along those lines. The problem in *Erechtheus* is the one confronted in *Poems and Ballads* and in *Atalanta in Calydon*—how to deal with the division in man's being caused by the desire for immortality and the certainty of death. Ross Murfin has perceptively noted that *Erechtheus* is a "dramatization of the psychic conflict between the human soul and the reality of death,"[35] and Erechtheus laments near the beginning that "no man's will and no desire of man's / Shall stand as doth a God's will" (IV, 373). The problem is precisely that of "Dolores": "our lives and our longings are twain." The earth, mother of Erechtheus, is, like Althaea, representative of all natural law and of natural life; she is, as should go without saying, the original earth mother: "Mother of life and death and all men's days" (IV, 371). Tightly fused images of seasonal change, birth, organic growth, fruition, and regeneration run throughout the play, always characterizing earth and the Athe-

---

[35] Murfin, p. 207.

nians, and the clear implication is that the Athenians represent the cyclical life of nature. The Thracians, on the other hand, are characterized by the sea, which Swinburne always uses as an image of eternality, and, as Murfin has shown, by devotion to gods who control their destiny. The Athenians stand for Althaea and Hertha, the Thracians for Meleager and Atalanta. The correspondences run consistently throughout the play. Athena, for example, represents Athens and earth because her gift to the new-found city was an olive tree, emblematic of organic nature, while Poseidon opposes Athens because his gift, a "well of bright strange brine" (IV, 390), was rejected.

Within this context the death of Chthonia can be more closely examined. Because she dies for the principle of cyclical life, earth-Athens-Hertha, Chthonia's acceptance of death is an acceptance of that order. The oracle has announced with strict, if inscrutable, justice that a maiden must die; the "under Gods"

> require
> For this land's life her death and maiden blood
> To save a maiden city.
>
> [IV, 384]

Significantly, the sacrifice is required by the under gods, the primitive gods of Althaea and of nature, for Swinburne is making the point that man must eventually acknowledge the eternal death represented by Proserpine. It is significant also that the gods require Chthonia, a maiden; for, like Atalanta, she represents the unnatural ideal of virginity, an evasion of the cyclical life of nature. Unlike Atalanta, however, Chthonia will surrender her maidenhood—her ritual acceptance of death at the altar is metaphorically described throughout the play as a marriage. The metaphor suggests the apocalyptic marriage of the maiden Church to Christ, the Midnight Bridegroom, but only to refute the Christian scheme of apocalypse and redemption. The marriage is an acceptance of cyclical nature—an abandonment of transcendental ideals rather than a culmination of them—and reveals that Swinburne has come to an appreciation of Proserpine as the goddess not only of death but of rebirth as well. Murfin has accurately described the meaning of Chthonia's death: "Chthonia . . . represents that choice always available to mankind of defeating the cruel powers of the gods (the sea) by recognizing that there is no divinity greater than that of the human soul—that there is no state of perfection beyond that which man can aspire to and that the only immortality in the universe is offered by Nature's eternal cycles of decomposition and regeneration."[36] The union of Chthonia with death, the transcendent ideal of Atalanta with the natural law of Althaea, represents man's acceptance of "The Garden of Proserpine." Once man has accepted death, his life and his longings are no longer twain.

The marriage to death, moreover, leads to a further consolation for mankind—a "Hesperia" phase for the race. Murfin has rightly observed that freedom from the tyranny of false gods and false ideals is one reward, but another is that the marriage produces progeny—not only is nature regenerated, but so is man. The play abounds with images of diurnal and seasonal variation to such an extent that every death implies a birth. The chorus, for example, at one point sings that "the season is full now of death or of birth, / To bring forth life, or an end of all" (IV, 434). According to Murfin, all of the play's imagery describes a time between times, the close of one cycle of history and the hoped-for beginning of another. As Erechtheus says at one point, "The time is full" (IV, 401). The chorus, seeing Chthonia slain, might well have wondered, like Eliot's Magi, whether they were witnesses to a death or a birth, for along with the images of marriage that describe the sacrifice is an abundance of images of childbirth.

Chthonia unquestionably loses her maidenhood to death. Swinburne conscientiously develops the phallic connotations of swords throughout the play. Males are synecdochically described as swords, and the birth of the race of Athenians from the intercourse of sun and earth develops the image of piercing:

None sowed us by land in thy [earth's] womb that conceived us and bore.
But the stroke of the shaft of the sunlight that brought us to birth
Pierced only and quickened thy furrows to bear us, O Earth!
With the beams of his love wast thou cloven as with iron or fire. . . .
[IV, 420]

These lines not only illustrate the extent to which man, nature, earth, and sun—all things, in short—are fused into unity by Swin-

[36] Murfin, p. 208.

burne's metaphors, but they also take part in the echo system of imagery that compels us to see Chthonia's death as a conception. Thus when she is pierced with the "sword's point," Chthonia is metaphorically impregnated and in the fullness of time will give birth.

In the simplest sense, Chthonia gives birth to the memory and fame of her own name. Like Meleager's, her name will be handed down from generation to generation, though the glory of her deed, of course, will live with a greater luster than that of Meleager's. Chthonia gives birth, however, to much more than the glory of her own name, as the images in Praxithea's speech to the chorus indicate:

> Give ear, O all ye people, that my word
> May pierce your hearts through, and the stroke that cleaves
> Be fruitful to them; so shall all that hear
> Grow great at heart with child of thought most high,
> And bring forth seed in season; this my child,
> This flower of this my body, this sweet life,
> This fair live youth I give you, to be slain,
> Spent, shed, poured out, and perish; take my gift,
> And give it death and the under Gods who crave
> So much for that they give; for this is more,
> Much more is this than all we; for they give
> Freedom, and for a blast, an air of breath,
> A little soul that is not, they give back
> Light for all eyes, cheer for all hearts, and life
> That fills the world's width full of fame and praise
> And mightier love than children's.
>
> [IV, 413–14]

This passage, half of a thirty-three line sentence, contains either explicitly or implicitly all of the major themes of the play. The most important point is that Chthonia's death, the death of an insignificant individual—an "air of breath"—produces freedom, light, cheer, and life for all men of all time. Her death, in fact, gives birth to Athens, the type of man's ideals, as the syntax of the chorus, addressing Chthonia, makes clear when referring to Athens as "thy child this city" (IV, 415).

Praxithea's speech is particularly striking, however, in its use of the images of piercing, fruitfulness, childbirth, and generational change in the context of the spoken word. The images are, in the first place, symptomatic of Swinburne's remarkable coalescence of imagery and indicate the extent to which he is able to bring all elements of his perception into imagistic as well as syntactic unity. Especially significant, however, is his addition of a new element—the word—to the complex system of correspondences. Swinburne is offering in *Erechtheus* not only the hope of freedom but the consolation for mortality that men's words can bear fruit in the minds of others. The word of Praxithea, carrying with it the significance of Chthonia's death, will "bring forth seed in season" in the minds of her countrymen and eventually grow to a flower—and the flower is Chthonia herself, resurrected: "this my child, / This flower of this my body." Her "name," as the chorus says elsewhere, "shall blossom" in the hearts of men (IV, 415). Chthonia gives birth to freedom and to Athens because, dying, she lives in the heart and spirit of Athenians and bolsters their will to freedom.

Praxithea's ability to impregnate the hearts of the chorus with a word implies that the word can live forever, perpetually regenerated as in the cycles of nature. The entire form of the play—in which words fuse the forms of nature and the acts of men and gods—implies that the word has power over all of these things; and even the choice of genre, Aeschylean tragedy, implies that the word can revivify the life of ancient Athens and the death of Chthonia. In fact, Swinburne's rendition of Praxithea's speech was, in large measure, inspired by Praxithea's speech as written by Euripides, proving that the word—in this case the word bearing the significance of Chthonia's death—can indeed be passed across the ages to bear fresh fruit in the thoughts of men.[37]

The idea of the word as salvation—and not the Christian salvation of Christ, the Word—is not only implicit in the form of *Erechtheus* but is implicitly developed with the echo system, or fused complex of images. The rape of Oreithyia by Boreas, associated with an earlier war against Athens, the cosmic power of the God of

---

[37] Swinburne admitted to introducing a substantial portion of Euripides' rendition of Praxithea's speech but said it was "so palpably and pitiably inferior to the rest" of the play that he "excised the sophist—wiped up and carted off his 'droppings'—only keeping a hint or two, and one or two of his best lines" (*Letters*, III, 99).

the north wind, and the elemental power of the wind itself, is also associated with the eternal song of the ages, as the chorus, the most sonorous and majestic one Swinburne ever wrote, makes clear:

> Out of the north wind grief came forth,
>   And the shining of the sword out of the sea.
> Yea, of old the first-blown blast blew the prelude of this last,
> The blast of his trumpet upon Rhodope.
>
> [IV, 393]

The image of a sword in connection with a rape is worth noting, but the association of song with the event is particularly important. The chorus later explains that the song is connected with the song of man and the transmission of memory:

> Of this hoary-headed woe
> Song made memory long ago;
> Now a younger grief to mourn
> Needs a new song younger born.
>
> [IV, 396]

The rape of Oreithyia is incumbent upon the present action as all things retained in memory and song are incumbent upon it. The choruses in *Erechtheus*, like Aeschylus' choruses, constantly recall the events of the past and hint at the events of the future, thus bringing all times into unity through song. One action, apparently unrelated to another, can be called its "prelude" because they are both part of the eternal song, which is the generational memory of man.

The sense of overwhelming, irresistible fate in Aeschylus is largely owing to the evocation of past events in the choruses. The suggestion of an ineluctable pattern of development is created by the carefully worked out juxtaposition of historical events around a few central images. Swinburne's technique in *Erechtheus* is exactly the same, but while Aeschylus had carefully shaped his dramas to portray an unquestionably genuine sense of a vast cosmic law, of a universal order shaped by transcendent forces, Swinburne carefully shaped his to create a sense of direction for the life of man and the life of mankind. In Aeschylus what matters is cosmic law; in Swinburne what matters is man's ability to transcend natural law both by the free choice of his deeds—particularly the freedom to choose

death—and by the memory of his deeds in song. The rape of
Oreithyia, the death of Procris, the earlier wars against Athens, the
founding of Athens, and all of the other events alluded to in the
play contribute to the song of man, which continually grows, every
event being the prelude of another. The song is, in short, Hertha,
man's ever-growing soul.

In *Erechtheus* the song is not to be equated with Hertha, of
course, but with Athens, described in the first epigraph to the play,
a fragment from Pindar, as "famous Athens, shining and violet
crowned and illustrious in song, stay of Hellas, city divine."[38]
Throughout the play the association of Athens with song is maintained. Athens's fame, says Athena, will be "The crown of all songs
sung, of all deeds done" (IV, 445), and the city is described by the
chorus as

> A maiden crowned with a fourfold glory
> That none from the pride of her head may rend,
> Violet and olive-leaf purple and hoary,
> Song-wreath and story the fairest of fame,
> Flowers that the winter can blast not or bend:
> A light upon earth as the sun's own flame,
>   A name as his name,
>   Athens, a praise without end.

> [IV, 375–76]

The main features of the city are the olive tree, representing wisdom, presented by Athena at its founding; its fame in song and
story; and its association with Apollo, god of song. The culminating
speech of the play, Praxithea's response to Athena (who clearly, as
Murfin has shown, represents not a transcendent goddess, but
human wisdom) makes the same associations:

> O queen Athena, from a heart made whole
> Take as thou givest us blessing; never tear
> Shall stain for shame nor groan untune the song
> That as a bird shall spread and fold its wings
> Here in thy praise forever, and fulfil
> The whole world's crowning city crowned with thee
> As the sun's eye fulfils and crowns with sight

---

[38] Translated by Rutland, p. 230.

> The circling crown of heaven. There is no grief
> Great as the joy to be made one in will
> With him that is the heart and rule of life,
> And thee, God born of God; thy name is ours,
> And thy large grace more great than our desire.
>
> [IV, 447]

This brilliant passage establishes, first of all, that the conflict of desire and necessity has been ended. Praxithea's heart is not divided but whole, and the last line of her speech refutes Erechtheus' statement at the beginning of the play that "what they [the gods] will is more than our desire" (IV, 373). The repetitions of the word "crown," moreover, conflate the ideas of the founding of wisdom in the birth of Pallas Athena from the forehead of Zeus, the death of the last crowned king of Athens by a thunderbolt to his forehead, the founding of Athens on a headland, the preservation of Athens by the bound brows of Chthonia, and the life-giving force of Apollo, described earlier as "Enkindling the waters and ways of the air / From thy forehead made bare" (IV, 432). Most of all, however, the word suggests the oft-repeated image of Athens as the "crown of song," and the passage as a whole suggests the displacement of the crowns of kingship with the crown of song. In addition the syntactic identification of the sun and song indicates that Swinburne is leaning heavily on Apollo's role as the god of song and suggests that we should think again about the oracle, the voice of Apollo, who ordered the death of Chthonia. The oracle must, at least metaphorically, be identified with the song of man, with the entire history of Athens. The role of the supernatural is eliminated from the play when we realize that the oracular demand is to be identified with the Hertha-like song, that it is a prelude to the death of Chthonia in the same sense as is the rape of Oreithyia. Thus the entire plot of the play may be understood as a song. Finally, the repeated use of the word *fulfill* in Praxithea's speech suggests, fairly emphatically, that the function of song may be understood as the filling of a void, that song creates meaning.

The form of *Erechtheus* is thus absolutely inseparable from its meaning. The one fault of the play, according to such critics as Gosse, Welby, and Rutland, is that the characters are not sufficiently individuated so that it has "a too marmoreal uniformity of dic-

tion."[39] The reason for this is that, despite John Addington
Symonds's remarkable comment that "Praxithea is as real and full in
personality as the Antigone of Sophocles," Swinburne was not trying to portray character but to blend all elements of his play into
lyric unity.[40] He is not interested, like Euripides, in the insignificant
emotions of individuals; he is attempting to create a lyric grammar
of inclusion, using syntax, imagery, meter, and sound itself to make
connections that will draw all of the disparate elements of the
mythic history of Athens into harmony. He is trying to recreate the
song of Athens, which fulfilled earth, sea, and land with meaning,
healing the cosmic division of nature and the psychic division
of man.

The astonishing form of the play, in which all of elemental nature
and man's actions are so merged that the life of one becomes the life
of another, reflects a pure mythopoeic perception. Swinburne is
not, as in *Atalanta in Calydon*, using the legends of a past
mythopoeic age to write mythological poetry, as Ovid and even
Euripides had done. He is recreating the myth from the mythopoeic
impulse that moved the original creators of the legends. He is, like
the primitive Greek, showing the unity of all things, and showing
also the personified life in nature and the natural (not supernatural)
life in man. And yet for all this, his verse, in *Erechtheus*, has not yet
become fully mythopoeic, for he does not, like Aeschylus, actually
perceive the unified life in the merging of man, society, and nature,
but in song, and his own song is not an independent creation of
myth but a recreation of someone else's myth. As long as he retained the forms and fables of another age, he was not wholly
creative—not creating from the void. Finally, *Erechtheus* is expressly
designed to bear a moral message, the message of Swinburne's
idealized republicanism and of the organic growth of man's soul in
nature. To the extent that this conceptual intention is perceptible in
the work, the near-perfect fusion of form and content in *Erechtheus*
remains only near-perfect. In short, the play is a masterpiece in all
respects—it is unrivaled as a recreation of the Greek spirit and
drama, nearly untouchable as a sustained lyric effusion, astounding

[39] Gosse, p. 232.
[40] Symonds, in *Academy*, 1876; rpt. in Hyder, ed., *Swinburne*, p. 166.

in its metrical variety, dazzling in its metaphoric representation, and even remarkable in its philosophical import—but it does not achieve the exalted standard Swinburne strove for; it does not create harmonious beauty and meaning from the sheer void, as a number of late lyrics would attempt to do, and a handful would succeed in doing.

IV

Swinburne's journey from the "Everlasting Nay" through the "Centre of Indifference" to the "Everlasting Yea" was made a reality in the decade that saw the production of *Atalanta in Calydon*, the republican songs, and *Erechtheus*. *Atalanta* represents the period of defiance and the trip into indifference; the republican poetry represents an entry—with a leap and a bound—into a period of affirmation. But Swinburne's turn to affirmation was too sudden, for he left his art behind him. *Songs of Two Nations* and *Songs before Sunrise* show the triumph of conceptualizing, even of Enlightenment rationality, over imagination. Form and content become separated, and art becomes the vehicle for a moral message. This is precisely the point at which most Victorian conversions arrived—Carlyle himself believed that art was the handmaiden of religion—and the point at which most ended. The most advanced thinkers of the mid-Victorian age struggled, in Robert Langbaum's terms, through eighteenth-century rationalism to an acceptance of the romantic ideals of the imagination, but they accepted romantic ideals, rather than creating them. Carlyle, in spite of himself, as well as Ruskin, Arnold and even, to an extent, Mill, came to make a religion of romanticism. The great Victorian prose writers removed Shelley's luminous wings and systematized Wordsworth, making a religion of culture and abandoning the attempt to create it. In *The Birth of Tragedy* Nietzsche wrote that

it is the fate of every myth to insinuate itself into the narrow limits of some alleged historical reality, and to be treated by some later generation as a solitary fact with historical claims. . . . For this is the manner in which religions are wont to die out: when of course under the stern, intelligent eyes of an orthodox dogmatism, the mythical presuppositions of a religion

are systematized as a completed sum of historical events, and when one
begins apprehensively to defend the credibility of the myth, while at the
same time opposing all continuation of their natural vitality and luxuriance;
when, accordingly, the feeling for myth dies out, and its place is taken by
the claim of religion to historical foundations.[41]

As the heirs of the Victorians, and particularly of Arnold, we are
loath to regard them as a school of euhemerists. Yet surely Arnold's
abandonment of poetry for criticism, his insistence that "prescrip-
tions of reason are absolute," that "epochs of concentration" must
alternate with "epochs of expansion," and that all things must be
judged historically, all indicate that he is of the school of orthodox
dogmatists who destroy the life of myth.[42] Similarly Ruskin's greatest efforts in the arts went into systematizing the creative imagination of J. M. W. Turner, Carlyle's into worship of the men
of an earlier age, and Morris's, both artistically and politically, into a
return to medievalism.

The phenomenon was nearly universal, and Swinburne suc-
cumbed to it in his republican verse, narrowing the scope of his
romantic idealism and creative imagination to serve the historical
realities of European republicanism. Swinburne, however, learned
to control his euphoric affirmation, to sublimate the external par-
ticulars in the service of creative art. Were *Erechtheus* merely the
culmination of the ideals expressed in *Songs before Sunrise*, as Welby
has said, it would be the work of typical mid-Victorian Socratism,
the soul separated from the sense, but it is also, in form and content, a creative myth in its own right. In this play Swinburne has
broken through to the "Hesperia" phase, in which the imagination
creates meaning. To see how far Swinburne differed from his fellow
Victorians in this, one need only compare his "Hesperia" and
Erechtheus with the roughly analogous work of Tennyson, the pro-
totypical Victorian, as in "The Hesperides" and the *Idylls of the King*.
"The Hesperides" is like "Hesperia" in the remarkable beauty of its
rhythms and in its celebration of the Blessed Isles of the West in

[41] Friedrich Nietzsche, *The Birth of Tragedy*, trans. William A. Haussmann (New
York, 1924), pp. 84–85.
[42] Matthew Arnold, "The Function of Criticism at the Present Time," in *Lectures
and Essays in Criticism*, ed. R. H. Super (Ann Arbor, Mich., 1962), pp. 264, 269.

terms of art. But Tennyson, unlike Swinburne, is not advocating a return to the land of the dead for the sake of inspiration; he is urging us to protect the cultural heritage of Western civilization, to hoard it:

> The golden apple, the golden apple, the hallowed fruit,
> Guard it well, guard it warily. . . .
>
> . . . . .
> Laugh not loudly: watch the treasure
> Of the wisdom of the West. . . .
>
> . . . . .
> If the golden apple be taken
> The world will be overwise.[43]

And the *Idylls of the King* ends with the dissolution of Western culture in that great final battle in the West. Tennyson's suggestion that redemption will come in the cycles of history only emphasizes his belief that the Victorian age is not a creative one. *Erechtheus*, in both form and content, repudiates Tennyson's pessimism. The battle for Athens against the great third wave is the final battle in the West, and the victory goes to the creative culture. The mythopoeic form of the poem proves that true creativity remains possible. Swinburne was, I believe, unique among the mid-Victorians in assimilating the optimism of affirmation with an unquestioning belief in the independent validity and viability of a truly creative imagination, and truly creative art.

[43] "The Hesperides," *The Poetic and Dramatic Works of Alfred Lord Tennyson*, ed. W. J. Rolfe (New York, 1898), p. 788.

Statement and Genesis of Myth
Poems and Ballads (Second
Series) and the Late Nature
CHAPTER 4 Poetry

PUBLISHED IN 1878, *Poems and Ballads* (Second Series) has been acclaimed by many of Swinburne's best critics as "the finest of his volumes of poems" and, unfortunately, as the last of his fine volumes. The book consists of lyrics written over the most tumultuous decade of Swinburne's life, the period from 1867 to 1877, when he lived in a state of chronic alcoholic dissipation and collapse. Alcohol seems to have had a sedative effect on his poetry, for no critic has failed to note the beautiful serenity of the verse. T. Earle Welby speaks of the "subdual and spiritualization of the hitherto clamorous music," John D. Rosenberg comments on its "chaste magnificence," Edmund Gosse observes that "no one would have guessed at the distracted and even alarming physical condition of the author from the serene volume," and Samuel Chew triumphantly sums it all up with a musical metaphor: "The tambourines, cymbals, kettledrums, timbrels and taborets of 1866 are heard no longer, nor the trumpet tones of 'Songs before Sunrise'; but in their place there sounds a new music, as of a flute, not less melodious but tenderer."[1] Yet for all the praise of its tender beauty, little of substance has been said about the volume.

The apparent conspiracy of silence about the ends and aims of what may be Swinburne's greatest single book of poems has had a

---

[1] *The Swinburne Letters*, ed. Cecil Y. Lang, I (New Haven, 1959), xix; T. Earle Welby, *A Study of Swinburne* (1926; rpt. New York, 1969), p. 122; John D. Rosenberg, ed., *Swinburne: Selected Poetry and Prose* (New York, 1968), p. xxii; Edmund Gosse, *The Life of Algernon Charles Swinburne* (New York, 1917), p. 239; Samuel Chew, *Swinburne* (Boston, 1929), pp. 141–42.

pernicious effect on our appreciation of all his work, for the themes of the 1878 *Poems and Ballads* are those that occupied Swinburne until his death. "The prevalent mood," says Chew, "is one of withdrawal from life around him into the intimate world of meditations and memories and into the ever-expanding world of books. The atmosphere is personal, reminiscent, elegiac, literary." These adjectives, particularly "literary," have been constantly used by critics not only to praise the 1878 volume but also to disparage the succeeding work. In one of the most damning comments ever made about Swinburne's late verse, A. E. Housman said that "Swinburne did worse than take books for his subject; he dragged this subject into the midst of all other subjects, and covered earth and sky and man with the dust of the library. He cannot watch a sunset at sea without thinking of Beaumont and Fletcher." [2] If the reasons for Swinburne's use of literature as a subject are properly understood, however, the literary quality of his verse becomes not a defect but a merit, embodying a profound mythic conception of man's relation to nature.

Because the poems in the volume were written over a period of ten years, *Poems and Ballads* is necessarily something of a miscellany, but Swinburne always took great care in structuring his books to form a coherent thematic pattern, and this one was no exception. The first poem, "The Last Oracle," provides the thematic key to all that follows. It is a pointed response to two of Swinburne's own earlier poems, the "Hymn to Proserpine," which epitomized the central concerns of *Poems and Ballads* (1866), and the "Hymn of Man," which epitomized the republican ardor of *Songs before Sunrise*. These earlier poems had sung the keynotes of the two previous phases of Swinburne's career, his negation of all values and his turn to euphoric affirmation; "The Last Oracle," which could as well have been called "Hymn to Apollo," sings the keynote of his third and final period, a period of creative alternative to despair.

In a letter to Watts-Dunton, Swinburne explicated the poem and in so doing clarified his intentions for the entire volume:

Starting from the answer brought back from Delphi to Julian by his envoy (A.D. 361), I go on to reinvoke Apollo to reappear in these days when the Galilean too is conquered and Christ has followed Pan to death, not as

---

[2] Chew, p. 141; Housman, "Swinburne," *Cornhill Magazine*, 177 (1969), 386.

they called him in Greece, merely son of Zeus the son of Chronos, but older than Time or any God born of Time, the Light and the Word incarnate in man, of whom comes the inner sunlight of human thought or imagination and the gift of speech and song, whence all Gods or ideas of Gods possible to man take form and fashion—conceived of thought or imagination and born of speech or song. Of this I take the sun-god and the singing-god of the Greeks to be the most perfect type attained, or attainable; and as such I call on him to return and reappear over the graves of intervening Gods.—This is the subject-matter; metre—twelve long trochaics followed by twelve shorter anapaestic lines, alternating through six stanzas of 24 verses.[3]

This extraordinarily pregnant paragraph concisely expresses or implies all of the most important themes of Swinburne's late poetry. The two most obvious points are that, as in the "Hymn to Proserpine," Swinburne clearly recognizes the inevitability of the genesis and death of gods in time's cycles and that, as Jerome McGann says, "the crucial thing is that Apollo and his children are not subject to these cycles."[4] What should be equally obvious is that the passage is a sort of manifesto of romantic mythmaking. The essential agnosticism of Swinburne's position could not be clearer. He has been repeatedly referred to as a pantheist, yet he dismisses Pan as cavalierly as he dismisses Christ: "Christ has followed Pan to death."[5] His alternative religion, worship of Apollo, the "sun-god and the singing-god of the Greeks," is clearly no more than a worship of man's power to create things to believe in, for he worships not gods but the power of making gods: "the gift of speech and song, whence all Gods or ideas of Gods possible to man take form and fashion." This worship of Apollo, the creative singing power in man, is a constant for the rest of Swinburne's career and is the key to understanding everything he wrote.

[3] *Letters*, III (1960), 137.

[4] *Swinburne: An Experiment in Criticism* (Chicago, 1972), p. 61.

[5] Swinburne was probably drawing on the Plutarchan tale of the mariners who heard a voice on the waters announcing the death of Pan, and the subsequent Christian interpretations that the Pan referred to was either a demon exorcised by Christ or Christ himself, the All. In either case the cyclical nature of history, the changing of the gods, is emphasized. See Patricia Merivale, *Pan the Goat-God* (Cambridge, Mass., 1969), pp. 12–16.

The tendency of Swinburne's critics to refer to him as a pantheist reflects a complicating factor in his worship of the god of song. Apollo cannot simply be reduced to the singing god—he is also the sun god. As in *Erechtheus*, and even "Hesperia," the natural element, the god, and its human significance are inseparable. In "The Last Oracle," sun, song, and Apollo are rhetorically interchangeable:

> Is the sun yet cast out of heaven?
>   Is the song yet cast out of man?
> Life that had song for its leaven
>   To quicken the blood that ran
> Through the veins of the songless years
> More bitter and cold than tears,
> Heaven that had thee for its one
> Light, life, word, witness, O sun,
> Are they soundless and sightless and hollow,
>   Without eye, without speech, without ear?
> O father of all of us, Paian, Apollo,
>   Destroyer and healer, hear!
>
>   [III, 7]

Modern criticism has, perhaps, been overinclined to interpret all poems as being about poetry, but with Swinburne there can be no alternative. Because his identification of man's song with nature is so strong, all of his poems about nature are about poetry also. As Housman said, he "cannot watch a sunset at sea without thinking of Beaumont and Fletcher"—or of Marlowe, Shakespeare, or Shelley—but before issuing a facile condemnation of his bookishness, it is worthwhile to examine the poems about poetry more clearly.

"In the Bay," second in the volume, is ostensibly about a sunset at sea. The first stanza sets the scene:

> Beyond the hollow sunset, ere a star
> Take heart in heaven from eastward, while the west,
> Fulfilled of watery resonance and rest,
> Is as a port with clouds for harbour bar. . . .
>
>   [III, 10]

Though they seem to be entirely about nature, these lines, especially the third, are primarily about poetry. The seascape, as we learn in the course of the poem, is "fufilled" with meaning because

of the "resonance," or "re-sounding" of the voices of long dead
poets in the ears of Swinburne. The poem goes on, not very successfully, for forty stanzas, developing the idea that the songs of all
poets live on in the natural scene, to be recreated in the minds of
later poets. It fails for a number of reasons, but primarily because
Swinburne insists on an elaborate allegory—by no better name can
it be called—in which the sun is a symbol of Shakespeare, the
morning star of Marlowe, the evening star of Shelley. The allegory,
which Swinburne returned to often, most notably in the *Sonnets on
English Dramatic Poets*, was wholly antithetical to mythopoeia, so
"In the Bay," along with "The Last Oracle," is more successful as a
manifesto than as a poem.

The suggestion that the resonance of the sea is the resonance of
generations of mortal singers, made explicit in the best line of "In
the Bay"—"All singing souls are as one sounding sea" (III, 15)—is
developed in some of the other, less didactic poems in the volume.
In the intensely beautiful "At a Month's End," for example, the
image is used brilliantly:

> With chafe and change of surges chiming,
>   The clashing channels rocked and rang
> Large music, wave to wild wave timing,
>   And all the choral water sang.
>
>   [III, 29]

"At a Month's End," however, is a poem not of joyous affirmation
but of sad farewell to the passion of youth; it represents not a new
singing-season, not a beginning, but an end, and as such it is more
typical of the volume than the thematically interesting but less
compelling poems we have been discussing. The image of a sounding, singing sea, however, implies a possible redemption. Swinburne's redemptive vision did not come easily—he had to see death
clearly and unblinkingly, and to continue seeing it. "A Forsaken
Garden," perhaps the most famous poem in the volume, and certainly one of the most beautiful in the language, expresses the
totality of death more emphatically than any poem I know. The
garden dies, lovers die, love, which should be eternal, dies, the
earth dies, and, in a triumph that is in every sense absolute, death,
with no more victims and still insatiable, turns upon himself:

Till the slow sea rise and the sheer cliff crumble,
    Till terrace and meadow the deep gulfs drink,
Till the strength of the waves of the high tides humble
    The fields that lessen, the rocks that shrink,
Here now in his triumph where all things falter,
    Stretched out on the spoils that his own hand spread,
As a god self-slain on his own strange altar,
        Death lies dead.

                                                    [III, 24]

The destruction of the land by the sea is the destruction that had
been avoided in *Erechtheus*—it is the complete annihilation of man
and all that man makes. The myth of eternal poetry put forth in
"The Last Oracle" and "In the Bay" mitigates the sense of doom, for
we recall that the sea is no longer, as in *Erechtheus*, antithetical to
man's creation, but is in harmony with it; yet the appalling vision of
"A Forsaken Garden" is not to be set aside so lightly, and we are left
with the uneasy feeling that the redemption is somehow premature,
that it has not been fairly earned. The new myth had been fully
articulated—perhaps too fully articulated—in the declamatory, allegorical poems, but it had not been fully realized.

The tone of *Poems and Ballads* seems strangely at odds with itself
because of this constant tension between rejoicing in the new Apollonian dispensation and despair at the inevitability of death. Most of
the poems are farewells to youth and elegies—mostly for other
poets—so the general mood of the volume is one of stoic acceptance. The redemptive vision in the elegies, of which "Ave atque
Vale" is thematically typical, is that the singers will live on in their
songs, but the real comfort is that their sorrows will be ended by
oblivion. In "Ex-Voto" Swinburne writes of his own twofold consolation for death. He knows that he will return to the sea but is
solaced by the knowledge that he is of the sea as song is of the sea:

        Yours was I born, and ye,
        The sea-wind and the sea,
        Made all my soul in me
            A song forever. . . .

                                                    [III, 86]

The more substantial emotional consolation, however, is still, as it
was in *Poems and Ballads* (1866) and in "A Forsaken Garden," that

oblivion will end the ever unsatisfied desire of life: "All fire of thirst that aches / The salt sea cools and slakes" (III, 88). Yet the mood of the volume is so strangely poised that in "A Song in Season," for example, Swinburne could contentedly affirm—in the face of the wholly opposite stance taken in "A Forsaken Garden"—that love lives forever, in song:

> Dust that covers
> Long dead lovers
> Song blows off with breath that brightens. . . .
>
> [III, 108]

As in all the other affirmative poems in the volume, the consolation is baldly stated, not poetically generated. The sentiment once again seems premature, the song oddly out of season. John D. Rosenberg comes close to a brilliant insight into the nature of the book when he notes the significance of the title of the poem "A Vision of Spring in Winter": "the volume itself is a prevision of Swinburne's long winter, seen from the last moment of his spring."[6] The volume, rather, anticipates, as Swinburne himself realized, a new creative spring for himself, and in the meantime his poems were

> As sweet desire of day before the day,
>   As dreams of love before the true love born,
>   From the outer edge of winter overworn
> The ghost arisen of May before the May. . . .
>
> [III, 100]

In *Songs of the Springtides*, published in 1879, he no longer needed to content himself with imposing a mythic structure on the meaninglessness of life but was able at last to generate his myth from the desperate void. "Thalassius," the first poem in the book, is not entirely successful, but, like "Hesperia" and the "Prelude" to *Songs before Sunrise*, it is one of the great turning points in Swinburne's poetry. It autobiographically sums up the poet's past and prophetically anticipates his future. The poem has been well and fully analyzed in two recent articles, both of which recognize its romantic roots. Richard D. McGhee, who notes the influence of Blake on the poem, has done a splendid job of analyzing the imagery, noting that

---

[6] Rosenberg, p. xxiii.

sun, sea, and wind are all images of song and that the aim of the singer is to become one with his song and therefore one with nature. The reading is unquestionably correct, as the famous lines that McGhee draws on in support of his argument clearly illustrate:

> Even so the spirit in him, when winds grew strong,
> Grew great with child of song.
> Nor less than when his veins first leapt for joy
> To draw delight in such as burns a boy,
> Now too the soul of all his senses felt
> The passionate pride of deep sea-pulses dealt
> Through nerve and jubilant vein
> As from the love and largess of old time,
> And with his heart again
> The tidal throb of all the tides keep rhyme
> And charm him from his own soul's separate sense
> With infinite and invasive influence
> That made strength sweet in him and sweetness strong,
> Being now no more a singer, but a song.
>
> [III, 327]

As in "Hesperia" and *Erechtheus* the images synesthetically merge so that disparate reality is fused into the monolithic vision of song. The description of the "resonant radiance" (III, 312) of the sun's car, for example, fuses images of light and sound and, in addition, suggests the re-singings of Apollonian poets. McGhee's closing comment on the poem, I think, perfectly expresses Swinburne's poetic intentions: "The pattern of imagery is integral with the myth, and the myth is identical with its pattern of imagery."[7]

Had Swinburne fulfilled his intentions, "Thalassius" would be a mythopoeic poem; as it is, the poem is still primarily mythological. The second half of McGhee's statement ignores the highly structured narrative line, which Kerry McSweeney has accurately described as "far too schematic and abstract."[8] Each verse paragraph has a more or less explicit external referent in Swinburne's life, and the poem is essentially an elaborate allegory of the growth of the poet's mind. McGhee praises the poem for what it achieves, and it

[7] Richard D. McGhee, "'Thalassius': Swinburne's Poetic Myth," *Victorian Poetry*, 5 (1967), 136.

[8] "Swinburne's 'Thalassius,'" *Humanities Association Bulletin*, 22 (1971), 55.

achieves much, but McSweeney finds it of interest chiefly for its prophecies of Swinburne's poetic development. The promise of future achievement is given by the oracular voice of Apollo in the last four lines of the poem:

> Have therefore in thine heart and in thy mouth
> The sound of song that mingles north and south,
> The song of all the winds that sing of me,
> And in thy soul the sense of all the sea.
>
> [III, 328]

The promise is of a poetry that will unite elemental nature and man's song entirely and inextricably, a mythopoeic poetry that will generate meaning from a sense of the unity of man and nature. McSweeney's opinion, and the opinion of most Swinburne scholars, is that Swinburne failed utterly to live up to his own prediction of greatness, but a close examination of his late nature poetry will show, I think, that he succeeded where his critics have failed—that his late nature poetry is in an extraordinarily complex mythopoeic mode that unsympathetic readers have simply failed to penetrate. The poem following "Thalassius" in *Songs of the Springtides*, "On the Cliffs," and a poem written two years later, "By the North Sea," will serve to demonstrate the astonishing complexities of his poetry of nature.

Swinburne's late lyrics, all of those written after he was "redeemed" by Watts-Dunton in 1879 and safely ensconced in Putney, have traditionally been dismissed with contempt by even his most friendly critics.[9] The resurrection of Watts-Dunton's character in recent years and the still more recent emergence of interest in some of the lyrics of the later period have not yet eradicated the notion that the last thirty years of Swinburne's life were a period of creative stagnation, during which "the waning fires of middle age were further damped and smothered by the brown blankets of No. 2 The

---

[9] The best critical work on the late poems, and on Swinburne generally, is Jerome McGann's, but his experimental dialogue format does not allow for close readings of individual poems. Few articles have been published about any of the late poems. No articles have appeared on "By the North Sea," and the only useful article on "On the Cliffs" is Meredith B. Raymond, "Swinburne among the Nightingales," *Victorian Poetry*, 6 (1968), 125–42.

Pines."[10] A. E. Housman, in a staggeringly ungracious remark, commented that "when Mr. Swinburne died, April 1909, at the age of 72, he might as well have been dead for a quarter of a century. For a quarter of a century and more he had written nothing that mattered." Even John D. Rosenberg, who finds "moments of astonishing strength in late Swinburne," laments that "the death of development in Swinburne may have been as large a loss to English poetry as the physical death of Keats."[11] An extremely sympathetic reader, Rosenberg still saw fit to print a mutilated version of "By the North Sea" in his *Swinburne: Selected Poetry and Prose.*

The general neglect caused by this attitude has resulted in the specific neglect of some of Swinburne's best poetry, notably such poems as "On the Cliffs" and "By the North Sea." With the exception of Jerome McGann, whose treatment of the poems is masterful, even those critics who have regarded them as exceptions to the general rule of mediocrity have declined to analyze them or even discuss their meanings.[12] Part of the reason for this has been the conviction that the late work is mere "nature poetry," unrewarding to close analysis. Samuel Chew, for example, noted the excellence of "By the North Sea" but characterized it as mere description, the "finest of Swinburne's nature-pieces," and wholly overlooked its real aim and accomplishment. E. K. Brown contended that it is upon *Songs before Sunrise* that Swinburne's "reputation as a prophet, an intellectual poet comparable with Shelley and Hugo, chiefly rests."[13] But the culmination and fullest expression of his thought is to be found in some of the later poetry. The general tendency which I have traced, the movement away from historical archetypes in "Faustine" and mythological archetypes in *Atalanta in Calydon* toward a genuinely mythopoeic poetry in *Erechtheus*, is completed in the creation of a myth of nature and poetry in the late works. The myth, which had been baldly stated in the mythological "The Last Oracle" and not quite successfully integrated in "In the Bay," finally

---

[10] Harold Nicolson, *Swinburne* (New York, 1926), p. 160.

[11] Housman, p. 382; Rosenberg, pp. xxxiii, xxxiv.

[12] McGann: for "On the Cliffs" see particularly pp. 75–79, 159–66; for "By the North Sea" see pp. 142–45.

[13] Chew, p. 159; Brown, "Swinburne: A Centenary Estimate"; rpt. in *Victorian Literature: Modern Essays in Criticism*, ed. Austin Wright (New York, 1961), p. 303.

becomes fully realized as poetry when treated in the manner foreshadowed by the closing lines of "Thalassius." The focus of this chapter is on the two poems that express this myth most fully, two of the three poems (the other is "Thalassius") which Jerome McGann has characterized as attempting "a full statement of Swinburne's artistic canon."[14] After clarifying just what that "canon" is, we will be able to view other late poems in a new light.

Perhaps the greatest fault charged to "On the Cliffs" and "By the North Sea," and certainly the most persistent, is what is charged to all of Swinburne's verse: that verbiage—wanton, excessive—obscures the meaning; that Swinburne has, as Arnold put it, a "fatal habit of using one hundred words where one would suffice."[15] This was considered a defect even in those poems written before the fire burned out, but, as Nicolson said, "when he approaches Nature directly the disabilities of his temperament become sadly apparent; his nature poems are diffuse, ecstatic, and marred by repetition." So complete is Nicolson's bias that he can link the worst of the late poems with the best in describing "some portentous dithyramb along the lines of 'By the North Sea'" and characterize that magnificent poem as one of "three long sea pieces, competent but wholly uninspired."[16]

No poem has been blamed for obscurity so persistently (or so understandably) as "On the Cliffs." Nicolson claimed that a "sense of tedium assails the reader of 'On the Cliff[s]'"; Chew described it as tenuous thought in a tide of verbiage; and William R. Rutland observed that it "might have been a great poem, had not Swinburne been content merely to let himself wildly go, and had he instead kept a grip upon his form and his thought." Unquestionably, it is extraordinarily difficult, "densely difficult," as Rosenberg puts it, and the reasons are apparent.[17] Most obviously, the extremely long sentences lose the reader in a syntactical maze of modifying clauses and phrases, forcing him into a conscious effort to find the main

[14] McGann, p. 143.

[15] Quoted in Clyde K. Hyder, ed., *Swinburne: The Critical Heritage* (New York, 1970), p. 117.

[16] Nicolson, pp. 170, 171.

[17] Ibid., p. 167; Chew, p. 156; William R. Rutland, *Swinburne: A Nineteenth Century Hellene* (Oxford, 1931), p. 321; Rosenberg, p. 249n.

subject and predicate. Less obvious, but just as bewildering, is the fact that the subject, once found, often has no immediately apparent referent; it is often a pronoun that could refer back to any of several things. The vocabulary of the poem also causes difficulty, since in many cases, as we shall see, our understanding of crucial phrases is dependent upon the recognition of a pun. In addition, Swinburne assumed that the reading public was as erudite as he was, that everyone, like himself, knew Aeschylus and Sappho by heart, so a major difficulty in understanding is simply to hold to the path in the labyrinth of literary allusion.

Perhaps the greatest reason for the difficulty, however, is that the strategy (even the very essence of the poem) requires that we be in continual doubt about any kind of meaning—not only that we not know the answer but also that we not know the question. The poem perfectly illustrates the death scene of Gertrude Stein, who, on regaining consciousness after grave exploratory surgery, asked: "Well, what is the answer?" When told that her condition was hopeless, she merely replied: "In that case, what is the question?" For the agnostic there is no sphinx or catechism to formulate a question; there is no framework of received myth within which to find an answer. Swinburne attempts in "On the Cliffs" to generate a myth from within the poem, so the question, as well as the answer, must be generated from within—it does not preexist, so it cannot simply be stated. My purpose in the reading of "On the Cliffs" which follows will be not only to explicate the meaning but to show that the complexities are functional and that both form and meaning reflect Swinburne's personal myth, still undergoing changes but nearing completion.

I

"On the Cliffs" is, as critics have charged, a nature poem, but it is a nature poem in the same sense as "Tintern Abbey" and "Frost at Midnight"; it is a meditative-descriptive lyric in which the description of nature is wholly subordinate to the thoughts the landscape inspires. Like "Tintern Abbey," "On the Cliffs" opens with a description of the natural scene, a description that can no more be characterized as merely ornamental nature poetry than can Wordsworth's description of the Wye Valley. The landscape is not objectively described as an independent entity to be exploited for comparisons with the poet's state of mind in the meditation that follows; it is imaginatively perceived, brought into unity with the poet's mind by that faculty called by Coleridge the esemplastic imagination. Swinburne half-creates and half-perceives the landscape, strictly conforming to the romantic conception of the best kind of "nature poetry" as described by his revered Coleridge: "Nature has her proper interest, and he will know what it is who believes and feels that everything has a life of its own and that we are all *One Life*. A poet's heart and intellect should be *combined*, intimately combined and unified with the great appearances of nature, and not merely held in solution and loose mixture with them, in the shape of formal similes."[18]

"On the Cliffs" takes place at twilight, "Between the moondawn and the sundown" (III, 329) as the poet stands on the cliffs overlooking the sea. His eyes are turned, however, not toward the sea, but toward the land, a vernal landscape showing signs only of death, with no hint of regeneration:

> Fiercely the gaunt woods to the grim soil cling
> That bears for all fair fruits
> Wan wild sparse flowers of windy and wintry spring
> Between the tortive serpent-shapen roots
> Wherethrough their dim growth hardly strikes and shoots
> And shews one gracious thing
> Hardly, to speak for summer one sweet word
> Of summer's self scarce heard.
> But higher the steep green sterile fields, thick-set
> With flowerless hawthorn even to the upward verge
> Whence the woods gathering watch new cliffs emerge
> Higher than their highest of crowns that sea-winds fret,
> Hold fast, for all that night or wind can say,
> Some pale pure colour yet,
> Too dim for green and luminous for grey.
> Between the climbing inland cliffs above

[18] Quoted by M. H. Abrams in *The Mirror and the Lamp* (New York, 1958), p. 294.

And these beneath that breast and break the bay,
A barren peace too soft for hate or love
Broods on an hour too dim for night or day.

[III, 329–30]

Swinburne's perception of the scene is of considerable biographical
interest, since it shows clearly his state of mind when the poem was
written, in July and August of 1879, just after he had been rescued
from London and alcoholic suicide and returned to his ancestral
home at Holmwood and just before he moved in with Watts-
Dunton to start a new life in Putney.[19] His bohemian youth having
finally ended at the age of forty-three, approaching the twilight and
autumn of his own life but still holding to it as the green held fast to
the high fields, Swinburne must have felt doubts about his creative
life, now "Too dim for green" but still too "luminous for grey." The
desolation of the landscape, its neutral tones, reflects his concern
that the wellspring of his creative life, his emotional life, may have
run dry, leaving him "A barren peace too soft for hate or love" and a
middle-age "too dim for night or day."

The central concern of the poem, as the opening description
implies, is the inevitability of death and the poet's doubts concerning any sort of resurrection or regeneration. The natural setting, a
high point of land overlooking the sea, has a long tradition in English poetry and had been often used as a starting point for an
exploration of the meaning of mortal life, since sea and cliffs present
such an imposing spectacle of the eternality of nature. In Chaucer's
"The Franklin's Tale," for example, Dorigen ponders the question why God had, in his "fair creacioun," included "grisly feendly
rokkes blake" to shipwreck sailors. Throughout the poem these
rocks are contrasted with a

gardyn ful of leves and floures;
And craft of mannes hand so curiously
Arrayed hadde this gardin, trewely,
That never was ther gardin of swich prys
But if it were the verray paradys.[20]

---

[19] Philip Henderson, *Swinburne: The Portrait of a Poet* (London, 1974), p. 218.
[20] "The Franklin's Tale," ll. 908–12, *The Complete Works of Geoffrey Chaucer*, ed.
Walter W. Skeat (Oxford, 1894), IV, 488.

Chaucer uses the contrast to illustrate the main theme of the poem, that man can make a paradise on earth through honesty and "gentilesse." In the famous cliff scene between Edgar and Gloucester in *King Lear* Shakespeare uses a similar setting to show that faith, even if it is illusory, makes life bearable. With the rediscovery of Longinus and the sublime in the late seventeenth and eighteenth centuries the conception of such scenes as an emblem of God's power became dogma, so when Wordsworth found his own god in the final book of *The Prelude*, he was, fittingly, looking out upon the sea from the top of Mount Snowden. The agnostic perception of such a scene has been poignantly presented by Hardy in "Beeny Cliff," where the landscape forces him to realize only that his dead wife will never return, and by Matthew Arnold, in "Dover Beach," where there is no hope of God, only a receding "Sea of Faith."

As we have seen, Swinburne himself had used the setting of cliffs by the sea in "A Forsaken Garden" to reflect his agnosticism, his belief that all earthly life, even the earth itself, is destined for oblivion. That this idea was present in Swinburne's mind when he wrote "On the Cliffs" becomes clear later in the poem, when he equates the suicide leap of Sappho with

> this grey north sea's half-sapped cliff-side
> That crumbles toward the coast-line, year by year
> More near the sands and near. . . .
>
> [III, 340]

The conflation of the death of the landscape and the death of Sappho, moreover, indicates a Coleridgean synthesis of both in the One Life and shows how central the poet's perception of nature is to his meditations upon mortality and upon the death of creativity.

Following the opening description, the poet begins to brood on the questions of mortality implicit in his perception of the twilight and the somber landscape. He seeks an answer, a "word," first from the wind and sea and finally in the song of a nightingale, but he receives no helpful reply. For the Christian, of course, the Word is Christ, the Redeemer, but Swinburne implicitly rejects the consolations of Christianity by seeking the "word" in nature. The unsatisfactory answer, the "one word . . . blown up usward ever from the sea" (III, 331), is never revealed to us, but Swinburne's insistence on its "unchangeable", "changeless" (III, 332) character indicates that it is apparently "death," the one constant in life. That the word *is* "death" becomes a certainty when we realize the extent to which "On the Cliffs" is a conscious recapitulation of and response to Whitman's "Out of the Cradle Endlessly Rocking." In Whitman's poem, as in Swinburne's, the poet, approaching middle age, stands alone on the "sterile sands" of the seacoast, questioning the sea and a bird, seeking the "word stronger and more delicious than any." Before the word can be given to him he must "A reminiscence sing" about his own youth and a song he had half-created, half-perceived of a bird that had lost its mate.[21] The reminiscence leads ultimately to an understanding of the ways of nature and of the poet's relation to nature, an understanding that releases creativity by allowing him literally to *reverberate* the song of nature in the song of himself: "already a thousand singers, a thousand songs, clearer, louder and more sorrowful than yours [the bird's], / A thousand warbling echoes have started to life within me, never to die." The revelation, the one word whispered by the sea, is "the low and delicious word death, / And again death, death, death. . . ."[22] Although Swinburne is not so explicit, the dynamic of "On the Cliffs" is identical to that of "Out of the Cradle." The perception of the landscape inspires essentially painful memories of childhood, "keen gusts of memory" that

> Heap the weight up of pain, and break, and leave
> Strength scarce enough to grieve
> In the sick heavy spirit, unmanned with strife
> Of waves that beat at the tired lips of life.

> [III, 332]

It is a sort of reverse Wordsworthian memory that leads not to intimations of immortality in youthful joy but to a conviction of mortality through recollections of youthful wretchedness.

---

[21] "Out of the Cradle Endlessly Rocking," ll. 4, 14, 22, *Leaves of Grass*, ed. Harold W. Blodgett and Sculley Bradley (New York, 1965), pp. 246–47. I am indebted to Professor McGann for pointing out that both this poem and, to a lesser extent, "When Lilacs Last in the Dooryard Bloomed" are important precursors of "On the Cliffs."

[22] Ibid., ll. 148–49, 168–69, p. 252.

Yet the grim realization of death, the message given by the sea, paradoxically leads, in Swinburne as in Whitman, to a celebration of life and song. The resolution of the paradox, which occupies Swinburne throughout the rest of the poem, involves the answer to a second question, a request for a second revelation, for he seeks

> what far other word
> Than ever of her [the sea] was spoken, or of me
> Or all my winged white kinfolk of the sea
> Between fresh wave and wave was ever heard,
> Cleaves the clear dark enwinding tree with tree
> Too close for stars to separate and to see
> Enmeshed in multitudinous unity?
>
> [III, 330]

An understanding of these difficult lines must take into account the double meaning of the word "cleaves," both in the sense of the word *cutting*, as of the flight of a bird cutting the air with its wings, and in the sense of causing adhesion, so as to bring all things into "multitudinous unity." In the second sense the question is simply, What word will bring all things into unity? This question remains, for the moment, unanswered. In the first sense the question is, What word is this I now hear cutting through the twilight and enwinding tree with tree to bring all things into multitudinous unity? The lines are to be appreciated in all their ambiguity as both seeking an answer and implying that it is present in the song of the nightingale, introduced for the first time four lines later: "What voice of God grown heavenlier in a bird" (III, 330).

The nightingale's song is so complex, Swinburne's language so precise, that it is necessary to step back for a moment to define the problems it presents and set forth a critical approach for dealing with them.

This poem must be viewed as a hermeneutic circle. The meaning of any work is elusive because the whole cannot be understood except through an understanding of the parts, and the parts cannot be understood except in relation to the whole. It is a gestalt theory of criticism which affirms that nothing can be comprehended except in relation to other things. In most poetry the problem is only theoretical, since meaning is arrived at through some sort of narrative progression so that the significance of each part is understood in relation to what preceded it, and once the parts are understood, so is the whole. "On the Cliffs," however, proves that the difficulties in theory can be difficulties in practice, for it arrives at its meaning, as McGann says, "not along a line but by accumulation and expansion." Each passage is densely filled with meaning that is communicated by puns and deliberate ambiguity, techniques that cause the words themselves to become Protean, their significations metamorphosing constantly according to how we perceive them in relation to the whole. The difficulties of comprehension are well expressed by McGann in his description of a specific passage:

The new organization of familiar materials moves us, as it were, into a wholly fresh relation toward the world of facts we thought we had known, or were beginning to know. But all those familiarities dissolve . . . transform themselves once more into mysterious signs with which we feel vaguely at home but which now acquire new suggestiveness. Their past associations only complicate the problem of understanding just because we expect these verbal counters to behave in certain ways and now find that they don't, or that they do so only imperfectly. Eager to know and understand them completely, in themselves and all their associations, they feed our desires still more. A certain few sets of symbolic relations will hold, but the rest are drawn into their ever-shifting patterns of beauty and glimpsed wholeness.[23]

The poem cannot be discussed in narrative fashion, and since we are unable to describe the whole without reference to the parts or the parts without reference to the whole, this analysis will use one short section as a sort of touchstone, discussing each line in all its ramifications and transformations when viewed in the ever shifting light of the context of the poem. The entire meaning of the poem will be found both in the "touchstone" passage and in the poem, so the focus will shift repeatedly from the part to the whole and back again.

Near the very center of "On the Cliffs" is a seven-line sentence of such density that it contains in capsule form all of the many complex motifs of the address to the nightingale. It is a perfect point to enter into the hermeneutic circle:

[23] McGann, pp. 143, 166.

> Love's priestess, mad with pain and joy of song,
> Song's priestess, mad with joy and pain of love,
> Name above all names that are lights above,
> We have loved, praised, pitied, crowned and done thee wrong,
> O thou past praise and pity; thou the sole
> Utterly deathless, perfect only and whole
> Immortal, body and soul.
>
> [III, 336]

The "name above all names," echoing Paul's discussion of Jesus in Philippians 2:9 ("Wherefore God also hath highly exalted him, and given him a name which is above every name"), suggests one of the central concerns of the poem, the displacement of Christianity by a new myth. Like most of the rest of the poem, these lines are addressed to the nightingale, whose song Swinburne hears carried on the wind. Within the context of the poem the nightingale is also Sappho, as Swinburne, continuing to address the bird, finally makes clear more than halfway through the poem: "I have known thee always who thou art, / . . . but inly by thine only name" (III, 337). Ovid had mythologized the nightingale for all of English literature from Shakespeare to Keats to Arnold until T. S. Eliot, characterizing the nightingale's song in two words borrowed from the Elizabethans, "jug, jug," finally demythologized it for the twentieth century. Swinburne, characteristically neither accepting received myth nor rejecting it entirely, remythologized it—metamorphosed, in a sense, the Ovidian tale. The nightingale is, according to Swinburne's "anti-Ovidian theory as to the real personality of that much misrepresented bird," an incarnation, or more appropriately, a metamorphosis not of Philomela but of Sappho.[24]

Though the reader could hardly be expected to perceive it without the more direct information noted above, the third line of the passage under consideration ("Name above all names that are lights above") clearly applies much more appropriately to Sappho than to the bird. The line alludes to the myth expressed in "In the Bay" as well as to that employed by Shelley in "Adonais," that poets, after death, become stars in the seventh heaven. Sappho, in Swinburne's opinion the greatest of all mortal poets, certainly merits the distinc-

---

[24] *Letters*, IV (1960), 78.

tion of being the "Name above all names" among these enskied poets.

The line is, however, ambiguous, for it also suggests Apollo, who deserves the distinction both in his role as god of the sun, the most important of all lights above, and in his role as god of song, surpassing all *mortal* poets. The identification of the bird with the god has been present from the moment it was first addressed: "God, if thou be God,—bird, if bird thou be,—" (III, 331). But if the technique of transformation of language is to be understood, it is important to notice that in the ambiguity of this one line all three figures, Sappho, the nightingale, and Apollo, are implied.

As Swinburne makes clear only near the end of the poem, the three together comprise a non-Christian Holy Trinity, a "treble-natured mystery," a "soul triune, woman and god and bird" (III, 341), in which Apollo replaces God the Father, the nightingale the Holy Ghost.[25] Sappho, as the human incarnation of the divinity, replaces Christ; mediating between the Apollonian immortality of song and the nightingale world of mortal love, she is "Song's priestess, mad with joy and pain of love, / Love's priestess, mad with pain and joy of song" (III, 336). As in the Christian Holy Trinity, not only are the three persons one God but each of them encompasses the other two. The very nature of the trinity is a primary cause of the main difficulty the poem offers its readers—the confusion of referents for ambiguous terms and the consequent difficulty of isolating any one meaning. Because the three are one, no matter which the poet addresses, he is addressing the other two as well. Thus this passage and the poem as a whole work on two levels, developing the idea of "multitudinous unity," the One Life, by deliberate ambiguity, while exploring the central theme with respect to the specific human incarnation of the godhead in the person of Sappho.

Having accepted the sea's message of the inevitability of death, the impossibility of immortality, Swinburne is given hope for

[25] The traditional representation of the Holy Ghost as a bird, a dove, strengthens the correlation of the nightingale with the Holy Ghost. In addition, the other traditional incarnation of the Holy Ghost, a tongue of fire, is invoked by Swinburne's frequent references throughout the poem to the nightingale in terms of fire.

another kind of immortality by the example of Sappho metamorphosed into a nightingale:

> We have loved, praised, pitied, crowned and done thee wrong,
> O thou past praise and pity; thou the sole
> Utterly deathless, perfect only and whole
> Immortal, body and soul.

Though the lines indicate that Sappho alone is immortal in both body and soul and that this salvation is inaccessible to Swinburne, a meager consolation is still possible. Unable to hope for Sappho's bodily resurrection, her metamorphosis into a living creature, Swinburne can nonetheless transcend time by reexperiencing the life and song of Sappho, by praising and pitying the life that lives on in the song. He has dismissed the Wordsworthian myth of memory, but in his own ode to a nightingale he turns to that of another of his romantic predecessors. He draws upon Keats's description of the continuing presence of the nightingale's song in all generations:

> Thou wast not born for death, immortal bird!
>   No hungry generations tread thee down;
> The voice I hear this passing night was heard
>   In ancient days by emperor and clown.
> Perhaps the self-same song that found a path
>   Through the sad heart of Ruth, when, sick for home,
>   She stood in tears amid the alien corn. . . .[26]

and says essentially the same thing:

> All ages call thee conqueror, and thy cry
> The mightiest as the least beneath the sky
> Whose heart was ever set to song, or stirred
> With wind of mounting music blown more high
> Than wildest wing may fly,
> Hath heard or hears,—even Aeschylus as I.

> [III, 341]

But Swinburne is willing to carry the idea further than Keats carried it, since his nightingale is also Apollo and Sappho, and its song is the cosmic song of the "soul triune" (III, 341). Elsewhere Swinburne

---

[26]"Ode to a Nightingale," ll. 61–67, *The Poems of John Keats*, ed. Miriam Allott (London, 1970), pp. 529–30.

echoes Keats's very syntax ("Thou wast not born for death") to proclaim the greater cosmic significance of his bird and to describe the greater intensity of his experience of the song:

> We were not marked for sorrow, thou nor I,
> For joy nor sorrow, sister, were we made,
> To take delight and grief to live and die,
> Assuaged by pleasures or by pains affrayed
> That melt men's hearts and alter; we retain
> A memory mastering pleasure and all pain,
> A spirit within the sense of ear and eye,
> A soul behind the soul, that seeks and sings
> And makes our life move only with its wings
> And feed but from its lips, that in return
> Feed of our hearts wherein the old fires that burn
> Have strength not to consume
> Nor glory enough to exalt us past our doom.
>
> [III, 333–34]

The poet, a singer himself, actually merges in the "soul behind the soul," which I take to be the song that they all—bird, god, woman, and poet—share. The song is, in a sense, a memory, because it recalls the past; unlike Wordsworth's memory, it unites the poet not merely with his own past but with all that has been, with the triune soul of the universe, the cosmic song of Apollo. It is, moreover, a Bergsonian "pure memory," which not only recalls the past but relives it, merging it with present experience. The poet is so completely at one with the song that he can describe the One Life of Apollo, the nightingale, and Sappho as "our life," completely merging his identity with theirs.

Yet this harmony is flawed; there is no ecstasy—Swinburne and the nightingale were not marked for sorrow, but neither were they marked for joy. The neutral tones of Swinburne's middle age take on no more individualized colors in the white light of eternity than in the oblivion of the sea. As we saw in discussing "Hesperia," eternality is, to human perception at least, no more reassuring than void. The problem is implied in the lines singled out for particular study, for though the opening lines seem to characterize Sappho in her life as a woman, experiencing pain and joy in their greatest intensity, the words "past praise and pity" make it clear that in her present incarnation as a nightingale she is beyond such mortal concerns. Her metamorphosis as described in the poem fills the world with song, but only, of course, through her death as a mortal woman, her plunge into the oblivion of the sea:

> Till the sea's portal was as funeral gate
> For that sole singer in all time's ageless date
> Singled and signed for so triumphal fate,
> All nightingales but one in all the world
> All her sweet life were silent; only then,
> When her life's wing of womanhood was furled,
> Their cry, this cry of thine was heard again,
> As of me now, of any born of men.
>
> [III, 342]

Sappho, as woman, is dead, and the song of Sappho as nightingale fills all nature but is a part of nature. The Wordsworthian memory that Swinburne rejects, because it brings him no joy, at least brings him human sorrow. But the song of the nightingale lacks even that:

> Nay, sad may be man's memory, sad may be
> The dream he weaves him as for shadow of thee,
> But scarce one breathing-space, one heartbeat long
> Wilt thou take shadow of sadness on thy song.
>
> [III, 332]

This may seem a positive attribute, but when we remember that Swinburne's plight is not sadness but the inability to feel anything, the song of the nightingale hardly seems like consolation.

The "soul triune," represented to Swinburne as the song of the nightingale, offers him no more solace than would Wordsworthian pantheism or the Coleridgean One Life. It offers no hope for any kind of personal immortality: all men, even singers, even Sappho, are "past praise and pity" when their mortal span is ended, when "all that lived and loved and sang and sinned / Are all borne down death's cold sweet soundless wind" (III, 336). Metamorphosis into a bird would seem to be no better than a Wordsworthian metamorphosis into a sod "rolled round in earth's diurnal course."

Just as Wordsworth in his youth was in such harmony with nature that he could not separate himself from it to hear the "still, sad music of humanity," so Swinburne has been too much in harmony with the song of the nightingale to separate the human passion of humanity, the love and pain of Sappho, from it. He has been responding to the song as he did when he was a child and she, for aught he knew, a mere bird:

> As brother and sister were we, child and bird,
> Since thy first Lesbian word
> Flamed on me, and I knew not whence I knew
> This was the song that struck my whole soul through,
> Pierced my keen spirit of sense with edge more keen,
> Even when I knew not,—even ere sooth was seen,—
> When thou wast but the tawny sweet winged thing
> Whose cry was but of spring.
>
> [III, 337]

Only about halfway through the poem does Swinburne begin to address the triune deity in its specifically human incarnation in the person of Sappho. Only then does he realize that Sappho, metamorphosed into the nightingale and made a part of the cosmic song, still retains her human identity, for death has conquered all but Sappho, all

> But one that wind hath touched and changed not,—one
> Whose body and soul are parcel of the sun;
> One that earth's fire could burn not, nor the sea
> Quench; nor might human doom take hold on thee;
> All praise, all pity, all dreams have done thee wrong,
> All love, with eyes love-blinded from above;
> Song's priestess, mad with joy and pain of love,
> Love's priestess, mad with pain and joy of song.
>
> [III, 336]

The context of the poem has altered the meaning of these last two lines, which no longer designate primarily the nightingale, as they did in the "touchstone" passage, but designate specifically the one mortal untouched by time and change, Sappho, addressed here and elsewhere in language suggesting invocations to the Virgin.

With the poet now addressing the human rather than the natural incarnation of the deity, the focus of the poem is subtly changed. Swinburne renews his questioning, now dismissing the pantheistic

notion of immersion in nature by seeking a significance in the song
that is not vouchsafed to nature, only to man:

> Hast thou none other answer then for me
> Than the air may have of thee,
> Or the earth's warm woodlands girdling with green girth
> Thy secret sleepless burning life on earth,
> Or even the sea that once, being woman crowned
> And girt with fire and glory of anguish round,
> Thou wert so fain to seek to, fain to crave
> If she would hear thee and save
> And give thee comfort of thy great green grave?
> Because I have known thee always who thou art,
> Thou knowest, have known thee to thy heart's own heart,
> . . . but inly by thine only name,
> Sappho—because I have known thee and loved hast thou
> None other answer now?

[III, 337]

This imaginative response to the song, this perception of the human
voice of Sappho in the song of the nightingale, is a sign of the
emotional and imaginative reawakening of the poet. He is no longer
in harmony with the song as in a "barren peace" with nature but is
responding to the human passions of Sappho as expressed in the
song.

Sapphic fragments, interpolated into the poem in Swinburne's
wonderful translations, are isolated in the song and characterized as
quite different from the whole song of the "soul triune":

> this that fires our northland night,
> This is the song that made
> Love fearful, even the heart of love afraid,
> With the great anguish of its great delight.
> No swan-song, no far-fluttering half-drawn breath,
> No word that love of love's sweet nature saith,
> No dirge that lulls the narrowing lids of death,
> No healing hymn of peace-prevented strife,—
> This is her song of life.

[III, 340]

The barren peace of the twilight landscape has been filled full of
human life, with anguish and delight and the intensity of Sappho's
love.

The joy and pain in the song of Sappho have been sublimed into the cosmic song of nature, the song of the nightingale, which is ideal for the child when nature is all in all to him, but for the adult, the singer, the "still, sad music of humanity," the unsublimed pain and joy of mankind, must be faced. In a brilliant passage that is remarkably parallel in thought to Wordsworth's famous description of the stages of growth in "Tintern Abbey," Swinburne makes it clear that knowledge of both the pains and joys of mortality are necessary to the singer:

> Through sleepless clear spring nights filled full of thee,
> Rekindled here, thy ruling song has thrilled
> The deep dark air and subtle tender sea
> And breathless hearts with one bright sound fulfilled.
> Or at midnoon to me
> Swimming, and birds about my happier head
> Skimming, one smooth soft way by water and air,
> To these my bright born brethren and to me
> Hath not the clear wind borne or seemed to bear
> A song wherein all earth and heaven and sea
> Were molten in one music made of thee
> To enforce us, O our sister of the shore,
> Look once in heart back landward and adore?
> For songless were we sea-mews, yet had we
> More joy than all things joyful of thee—more,
> Haply, than all things happiest; nay, save thee,
> In thy strong rapture of imperious joy
> Too high for heart of sea-borne bird or boy,
> What living things were happiest if not we?
> But knowing not love nor change nor wrath nor wrong,
> No more we knew of song.
>
> [III, 343]

It is therefore necessary for Swinburne to hear the "music of humanity" in the cosmic song, and he does, by imaginatively metamorphosing the song of the nightingale back to the actual song of Sappho, her passionate outcry of love and suffering. This passage, in a sense, represents the "elegiac turn" in the poem, for the verse "Look once in heart back landward and adore" recalls the turning point in "Lycidas"—"Look homeward angel now, and melt with ruth." Though "On the Cliffs" is not an elegy or even elegiac, it is, as Swinburne said, written in "the irregular Italian metre of Lycidas,"

so it is reasonable to suppose that he had Milton's poem in mind.[27]
Perhaps the reason the poem is not elegiac is that the "turn" has
been implicit from the beginning. Unlike Arnold, who looks out to
a receding "Sea of Faith" in "Dover Beach," Swinburne is already
looking back toward the land as the poem begins. This pattern of
latent meaning becoming manifest is consistent with the strategy of
the poem, for just as the nightingale is gradually revealed as Sappho, so the apparently impersonal song is gradually shown to have
human significance and to give meaning to the natural landscape.

Sappho has passed her song not just to nightingales but to all
generations of mortal singers. She has passed it on, in particular, to
Swinburne, who is shaken out of his uncreative twilight slumber by
a renewal of his emotional life through his participation in her
love and wrath. Through her life and love and death she has metamorphosed such sea mews as Swinburne into nightingales. She is
therefore reincarnated not just in nature, in the bird, but spiritually in man, in Swinburne and other singers. In "On the Cliffs"
Swinburne, inspired by the song of the nightingale, of the triune
soul of nature, finally arrives at an apprehension of Sapphic intensity of life; his song becomes part of her song if

> it be not sin
> To hold myself in spirit of thy sweet kin,
> In heart and spirit of song;
> If this my great love do thy grace no wrong,
> Thy grace that gave me grace to dwell therein;
> If thy gods thus be my gods, and their will
> Made my song part of thy song—even such part
> As man's hath of God's heart—
>
>   [III, 338]

Wittily echoing Ruth's address to Naomi ("thy people shall be my
people, and thy God my God"), Swinburne is once again transform-
ing Biblical language into an aesthetic creed and traditional theology into a personal dogma. Swinburne becomes, in spirit, a nightingale, so that Sappho is spiritually reincarnated in him as he sings;
Sappho's spirit lives again in Swinburne, lives therefore in man, not

---

[27] *Letters*, IV, 109.

just in nature. Further, as a nightingale, Swinburne is serving Apollo just as Sappho did, for just as she alone answered Apollo at the dawn of time, answered "the old reconquering ray" with her "strange manlike maiden's godlike note" (III, 342), so Swinburne, at twilight, answers her. His is the "cry of song by night" that shoots "fire into the cloud-constraining light" (III, 342). Both songs are a part of the same song, the song of Apollo reechoed down the ages.

It is possible, with this fuller knowledge of the meaning of the whole of the poem, to circle back to the verses isolated as a "touchstone" and find still more latent meaning in the lines

> thou the sole
> Utterly deathless, perfect only and whole
> Immortal, body and soul.

Sappho is unique in being the only mortal to live on in bodily form, reincarnated in generations of nightingales; but her soul, her mortal identity, lives on more truly in incarnations of generations of poets. Swinburne's Bergsonian memory of literature conflates past and present, Sappho and Swinburne, in the present moment. His essential argument, stripped of its mythic structure, is that Sappho's poetry enabled him to relive Sappho's emotions, that this renewal of emotional life enabled him to write a poem; that because Sappho's life has become a part of his life, his song is also Sappho's song. All of this becomes clear in the triumphant finale of the poem, a single sentence of twenty-one lines:

> Song, and the secrets of it, and their might,
> What blessings curse it and what curses bless,
> I know them since my spirit had first in sight,
> Clear as thy song's words or the live sun's light,
> The small dark body's Lesbian loveliness
> That held the fire eternal; eye and ear
> Were as a god's to see, a god's to hear,
> Through all his hours of daily and nightly chime,
> The sundering of the two-edged spear of time:
> The spear that pierces even the sevenfold shields
> Of mightiest Memory, mother of all songs made,
> And wastes all songs as roseleaves kissed and frayed
> As here the harvest of the foam-flowered fields;

But thine the spear may waste not that he wields
Since first the God whose soul is man's live breath,
The sun whose face hath our sun's face for shade,
Put all the light of life and love and death
Too strong for life, but not for love too strong,
Where pain makes peace with pleasure in thy song,
And in thine heart, where love and song make strife,
Fire everlasting of eternal life.

[III, 343–44]

The "two-edged spear of time" recalls the "two-edged spear" which earlier in the poem was said to have sundered Cassandra; Cassandra, having refused to submit to Apollo, was "sundered" from life not in the literal sense that she was killed but in the sense that her prophesies could not be believed, her songs could not influence further generations. Even "mightiest Memory" cannot save from oblivion those poets who refuse to submit to Apollo—those poems, in effect, written outside the "tradition," those songs which do not reecho the eternal song of Apollo and Sappho. Their song is immortal; time's spear cannot "waste" it. Theirs is the one song of the One Life, the "word" that cleaves all things in "multitudinous unity." Swinburne has heard in the song of the nightingale more than merely the voice of nature, more even than the "fire eternal" of Apollo's song; he has heard the voice of human passion, of love too strong for death.

By adding the dimension of human song to the Coleridgean and Wordsworthian notion of the One Life, Swinburne is doing more than stating a theory of poetic influence—he is demonstrating, though not by design, how it works in practice. He is very nearly restating the pantheistic theory of Wordsworth as expressed in "Tintern Abbey":

I have learned
To look on nature, not as in the hour
Of thoughtless youth; but hearing oftentimes
The still, sad music of humanity,
Nor harsh nor grating, though of ample power
To chasten and subdue. And I have felt
A presence that disturbs me with the joy
Of elevated thoughts; a sense sublime

> Of something far more deeply interfused,
> Whose dwelling is the light of setting suns,
> And the round ocean and the living air,
> And the blue sky. . . .[28]

Wordsworth, however, does not mean the phrase "music of humanity" literally—Swinburne does. For Wordsworth, the informing force in nature is a mysterious pantheistic deity; for Swinburne, it is poetry—the god, Apollo, is "man's live breath." For Swinburne the "sense sublime / Of something far more deeply interfused" in all of nature is the sense of centuries of poetry stemming from Sappho and subliminated in his perception of the landscape. Like Wordsworth, he half-creates and half-perceives the scene, but the rest of his creation and perception is supplied not by nature but by his reexperiencing of the human pain and joy of Sappho.

Swinburne is not a pantheist, for there is no deity in nature but Apollo, and Apollo is simply a personfication of poetry, "man's live breath." It is poetry that fills all nature and unites all things by its "ruling song":

> Hath not the clear wind borne or seemed to bear
> A song wherein all earth and heaven and sea
> Were molten in one music made of thee [Sappho]. . . .
> [III, 343]

It is, however, of crucial importance to note the phrase "seemed to bear," for Swinburne was a complete agnostic, though his constant emphasis in this poem on the unity of all in nature seems, without this qualification and the appository definition of Apollo at the very end, to suggest that he was a pantheist. As this verbal precision indicates, he has been consciously generating a myth about the "soul triune," for he is entirely aware that the only thing unifying the landscape is his perception of it—his perception, that is, as modified by his reexperiencing of Sappho's emotional life. He perceives the landscape both as himself and as Sappho. As often in Swinburne, the ambiguity of the word "fulfilled" suggests how his agnostic myth works:

[28] "Tintern Abbey," ll. 88–99, *The Poetical Works of William Wordsworth*, ed. Ernest de Selincourt, II (Oxford, 1944), 261–62.

> thy ruling song has thrilled
> The deep dark air and subtle tender sea
> And breathless hearts with one bright sound fulfilled.
>
> [III, 343]

Nature is indeed full of song, but only because Sappho's song, which is, as we have seen, Swinburne's song as well, has filled it full.

This does not mean, however, that his work is "founded on litera-ture, not on nature," as Morris said,[29] for Swinburne would not agree with Wilde's statement that "nature is no great mother who has borne us. She is our creation. It is in our brain that she quickens to life. Things are because we see them, and what we see, and how we see it, depends on the arts that have influenced us. To look at a thing is very different from seeing a thing. One does not see any-thing until one sees its beauty. Then, and only then, does it come into existence." Rather, he falls between the two poles of Wordsworth's inspiration as described by Wilde: "Wordsworth went to the lakes, but he was never a lake poet. He found in stones the sermons he had already hidden there. He went moralizing about the district, but his good work was written when he returned not to Nature, but to poetry."[30] Swinburne goes to nature and, in a sense, finds the sermons hidden there, but the sermons were hidden not by him alone but by all generations of poets—he returns to both nature and poetry. Further, the original landscape is the natural landscape, essentially the same landscape that Sappho had seen and been inspired by; and seeing it, seeing the "sermon" hidden in it, is only the first step. He is not, like Wilde, merely achieving aesthetic appreciation, but by reliving Sappho's experience of nature, he is sharing in her creation, her creative perception of it. For the first time in his poetry, Swinburne is truly "now no more a singer, but a song."

Because he is sharing in Sappho's song, the "word" that brings all things into "multitudinous unity," Swinburne's song is genuinely mythopoeic—it finds significance and structure in a seemingly ran-dom universe. All of the poetic techniques that have served to

---

[29] Quoted in Hyder, ed., *Swinburne*, p. 123.
[30] "The Decay of Lying," in *The Artist as Critic: Critical Writings of Oscar Wilde*, ed. Richard Ellmann (New York, 1969), pp. 312, 301.

make the poem inaccessible to generations of readers serve Swinburne's mythopoeic purpose. The puns and ambiguity that make words take on a variety of different meanings, the multiple referents of pronouns, and even the extraordinarily long sentences, which, by the inclusion of multiple phrases and clauses, incorporate diverse thoughts and images into syntactical unity, all fit the pattern of what Northrop Frye has called "mythical imagery": "a world of total metaphor in which everything is potentially identifiable with everything else, as though it were all inside a single infinite body."[31]

Finally, the frequent literary allusions and the incorporation of whole passages from Aeschylus and Sappho demonstrate the central premise—that the poetry of all generations impinges on the poetry of the present. Eliot, in "The Waste Land," tried to revive the dying tradition of poetry with fragments shored against his ruins but had failed because the fragments remained fragments. The cultural memory was no longer capable of bringing the uninterrupted stream of the poetic tradition to bear on the present moment. Where Eliot failed, Swinburne succeeded, for his Bergsonian, pure memory of the poetry of all ages flows in a continuous stream, engulfing and incorporating the present moment and the present song in the eternal Apollonian song of the ages. His poem, as a result, is not fragmented like Eliot's, but presents a Coleridgean synthesis of the One Life, or, in Swinburne's terms, the One Song. All of the complex verbal and syntactical effects combine to reinforce the central idea of multeity in unity. Thus "On the Cliffs" achieves its meaning in two distinct ways. The prose meaning of the poem, insofar as it can be isolated, sets forth a myth of poetry as redemption; the poetic form illustrates the premise of the myth— that poetry can give significance to life. Finally, the "truth" of Swinburne's mythic perception is attested to by Thomas Hardy's tribute to him in "A Singer Asleep." Just as Swinburne recreated the song of Sappho in himself, so Hardy recreates, in his own mind, the song of Sappho in Swinburne:

> One dreams him sighing to her spectral form:
> "O teacher, where lies hid thy burning line,
> Where are those songs, O poetess divine

[31] *Anatomy of Criticism: Four Essays* (Princeton, 1957), p. 136.

Whose very orts are love incarnadine?"
And her smile back: "Disciple true and warm,
      Sufficient now are thine."[32]

Sappho, her disciple, and now her disciple's disciple are fused in
song. In a sense Hardy's song now suffices to bring to us the whole
song of the generations of man.

II

"By the North Sea" has suffered at least as much from the tag
"nature poetry" as "On the Cliffs," and though it has never been
condemned for obscurity, it has never been fully understood. The
poem has been commonly supposed to be one of the earliest results
of Watts-Dunton's program to persuade Swinburne to devote himself to "morally safe" subjects—landscapes and seascapes.[33] If Watts
was looking for "morally safe" poems, however, he must have been
exceedingly imperceptive to think this the best poem Swinburne
had ever written, as he claimed to have done.[34] The natural setting,
as Swinburne described it in a letter to Benjamin Buisson, suggests
that the not terribly safe subject of the poem is Swinburne's vehe-
ment anti-Christianity; it is

une étrange et lente ruine . . . la ville de Dunwich, en Suffolk, autrefois
métropole de province ayant six grandes églises dont une cathédrale, n'est
plus qu'un petit village qui ne sera probablement plus rien en moins d'un
siècle. La mer a mangé tout le reste; elle ronge encore les ruines. Un débris
de la grande église se tient encore debout sur la dune auprès des restes
d'un grand monastère hospitalier ou l'on recueillait les pauvres in-
firmes. . . . j'ai vu du côté de la plage les ossements des morts qui trouaient
les sables de la dune-cimitiere qui s'eleve en haut des marais salés—vastes
landes qui n'appartient ni à la terre ni à la mer et qui s'émiettent littérale-
ment dans les flots de la mer toujours croissante. Jamais, même dans la

[32] "A Singer Asleep," *The Complete Poems of Thomas Hardy: New Wessex Edition*,
ed. James Gibson (London, 1976), p. 265.
[33] Welby, pp. 131–32.
[34] *Letters*, IV, 158.

maremma siénoise dont parle Dante, je n'ai rien vu de si lugubrement magnifique et fatal.[35]

This prose painting of the landscape falls far short of the poetic one. In a ghastly parody of Gray's "Elegy" the poet meditates upon a church graveyard and surveys a desolate landscape as surreal as anything in "Childe Roland"—a seacoast where winds lack breath and no birds sing. As in "On the Cliffs" and "A Forsaken Garden," the cliffs are slowly disintegrating, crumbling into the sea, but here they are bringing with them the dead in their graves. As the cliffs crumble, Dunwich's six churches and cathedral fall toward the sea, and with them the graveyards—tombstones, coffins, and the very corpses tumble down disintegrating sea banks. Like a mad army of ghouls, the dead, divested of burial shrouds, their "bare white piteous bones" (V, 107) protruding, crumble row by row and line by line into the thirsty sea. Worse yet, even Swinburne's eroticism pervades the poem. Personified death, gray and hoary, couples lasciviously and incestuously with the scurvy yellow sea, polluted and corrupted with dead men's bones.

The action of "By the North Sea" is, as Swinburne said in the letter to Buisson "sans catastrophe actuelle ni coups de théâtre"; it consists simply of the erosion of the Dunwich coast by the North Sea. As in *Erechtheus*, the theme is the eternal warfare of sea and land. The personifications, however, suggest that his mythopoeic technique has changed considerably since *Erechtheus*. There are no longer human figures who represent mythic forces; the elemental forces themselves have become the actors. Swinburne has solved the problem that he saw as plaguing Blake—the need to invent confusing names and characters as intermediaries to the mythic perception—by simply leaving out the intermediaries. Even in "On the Cliffs" he had found it necessary to posit a mediator, Sappho, between mortality and eternity, but in "By the North Sea" the mythic structure is stripped to its bare essentials—nature and the perceiving poet.

The eroding coast is an emblem of change and destruction, of the triumph of time, where death and the eternal sea are the deathless lords of the land. Because the land is under the dominion of death,

[35] Ibid., IV, 176.

Swinburne suggests in Part I, it is a wasteland where "the winds lack breath," the birds are songless, and

> Where, hardly redeemed from the waves,
>   Lie thick as the blades of the grasses
>   The dead in their graves.
>
> [V, 87]

This view of the shore, that liminal area that is neither sea nor land, is a constant in the poem, achieving its clearest statement in Part V, where Swinburne describes the sea inshore:

> The grime of her greed is upon her,
>   The sign of her deed is her soil;
> As the earth's is her own dishonour,
>   And corruption the crown of her toil:
> She hath spoiled and devoured, and her honour
>   Is this, to be shamed by her spoil.
>
> [V, 102]

The shore is an emblem of mortal life; its constant erosion represents the inevitability of death and change. Yet despite his unwavering awareness of death and corruption, Swinburne finds hope and even joy in the process of writing the poem, and the perspective gradually turns from "A land that is lonelier than ruin; / A sea that is stranger than death" (V, 85), in the opening lines, to

> The hills and the sands and the beaches,
>   The waters adrift and afar,
> The banks and the creeks and the reaches,
>   How glad of thee all these are!
> The flowers, overflowing, overcrowded,
>   Are drunk with the mad wind's mirth:
> The delight of thy coming unclouded
>   Makes music of earth.
>
> [V, 109–10]

As the juxtaposition of these lines suggests, the land is no longer perceived as lonely, nor the sea as a stranger to the land, because land and sea have been brought into unity by the elemental forces common to both, the sun (the "thee" addressed in the lines cited) and the wind.

In the course of the poem we come to realize that "lonelier" and "stranger" of the first two lines are extremely precise terms used to mark a radical division between sea and land, and to suggest the possibility of unity. The opening section of the poem emphasizes that time is lord of the land, where "year upon year dawns living, / And age upon age drops dead" and that the sea is eternally devouring the land: "And his [death's] hand is not weary of giving, / And the thirst of her [the sea's] heart is not fed" (V, 87). The implication is that the radical division between sea and land is that between eternity and process, between life and death. This implication is enhanced when Swinburne compares the border of sea and land with the ditch of blood that separated the living Odysseus from his dead mother in the *Odyssey*. But the divisive factor is not death, for the eventual reunion of sea and land is, as I have said, accomplished in the face of an unblinking realization that death rules the shore.

As in Blake's myth of the Eternal Man—or the myth of Christianity, for that matter—the division, the fall into disunity, proceeds from a flaw in man himself. This flaw is man's inability to realize that death itself is eternal, his delusive belief that he might not be sundered utterly from the earth of which he consists. Odysseus' attempt to embrace Anticleia represents an effort to reunite the dead with the living, and represents it as futile. Swinburne, however, goes beyond the Homeric idea of division of the corporeal body of the living from the shadowy body of the dead. While he realizes the temptations of the Greek idea of personal immortality—"All too sweet such men's Hellenic speech is" (V, 96)—he realizes also that it is a delusion; that this northern Hades is "Ghostless, all its gulfs and creeks and reaches, / Sky and shore, and cloud, and waste, and sea" (V, 96). All that remains, all that is eternal, is the landscape, or, more accurately, the elements that constitute it.

The church steeples and the graves along the coast illustrate the more modern delusion about death, the Christian belief in the immortality of the soul. Swinburne, agnostic rather than atheistic, knows that "Prayers nor curses prove not nor disprove thee, / Move nor change thee with our change of cheer" (V, 105), but his emphasis on what we can know, the elemental forces of sea, wind, and sun, suggests the foolishness of believing in what we cannot. The very situation—in which the church, where man "Hailed a God more merciful than Time" (V, 106), and the graves, where the dead

"awaited / Long the archangel's re-creating word" (V, 107), fall into
the sea—indicates the inadequacy of Christianity. Swinburne's language also contributes to the debunking of the Christian myth, for
he suggests the inadequacy of both Christ ("more merciful than
Time") and God the Father, the avenging Jehovah. The "word"
which the dead await, moreover, probably refers, as in "On the
Cliffs," to Christ and, also as in that poem, fails to appear. Time, not
the word, triumphs, as all the Christian corpses are cast into the sea.
The sea alone remains eternal, where "Earth, and man, and all their
gods wax humble / Here, where Time brings pasture to the sea" (V,
107). Man, his gods, and even the earth that made them are reduced
to fodder for the ever devouring sea.

The return from fragmentation to unity is achieved when all
things are unified in the all-embracing sea—the mythic cycle from
unity to fall to unity again is completed. Like Blake's, Swinburne's
mythic battleground is a war of contraries, in this case the land and
mortal life against the eternal sea and death:

> The waves are as ranks enrolled
>   Too close for the sun to sever:
> The fens lie naked and cold,
>   But their heart fails utterly never:
> The lists are set from of old,
>   And the warfare endureth forever.
>
> [V, 92]

But though the warfare never ends, the battleground continually
shifts as the sea swallows the land and moves on—eventually this
particular shoreline will be far out to sea where there is no conflict:

> afar where pollution is none
>   Nor ensign of strife nor endeavour,
> Where her heart and the sun's are one,
>   And the soil of her sin comes never,
> She is pure as the wind and the sun,
>   And her sweetness endureth forever.
>
> [V, 103]

The echo of "warfare endureth forever" in "sweetness endureth
forever" demonstrates the "antiphonal effect" of the poem that

Swinburne spoke of in a letter to Edmund Gosse.[36] As elsewhere in this intricately structured poem, the slight variation of a line indicates a significant change in meaning and tone.

The purpose of all myths of salvation is to slay death, but Swinburne demonstrates that natural law does this, that no myth is necessary. The situation is precisely the same as that at the end of "A Forsaken Garden." Unlike the Christian cycle, however, the movement is not from life through death to a higher form of life, but from nonbeing through life and back to nonbeing.

There is, nevertheless, a consolation for mortality that man's delusive belief in eternal life prevents him from discovering—a consolation that proceeds from a recognition of the eternality of death. The only immortality we achieve is the eternality of the elements to which we return. This is a strictly reductive immortality consisting of no more than the realization that after the first death there is no other:

> And sweeter than all things and stranger
> The sense, if perchance it may be,
> That the wind is divested of danger,
> And scatheless the sea.
>
> [V, 88]

The merger with elemental forces is neither more nor less than oblivion. Until this enormously reductive idea of man's significance is appreciated, all of his pain in mortality is muted by his false self-appraisal, by the false notion that he is anything more than atomically immortal. As we saw in "On the Cliffs," the negation of pain, or of any kind of emotional intensity, is precisely what Swinburne wants to avoid.

The return to the elements, the oblivion after death, is, moreover, a positive good throughout Swinburne's poetry. Though pain is necessary to creation, and creation necessary to the only type of human survival envisaged by Swinburne—participation in the Apollonian song—oblivion is welcomed because it ends pain as it ends life. This is the subject of what may be the most famous passage in Swinburne, the lines from "The Triumph of Time":

---

[36] *Letters*, IV, 176.

I will go back to the great sweet mother,
　　Mother and lover of men, the sea,
I will go down to her, I and none other,
　　Close with her, kiss her and mix her with me.
Cling to her, strive with her, hold her fast:
　　O fair white mother, in days long past
Born without sister, born without brother,
　　Set free my soul as thy soul is free.

[I, 48]

The triumphant conclusion of *Tristram of Lyonesse* provides an exact
corollary to the dead in their graves of "By the North Sea." Like
them, the lovers' "coffined bones" are swallowed by the all-
devouring sea, but their souls, troubled in life, are finally at rest:

peace they have that none may gain who live,
And rest about them that no love can give,
And over them, while death and life shall be,
The light and sound and darkness of the sea.

[IV, 163]

Death and oblivion cut off the pains of life. This is some consolation—it is the consolation which Matthew Arnold, who provides a
clear contrast with Swinburne, had arrived at in his version of the
Tristram legend. The tale of Merlin and Vivien, which concludes
Tristram and Iseult and provides its moral, shows Merlin escaped
from the "gradual furnace of the world" by being imprisoned "till
the judgment-day" in a quiet grove—"No fairer resting-place a man
could find." [37] Arnold's reliance on escape into elemental nature is
even more clearly expressed in the resolution to *Empedocles on Etna*,
where Empedocles leaps into the mouth of the volcano. Though
Empedocles is hoping for some kind of survival—"Not to die
wholly"—the final stanza of the poem, Callicles' rendition of the
Muse's hymn to Apollo, sums up Arnold's main argument by implicitly contrasting Empedocles in life and in death:

The day in his hotness,
The strife with the palm;

[37] *Tristram and Iseult*, Part III, ll. 119, 222, 210, *The Poetical Works of Matthew
Arnold*, ed. C. B. Tinker and H. F. Lowry (London, 1950), pp. 152, 155, 156.

> The night in her silence,
> The stars in their calm.

"Calm," here as everywhere in Arnold, is a key word. His message is everywhere the same, that resignation, acceptance of life as it is, is the only way to find peace, to escape the "gradual furnace of the world." This passive acceptance of life, which mutes emotional intensity even more than Christianity, is, of course, anathema to Swinburne. It is of the greatest significance that Arnold's Epicurean view of life rejects not only emotional intensity but poetry as well. Empedocles, before leaping into the volcano, abandons poetry ("lie thou there, / My laurel bough!") just as Arnold himself later abandoned it and resigned himself to a life of prose.[38]

Though finding solace in the idea of eventual oblivion, Swinburne clearly could not accept the Arnoldian ethic of resignation and escape. He had, moreover, already rejected the idea of a pantheistic return to harmony with nature in "On the Cliffs," and, as in the earlier poem, he finds it necessary not to reject passion and poetry but to embrace passion for the sake of immortal poetry. Arnold's Empedocles had hoped "not to die wholly." Swinburne, in "Thalassius," insists that a man dies "not wholly as all men" if any "deed or word" of his lives on as a result of his having been "kindled" by the "love / That life and death are fashioned of" (III, 315). The juxtaposition of comfort in the fact of eventual oblivion with the idea of the salvation of human existence through poetry had been central in *Poems and Ballads* (Second Series) and had been expressed as early as 1867, in "Ave atque Vale." The greatest consolation for Baudelaire, as the concluding lines state, was that he had escaped from his wretched existence:

> Content thee, howsoe'er, whose days are done;
> There lies not any troublous thing before,
> Nor sight nor sound to war against thee more,
> For whom all winds are quiet as the sun,
> All waters as the shore.
>
> [III, 60]

---

[38] *Empedocles on Etna*, Act II, ll. 406, 465–68, 191–92, *Poetical Works*, pp. 441, 443, 434.

There is also, however, more than a suggestion of the apostolic succession of poets, the impingement of all poetry on the present, which found its first full expression in "On the Cliffs":

> Not thee, O never thee, in all time's changes,
>   Not thee, but this the sound of thy sad soul,
>   The shadow of thy swift spirit, this shut scroll
> I lay my hand on, and not death estranges
>   My spirit from communion of thy song—
>   These memories and these melodies that throng
> Veiled porches of a Muse funereal—
>   These I salute, these touch, these clasp and fold
>   As though a hand were in my hand to hold,
> Or through mine ears a mourning musical
>   Of many mourners rolled.
>
> > [III, 56]

Swinburne's emphasis in "Ave atque Vale" and generally throughout the second series of *Poems and Ballads* was on the consolation—that oblivion ends mortal pains—so there was no clear implication that he considered Arnoldian resignation or the Christian faith in an afterlife as necessarily limiting.

By the time he wrote "By the North Sea" in 1881, however, the balance had clearly shifted, for in that poem more clearly than in any of his earlier works Swinburne suggests that our Christian faith in immortality proceeds from a fear of acknowledging a reductive view of man's limits:

> Change of change, and death of death begotten,
>   Darkness born of darkness, one and three,
> Ghostly godhead of a world forgotten,
>   Crowned with heaven, enthroned on land and sea,
> Here, where earth with dead men's bones is rotten,
>   God of Time, thy likeness worships thee.
>
> > [V, 104]

God is born of man when man refuses to acknowledge death; He is begotten of the "death of death." Here, as elsewhere in the poem, and as in "On the Cliffs," Swinburne is echoing the language of Christianity to suggest the inanity of a vocabulary divorced from the world we can perceive. In this case he is using his remarkable gift for parody, for, just as clearly as he inverted the Litany to parody the Virgin in "Dolores," he is inverting the Nicene Creed to undercut the Christian's blind faith in the Holy Trinity:

> Change of change, darkness of darkness, hidden,
>   Very death of very death, begun
> When none knows,—the knowledge is forbidden—
>   Self-begotten, self-proceeding, one,
> Born, not made—abhorred, unchained, unchidden,
>   Night stands here defiant of the sun.
>
> [V, 104]

He is not, however, content merely to parody. By first emptying the language of its traditional meaning and then refilling it with his own terms, Swinburne is able to suggest a profane alternative to Christianity. Earth, sea, and wind, he suggests, are the only immortal trinity we can truly know. Only if we can accept them for what they are and no more, cease to construct transcendent gods from fear of mortality, can we begin to live life in all its passionate intensity. The Christian God, then, is a god of ignorance, a god of the night, and as long as man believes in him he is not living up to his utmost potential.

For Swinburne the ultimate god is truth, achieved through knowledge and wisdom, and especially through the apotheosis of human endeavor, poetry. In "By the North Sea," as in "On the Cliffs," "Thalassius," and all of the 1878 *Poems and Ballads*, truth and poetry are represented by the "lord of the day," the sun:

> Time, haggard and changeful and hoary,
>   Is master and God of the land:
> But the air is fulfilled of the glory
>   That is shed from our lord's right hand.
> O father of all of us ever,
>   All glory be only to thee
> From heaven, that is void of thee never,
>   And earth, and the sea.
>
> [V, 108–9]

The issue is confused by the fact that Swinburne seems, though inconsistently, to use the word "land" to speak of what is mortal and subject to time, and "earth" to speak of the eternal material element, which, however it may shift its shape, like sea or wind, does not fundamentally change. It is, nevertheless, clear that the sun brings the profane trinity of heaven, earth, and sea into unity by the "glory," used both in the conventional sense and in the sense of an effusion of light, which is spread through the elements. The replacement of the unity in trinity and trinity in unity traditional in the Christian church by an elemental alternative is even more striking in the preceding stanza:

> Where the horn of the headland is sharper,
>   And her green floor glitters with fire,
> The sea has the sun for a harper,
>   The sun has the sea for a lyre.
> The waves are a pavement of amber,
>   By the feet of the sea-winds trod
> To receive in a god's presence-chamber
>   Our father, the God.
>
> [V, 108]

The three elements are united in enlightenment by the fourth element, the sun, which thus becomes Swinburne's replacement for the one god which encompasses the three: "Thou, Lord, art God of the day. / Thou art father and saviour and spirit" (V, 109). The replacement of the Christian God by the elements is complete: earth, wind, sun, and sea, or, in their more familiar elemental names, earth, air, fire, and water, have become the only possible objects of worship. The radical division, moreover, between sea and land is healed by the unifying power of the sun, and, in more human terms, consolation for mortality is achieved by recognition of the eternally true rather than by retreat in a lie.

The situation is, however, somewhat more complicated than the replacement of Christian by elemental forces implies. Swinburne's exaltation of the elemental unity is not pantheistic; he is not simply replacing one god by another. A subtle ambiguity in the first two lines of the dedicatory sonnet indicates that Swinburne's vision is truly agnostic, not pantheistic: "Sea, wind and sun, with light and sound and breath / The spirit of man fulfilling—" (V, 84). The elemental forces fulfill the spirit of man, but only because, as the subtle ambiguity suggests, the spirit of man fulfills the elements. The question of whether man created or perceived the power in nature had been a chronic problem for the earlier romantics. Wordsworth never solved it, and his poetry contains innumerable contradictions on the subject. Shelley, characteristically, faced the question head-on, as he pondered at the end of "Mont Blanc" whether power is in nature or is given to nature by the mind of man:

> The secret Strength of things
> Which governs thought, and to the infinite dome
> Of Heaven is as a law, inhabits thee!
> And what were thou, and earth, and stars, and sea,
> If to the human mind's imaginings
> Silence and solitude were vacancy?

Shelley never settled the question and was consistently ambivalent about it in his poetry. In the "Lines Written among the Euganean Hills," he poses the problem in exactly the same way as Swinburne does in "By the North Sea," for the question is whether the sun or the poetic imagination brings all things into multitudinous unity, for all things

> Interpenetrated lie
> By the glory of the sky:
> Be it love, light, harmony,
> Odour, or the soul of all
> Which from Heaven like dew doth fall,
> Or the mind which feeds this verse
> Peopling the lone universe.[39]

For Swinburne, however, the problem reduces to a tautology, since the sun is the poetic imagination, since Apollo is "man's live breath." The fulfilling power is poetry.

But it is unnecessary to refer back to "On the Cliffs" to find Swinburne's myth of poetry in "By the North Sea," for it is set forth fully in the latter poem. The allusion to the *Odyssey* in Part III serves much the same purpose as the song of Sappho in "On the Cliffs." Swinburne's meditations in Parts I and II and through the first seven stanzas of Part III had been of unrelieved melancholy inspired by

---

[39] "Mont Blanc," ll. 139–44; "Lines Written among the Euganean Hills," ll. 313–19, *Shelley: Poetical Works*, ed. Thomas Hutchinson, corrected by G. M. Matthews (Oxford, 1970), pp. 535, 557.

the bleak landscape. Finally in Part III he poses a question: "but yonder, / See, what sign of life or death survives?" (V, 94). The answer involves eight stanzas about Odysseus and Anticleia and the unbridgeable abyss between the dead and the living. The allusion suggests, as I have said, the misery inspired by believing in personal immortality, the "bitterest of derisions," but it also suggests a consolation, for though no ghost of Anticleia or Odysseus survives, their love does:

> Love that lives and stands up re-created
>   Then when life has ebbed and anguish fled;
> Love more strong than death or all things fated,
>   Child's and mother's, lit by love and led;
> Love that found what life so long awaited
>   Here, when life came down among the dead.
>
>   [V, 96]

What survives of life or death is love and the passionate intensity with which Odysseus sought his mother. After realizing that the love of mother and son, as recorded by Homer, invests the scene with meaning, Swinburne's thoughts begin to become more positive.

"By the North Sea" opens with the eerie quatrain

> A land that is lonelier than ruin;
>   A sea that is stranger than death:
> Far fields that a rose never blew in,
>   Wan waste where the winds lack breath.
>
>   [V, 85]

Now, in Part IV, at exactly the midpoint of the poem, he subtly and significantly introduces an antiphonal variation on the initial theme:

> A land that is thirstier than ruin:
>   A sea that is hungrier than death;
> Heaped hills that a tree never grew in;
>   Wide sands where the wave draws breath.
>
>   [V, 98]

The significant changes are the substitution of the words *thirstier* and *hungrier* for *lonelier* and *stranger*, changes which suggest a movement from division toward unity, and the substitution of

"where the wave draws breath" for "where the winds lack breath."
The winds have been described as active, "relentless and sleepless"
(V, 86) from the beginning, but now, for the first time, they have
breath, and further, the sea shares in the breath. Not only are two of
the elements brought into unity by the shared breath, but "breath"
itself is, as we have seen, a key word in Swinburne, for it not only
personifies sea and wind but suggests that they are fulfilled with
poetry. The solace, as in "On the Cliffs," is the perception of human
passion in nature—the literal inspiration in the landscape.

As the next ten stanzas suggest, the "breath" is connected to the
memory of Homer's poetic account of love. The wind is characterized with the ambiguous antecedents leading us to think the
characterization is of man, as a continual striving, never either
satisfied or weary, a force whose

> doom is for ever
> To seek and desire and rejoice,
> And the sense that eternity never
> Shall silence his voice.
>
> [V, 99]

The eternal strife of the wind, like that of human hearts, achieves
immortality through its forever unwearied voice. It is this voice of
the wind that man shares in, this voice that literally inspires man
with song:

> There are those too of mortals that love him,
> There are souls that desire and require,
> Be the glories of midnight above him
> Or beneath him the daysprings of fire:
> And their hearts are as harps that approve him
> And praise him as chords of a lyre
> That were fain with their music to move him
> To meet their desire.
>
> [V, 100–1]

Through sharing in the eternal voice of the wind, through song,
man shares in eternity:

> For these have the toil and the guerdon
> That the wind has eternally: these

> Have part in the boon and the burden
> Of the sleepless unsatisfied breeze. . . .
>
> [V, 101]

The puns on "require" and "burden" emphasize how closely Swinburne is associating the wind with man's song, but we must be careful to avoid equating his view with the pantheistic Wordsworthian and Coleridgean idea of man's soul as an aeolian harp played upon by the wind.[40] The ambiguity of "fulfilling" in the dedicatory sonnet, the fact that it is the breath of Homer that inspires Swinburne, and the fact that the wind is "Filled and thrilled with its perpetual story" (V, 106) all suggest that the wind is inspiring because inspired by man. That is, the song of Homer, metaphorically carried on the wind, is rechoired in the wind by Swinburne, who, in "By the North Sea," is singing the "burden" to the song of Odysseus and Anticleia. He is striving for unity with his mother, the sea, just as Odysseus sought reunion with Anticleia.

The idea of man's song becoming, in effect, a part of nature, is not new in Swinburne but was expressed as early as 1867 in "Anactoria," where Swinburne had proclaimed Sappho's immortality on the basis that whenever man perceived eternal nature "Memories shall mix and metaphors of me [Sappho]" (I, 70). As we have seen, the same idea was expressed in "On the Cliffs," and the idea of an apostolic succession of poets had been set forth as early as "Ave atque Vale." "By the North Sea," however, presents the fully developed myth of nature and poetry for the first time, and presents it in the form of traditional myth.

Swinburne expresses this myth not only by means of the antiphonal structure and by substituting pagan for Christian deities within the structure of Christian language but also by employing the Greek method of interpreting nature, as described by Henri Frankfort: "an ordered view of the universe was obtained by bringing its elements in a genealogical relationship with one another."[41] In Swinburne's, as in most pagan mythologies, creation occurs when the sky god and earth goddess arise from chaos and reproduce. In

---

[40] McGann, p. 142. McGann uses the pun on "require" as an entrance into his discussion of "By the North Sea."

[41] Henri Frankfort, Mrs. H. A. Frankfort, John A. Wilson, and Thorkild Jacobsen, *Before Philosophy* (London, 1949), p. 249.

the opening of "By the North Sea," "Death's self" (V, 103), described in terms of the sky, couples with the sea, at a point where it
is neither wholly sea nor land, but a combination of both. This
liminal area may be regarded as analogous with the pagan earth
goddess. All of the central concerns of the poem are latent in the
description of the coupling of this pair:

> In the pride of his power she rejoices,
>   In her glory he glows and is glad:
> In her darkness the sound of his voice is,
>   With his breath she dilates and is mad:
> "If thou slay me, O death, and outlive me,
>   Yet thy love hath fulfilled me of thee."
> "Shall I give thee not back if thou give me,
>   O sister, O sea?"
>
> [V, 86]

The coastal area, filled with dead men's bones, is, here and throughout the poem, an emblem of the world of process, the world of
change. By coming to terms with death, this area is "fulfilled," or
impregnated, with love. Thus, in cryptic and greatly abbreviated
form, the stanza suggests the central theme of the poem, that man's
recognition of his mortality fulfills the world of process with love.
The birth of the two other gods, moreover, is suggested by the
language of the stanza, for death, in union with the sea, "glows" in
her "glory," suggesting the sun, the god of poetry, and the sea dilates
with death's "breath," suggesting the wind, the vehicle of poetry.
    In addition, the two primeval gods are reminiscent of the parents
of Apollo in the Greek cosmogony. Death, characterized as an
overcast sky, is comparable to Zeus, the storm god, and the coast,
which is neither sea nor land, is comparable both to Delos, Apollo's
birthplace, an island that floated in the sea, and to Latona, who was
an outcast from all the elements, who, as Ovid said, in *Metamorphoses,*

> maxima quondam
> exiguam sedem pariturae terra negavit!
> nec caelo nec humo nec aquis dea vestra recepta est:
> exsul erat mundi. . . .[42]

[42] *Metamorphoses* VI. 186–89. The Loeb translation renders the lines "to whom
the broad earth once refused a tiny spot for bringing forth her children. Neither

Suggesting that Apollo was begat of death on the sea is not so farfetched an interpretation as it might appear, both because Swinburne chronically overestimated the erudition of his readers and because Ovid's reference to Latona is in Book VI of the *Metamorphoses*, which Swinburne was intimately acquainted with, since it contains the story of Philomela, refuted in "On the Cliffs," as well as the rape of Oreithyia by Boreas, alluded to in "On the Cliffs" and narrated in *Erechtheus* in perhaps the greatest of all Swinburne's choruses. The clear implication of the genealogical connection latent in this stanza, the birth of the god of song from the union of death and change, is that man's full recognition of death, of his eventual oblivion in the sea, fulfills the world with poetry as well as love. That the coupling which produces Apollo, the beautiful god of song, is both repulsive and lascivious should not be surprising. Swinburne insists throughout the poem that the ability to sing is dependent upon a full recognition of the true nature of mortal life, and generation, always essentially lascivious, is as necessary a part of change as death is. Truth may be repulsive to the sentimental, conventional, tradition-ridden victim of received doctrine, and this particular truth is particularly grim and ugly, but it must be recognized in all its ugliness.

Finally, the apostolic succession of poets, which we have noted in other poems, is set forth in "By the North Sea" in genealogical terms. As in "Thalassius" Swinburne declares himself the child of the sun ("Our father, the god" [V, 108]) and the eternal sea ("My mother, my sea" [V, 98]) who unite

> afar where pollution is none,
>   Nor ensign of strife nor endeavour,
> Where her [the sea's] heart and the sun's are one,
>   And the soil of her sin comes never,
> She is pure as the wind and the sun,
>   And her sweetness endureth forever.
>   [V, 103]

Far out to sea, where the war of contraries is unheard of, and death is complete and utter, the sea and the sun are one. Poetry and

---

heaven nor earth nor sea was open for this goddess of yours; she was outlawed from the universe."

eternal oblivion are inseparable, because the true poet must see eternal truth, though it means seeing his own insignificance in the cosmic order. Death is the mother of beauty, the mother of Apollo and all his line, the mother, therefore, of Swinburne.

That a full realization of personal mortality is the way to the only kind of human immortality possible, the immortality of poetry, is deliberately paradoxical—but it is merely paradoxical. The immortality of the song, of course, does not affect the mortality of the singer. Swinburne had become one with the deathless song of Sappho in "On the Cliffs" and in "Thalassius" had said that sun and wind and sea take hold of the poet, making him a part of the cosmic song of nature, they

> charm him from his own soul's separate sense
> With infinite and invasive influence
> That made strength sweet in him and sweetness strong,
> Being now no more a singer, but a song.
>
> [III, 327]

The idea that each man must die but that in accepting his death may participate in eternity by becoming a part of what eternally lives, is, moreover, perfectly consistent with the theme of Swinburne's republican poetry. His devotion to liberty and his devotion to poetry merge, because both are part of the great cosmic order. Thus in "Super Flumina Babylonis," as we have seen, Swinburne expresses precisely the same paradox of immortality achieved by acceptance of mortality: "Whoso takes the world's life on him and his own lays down, / He, dying so, lives" (II, 38). In "By the North Sea" it is only Homer's song that survives, not Homer, and only the love of Odysseus and Anticleia, not their shades. As the final stanza implies, Swinburne's song too will survive, and his love for his mother, the sea:

> I, last least voice of her [earth's] voices,
>   Give thanks that were mute in me long
> To the soul in my soul that rejoices
>   For the song that is over my song.
> Time gives what he gains for the giving
>   Or takes for his tribute of me;
> My dreams to the wind everliving,
>   My song to the sea.
>
> [V, 110]

The "song that is over his song" is the song of Homer, the song of
Sappho; it is the song of the sun, of all of nature. His song to the
sea, at once his mother and his promise of oblivion, becomes a part
of the wind ever-living, the eternal song of man in nature. Swinburne provides the latest antiphon to all generations of poets, just
as this last stanza provides the final antiphon to the poem. The
cryptic line "Time gives what he gains for the giving" is an antiphonal response to the question asked by death of the sea in Part
I: "Shall I give thee not back if thou give me, / O sister, O sea?" (V,
86). Time, or death, takes love from the world of mortality, but
takes it only to return it to the mortal world in song. The offering of
song, like any sacrificial offering, is ultimately an offering to death.
Finally, in an antiphonal response to the last line of the first stanza,
"To strive with the sea" (V, 85), and of the last line of the stanza on
which the poem turns, "My mother, my sea" (V, 98), the poem
concludes movingly with "My song to the sea" (V, 110). Of the
seven stanzas of the poem, all but the second and fifth (which are
themselves contrapuntal) end in the word *sea*, and the last lines of
these five sections in themselves are a wonderful epitome of the
whole. The pattern of antiphonal response reflects the movement
of the poem from strife with the mortal condition to acceptance of
it and finally to celebration of it in song. Moreover, the antiphonal
structure is itself a way of asserting order in chaos. Walter Pater,
discussing the Heraclitean doctrine of continual change—a doctrine
which, we have seen, Swinburne subscribed to—insisted that there
is another side to that doctrine also, a "search for and . . . notation, if
there be such, of an antiphonal rhythm, or logic, which, proceeding
uniformly from movement to movement as in some intricate musical theme, might link together in one of those contending, infinitely
diverse impulses." Such a search, Pater continues, is "an act of recognition, even on the part of a philosophy of the inconsecutive, the
incoherent, the insane, of that Wisdom which, 'reacheth from end
to end, sweetly and strongly ordering all things.'"[43] In Swinburne
the source of order, of antiphonal music, is the human mind, the
creative imagination; the intricate music is the song of one man and
of all men.

[43] *Plato and Platonism* (London, 1910), pp. 17–18.

Swinburne may be the preeminent poet of paradox in all English poetry. In "Hertha" he used a technique of stasis to describe growth, and certainly one of the characteristic strengths of "By the North Sea" is his reliance on the language of artifice (vocabulary, syntax, and metrics as well as structure) to render the natural, his reaching to the very limits of verbal beauty to set forth the starkest, bleakest vision imaginable in a language that is yet hopeful and consolatory. Also paradoxical, and also characteristic, are his summoning of a personal myth to combat the received myth of Christianity and his parody and simultaneous use of received theological language.

In the perfection of its structural and thematic development, its ordered progression from crisis to resolution in precisely modulated language, the playing-off of iambic and anapestic movements, of six-line against eight-line stanzas, the mathematical symmetry of sections (articulated so that four duplicates one, five duplicates two, and six three), "By the North Sea" exemplifies—in fact, *becomes*—its very subject (growth, change, quiescence, celebration) as elegantly, scrupulously, and efficiently as any poem known to me. In the truest sense it aspires to the condition of music.

III

Swinburne's turn to "nature poetry" late in his career in such poems as "On the Cliffs" and "By the North Sea" was not, as has been said, an abandonment of his creative gifts, but the fulfillment of them. His earliest successful poetry, *Atalanta in Calydon* and the first series of *Poems and Ballads*, was, as we have seen, primarily mythological and archetypal; in *Erechtheus* he moved closer to the mythopoeic origins of Hellenic myth, but he remained within the mythological tradition; and in *Songs before Sunrise* and even in the second series of *Poems and Ballads*, though he set forth his personal myth, the primary mode of thought was abstract and speculative. In all of these earlier works, the finished poem represents a conclusion rather than a process of experience. Even in "Hertha," a poem expressing Swinburne's Heraclitean belief in eternity as process, in change as the one constant, the speaking voice is bardic or pro-

phetic, as though presenting an established truth rather than perceiving and creating truth:

Though sore be my burden
    And more than ye know,
And my growth have no guerdon
    But only to grow,
Yet I fail not of growing for lightnings above me or deathworms below.

                                                              [II, 79]

The idea is perfectly consistent with the notion of the eternal
growth of the cosmic song of man in "On the Cliffs" and "By the
North Sea," but it is expressed as the end product of a speculative
philosophy.

   The nature poems, on the other hand, are not speculative but
mythopoeic; they present not conclusions but lived experiences.
The mode of thought expressed in these poems perfectly fits Henri
Frankfort's succinct summary of the primitive mythopoeic mode:
"Myth is a form of poetry which transcends poetry in that it proclaims a truth; a form of reasoning which transcends reasoning in
that it wants to bring about the truth it proclaims; a form of action,
of ritual behavior, which does not find its fulfillment in the act but
must proclaim and elaborate a poetic form of truth." Both poems
follow essentially the same pattern: the poet, standing alone, faces a
barren landscape and a seemingly dead nature which, in the course
of the poem, comes to life through the poetic imagination. Once
this happens, Swinburne experiences nature as primitive, mythopoeic man did, not as an "It" but as a "Thou":

The world appears to primitive man neither inanimate nor empty but
redundant with life; and life has individuality, in man and beast and plant,
and in every phenomenon which confronts man—the thunderclap, the
sudden shadow, the eerie and unknown clearing in the wood. . . . Any
phenomenon may at any time face him, not as "It," but as "Thou." In this
confrontation, "Thou" reveals its individuality, its qualities, its will. "Thou"
is not contemplated with intellectual detachment; it is experienced as life
confronting life, involving every faculty of man in a reciprocal relationship.[44]

[44]Frankfort et al., pp. 16, 14.

Like the primitive mythmaker, Swinburne confronts nature directly, particularly in "By the North Sea," and earth, sea, wind, and sky present themselves as living, individualized entities. The difference between mythopoeic and philosophical logic, moreover, explains why the two poems are so difficult for the logical intellect to follow, why the "thought" does not move in a logical, linear narrative, but is conveyed, as McGann says, by "accumulation and expansion." The whole soul of Swinburne responds to the whole soul of nature. The language used to express the immediate, subjective experience is itself immediate and subjective. The multileveled imagery that presents itself to "every faculty of man in a reciprocal relationship" with nature is allowed to stand in all its complexity.

The myth, which must be constructed by the reader from the imagery, is essentially that nature is alive because fulfilled with the ever growing, ever changing song of man. Because the song undergoes continual metamorphosis, changing with each new singer, eternal nature is still seen as a Heraclitean process of continual change and growth. This is evidenced by the poems themselves since, as we have seen, "On the Cliffs" is, in a sense, a metamorphosis of the song of Sappho, the plays of Aeschylus, Wordsworth's "Immortality Ode," and Keats's "Ode to a Nightingale"; "By the North Sea" is an extension of the Homeric song of Odysseus and Anticleia, and also a continuation of the romantic song of nature, of the question whether god or man makes it live. Further, both poems are metamorphoses of the Christian myth of the trinity.

The myth not only brings nature to life but also fulfills one of the basic requirements man makes of a religion by guaranteeing a certain kind of immortality. The spirit of all mankind lives on in nature, but, more than this, the spirit of the individual poet lives on, metamorphosed, like Sappho, in the minds of future generations. W. H. Auden expressed a similar idea in "In Memory of W. B. Yeats," for when Yeats died,

> The current of his feeling failed: he became his admirers.
>
> Now he is scattered among a hundred cities
> And wholly given over to unfamiliar affections;
> To find his happiness in another kind of wood

> And be punished under a foreign code of conscience.
> The words of a dead man
> Are modified in the guts of the living.[45]

Conceivably, the words of Swinburne are modified in the guts of Auden.

The authenticity of the myth is not affected by the fact that Swinburne was intellectually aware that he was, himself, imaginatively creating the life in nature, because the mythopoeic experience is not merely intellectual but is a response of the entire being. Emotionally, there is every reason to assume, Swinburne believed in the myth; the intellectual detachment that follows the mythopoeic experience does not negate the truth of the experience itself. In any case, "the science of myth," as Joseph Campbell has said, "is concerned precisely with the phenomenon of self-induced belief"; there is "a shift of view from the logic of the normal secular sphere, where things are understood to be distinct from each other, to a theatrical or play sphere, where they are accepted for what they are *experienced* as being, and the logic is that of 'make-believe'—'as if.'"[46] This is not to say that the mythmaker is indulging in whimsical fantasy, but that the emotional involvement is sufficiently intense to override intellectual reflection. In his classic study of the psychology of religion, *The Varieties of Religious Experience*, William James argues that the subjective, emotional, egotistic reality of experience is at least as important as the objective, scientific reality of speculative thought:

it is absurd for science to say that the egotistic elements of experience should be suppressed. The axis of reality runs solely through the egotistic places,—they are strung upon it like so many beads. To describe the world with all the various feelings of the individual pinch of destiny, all the various spiritual attitudes, left out from the description—they being as describable as anything else—would be something like offering a printed bill of fare as the equivalent for a solid meal.[47]

---

[45] "In Memory of W. B. Yeats," ll. 17–23, *The Collected Poetry of W. H. Auden* (New York, 1945), p. 49.

[46] Joseph Campbell, "The Historical Development of Mythology," in *Myth and Mythmaking*, ed. Henry A. Murray (Boston, 1969), p. 34.

[47] *The Varieties of Religious Experience* (1902; rpt. New York, 1958), p. 377.

In his republican poetry, in "Hertha," Swinburne had presented the bill of fare; in "On the Cliffs" and "By the North Sea" he offers the experience itself, with all the complex feelings and spiritual attitudes of the mythopoeic moment left intact.

Swinburne's emphasis on what Carlyle called the "felt indubitable certainty of Experience," his affirmation of its greater reality than objective speculation, puts him at the very heart of romanticism.[48] As Robert Langbaum has said, the "essential idea" of romanticism is "the doctrine of experience—the doctrine that the imaginative apprehension gained through immediate experience is primary and certain, whereas the analytic reflection that follows is secondary and problematical."[49] Swinburne's analytic reflection is purely agnostic, but his emotional apprehension of reality is essentially religious and mythopoeic. He knows, intellectually, that life is given to nature by man, but he experiences, emotionally, the reality of that life in nature.

William James argues that objective perception of reality is achieved by the conscious mind and that religious, subjective experience is founded in the subconscious.[50] Swinburne, without using such scientific terminology, seems to be saying much the same thing. The songs of all singers operate within the recesses of his mind to influence his perception of nature so that in "On the Cliffs" he can refer to his Bergsonian memory of the songs as "A soul behind the soul" (III, 334). But the songs are also, by the logic of experience, a part of external nature, so that in "By the North Sea" he can have it both ways, placing the cosmic song of all singers both within and above his own soul, speaking of "the soul in my soul that rejoices / . . . the song that is over my song" (V, 110). Thus for Swinburne the perception of reality is both religious and experiential. The central problem of the nineteenth century was to find room for religious experience after science had destroyed God. Tennyson struggled to make religion and science compatible; Arnold tried to act as a mediating priest between culture and man;

---

[48] Thomas Carlyle, *Sartor Resartus* II.ix, "The Everlasting Yea," ed. Charles Frederick Harrold (New York, 1937), p. 196.

[49] *The Poetry of Experience* (New York, 1957), p. 35.

[50] James, pp. 386–88.

Browning tried to find experiential reality, but rarely in his own person. For Swinburne alone the evidence of experience was at least as real as the evidence of science; he alone was able to generate a saving personal myth. The contrast with Arnold is particularly revealing, for if Arnold was the high priest of culture, he was a high church high priest, laying down truths of culture as dogma. Swinburne, on the other hand, was evangelical, allowing each man to meet the divinity on his own terms. Arnold grew out of personal poetry, rejecting "Empedocles on Etna" from his *Poems* (1853) on the grounds that it lacked the "disinterested objectivity" of the Greek genius;[51] Swinburne grew into personal poetry, finding that experience is self-validating. Arnold's criticism is objective and scientific, even going so far as to use "touchstones" as a scientific measure of the worth of a poetic line; Swinburne's is subjective and impressionistic, valuing the experience of a work of art above any abstract aesthetic principle.

By 1879 and 1881, then, Swinburne was both agnostic and religious. With a religious temperament and a mythopoeic imagination he created a genuine myth of man, nature, and poetry. But with an objective critical eye he perceived that the deity he worshipped was still, as in the republican poetry, man himself.

[51] Matthew Arnold, "Preface to First Edition of *Poems*," in *On the Classical Tradition*, ed. R. H. Super (Ann Arbor, Mich., 1960), p. 1.

The Putney Period
CHAPTER 5   Solipsism without Fear

THE ENORMOUS BULK of the poetry written in the last thirty years of Swinburne's life has been greeted with almost unmitigated disdain by the few readers who have gone to the trouble of looking at it. Swinburne, it is routinely said, devoted more than half of his creative life to the production of fatuous effusions of baby worship, political poems savoring of the rankest kind of imperialism, and nature poetry of the travel-book variety. The charges have been made so persistently that they must be met head-on, and, indeed, there is a certain amount of truth in them. The nature poetry, which makes up the bulk of the late verse and is of a far higher order than has been acknowledged, will be discussed separately and at some length, but the poems of baby worship and imperialism may be dismissed without extended comment—and without disdain. They are far fewer than Swinburne's detractors would have us believe, and those in praise of babies, are inoffensive at worst and even, for the most part, lovely. The baby poems may, in a very limited way, be attributable to Swinburne's general tendency to celebrate regeneration in all things—sunrises, spring, flowering, and so on—but must be mainly attributed to a not unattractive foible, an aging and lonely man's love for children. Continuing to misread Blake, moreover, he probably felt that the precedent of *Songs of Innocence* sanctioned his adoption of the subject, and he must also have been encouraged by the example of Christina Rossetti's children's poems, which he loved. Though these poems do not attain to the level of high art, they hardly deserve the uninformed contempt they have received.

The imperialist poetry, unfortunately, is a different matter, and has fully earned its share of scorn. Nevertheless, though this rant cannot be excused, it can be briefly explained in terms of Swinburne's development and the development of his myth. His mythmaking had always extended from ancient myth to actual history, particularly English history—Mary Stuart, in the *Chastelard, Bothwell, Mary Stuart* trilogy, is a giantess à la Dolores and Faustine—and ultimately he created his own myth of British history. Cecil Lang has observed that

it was Swinburne's insularity, his very *Englishness*, that came to dominate his thinking. The most cosmopolitan of English poets was transformed into the most parochial and chauvinistic of British jingoes. The republican-turned-"English Republican" became English first and last, and remained republican only by a semantic sophistry that would be as much at home in *1984* as in *Through the Looking Glass*. "People nowadays seem to forget . . . ," he wrote to his mother in 1886, "that the first principle of a Republican is and must be Unity (without which liberty can only mean license—or pure anarchy—or pretentious hypocrisy) and that Republican right is common consistency and honesty to the first to protest against a party of anarchists and intriguers whose policy is to break up the state."[1]

This is, to be sure, sophistry, but it is perfectly consistent with the political philosophy of "Hertha," only brought out of the realm of abstraction into the realm of practice. All of Swinburne's mythmaking is aimed at unifying the human race under the aegis of love and art—the Apollonian song, after all, was the song of the *whole* of mankind. The organic metaphor of the tree in "Hertha" implies that there can be only one seed which will grow into the world-soul. For Swinburne, in effect, the tradition was all, and tradition, civilization, was more highly developed in England than elsewhere. As Oswald Spengler aphoristically put it, "Imperialism is Civilization unadulterated,"[2] and unadulterated civilization is precisely what Swinburne had always sought. The switch from republicanism to imperialism was not so radical a transformation as it appears, if only because the theory behind the former had always actually been

[1] *The Swinburne Letters*, ed. Cecil Y. Lang, I (New Haven, 1959), xxviii–xxix (see also V [1962], 192–93).

[2] *The Decline of the West*, trans. Charles Francis Atkinson (New York, 1926), p. 36.

more conducive to the latter. The jingoism of the late years, to use the metaphor of "Hertha," grew inevitably from the seeds of cultural monism apparent even in *Songs before Sunrise*. However deplorable we find poems like "The Commonweal," "The Armada," and "England: An Ode," they are consistent with Swinburne's political growth. Despite the praise that has been lavished on *Songs before Sunrise*, politics had never been Swinburne's strong point.

His strong point had, in fact, always been the poetry of the life of man confronting the life of nature, and it is to the late nature poetry that we must turn to find the unadulterated strength of the aging Swinburne. The critical contempt for this poetry, written under the auspices of Watts-Dunton at the Pines in Putney, has been so universal that one would think, with Samuel Chew, that the critic's job should be simply to "call attention to the comparatively few pieces that have some lasting interest, attractiveness and individuality." The judgment of Chew and his contemporaries has echoed down the decades, like the Apollonian song, finding its most recent expression in Kerry McSweeney's article on "Thalassius": "From 1880 to his death in 1909 Swinburne wrote a great amount of nature poetry, the vast majority of the merely decorative or travel-book variety. Only infrequently do we find poems describing the naked encounter of poet and natural world. When we do find this, as in 'A Nympholept' (1894) and 'The Lake of Gaube' (1904), the results are two of Swinburne's greatest poems."[3] Yet the problem of dealing with the huge bulk of Swinburne's poetry in these last thirty years is not, in fact, a paucity of good poems but a plethora; the problem is not to sort the grain from the chaff but to choose examples from an embarrassment of riches. And despite McSweeney's implication that little of the late poetry can be truly mythopoeic, a substantial portion of the nature lyrics is just that—the life of man confronting the life in nature. While it is true that such poems as "A Nympholept" and "The Lake of Gaube" stand out as supreme achievements in Swinburne's canon, many other exquisite poems should not be slighted, lyrics like "To a Seamew," "Neap-tide," "Off Shore," "Evening on the Broads," "Adieux à Marie Stuart," "A Mid-

---

[3] Chew, *Swinburne* (Boston, 1929), p. 280; McSweeney, "Swinburne's 'Thalassius,'" *Humanities Association Bulletin*, 22 (1971), 54.

•

summer Holiday," "A Ballad of Sark," "Dedication: To William Morris," many poems of the lovely *Century of Roundels*, "Astrophel," "On the South Coast," "A Swimmer's Dream," "Loch Torridon," "The Palace of Pan," "A Channel Passage," "The Promise of the Hawthorn," "Hawthorn Tide," "The Passing of the Hawthorn," and a long list of others. All of these poems, beautiful by any standards, exhibit Swinburne's powers of mythmaking and body forth the tenets of the achieved myth.

The most notable exception to what has been called the "rule of mediocrity" in the late verse is not a lyric at all, but the magnificent narrative *Tristram of Lyonesse* (1882), by far the best modern rendering of the Tristram legend. Both the "Prelude," written as early as 1869, and the rest of the enormous narrative, not produced until the 1880s, reflect all of the achievements—technical and thematic—of his best mythopoeic poetry. Jerome McGann has compared the rhetorical structures of *Tristram* to those of "On the Cliffs," and the extraordinary inclusiveness of the syntax may even surpass that of "On the Cliffs." [4] The overall structure, moreover, is antiphonal in the same sense as that of "By the North Sea." In addition to the awesome antiphonal response of the first forty-four lines of the "Prelude" in the first forty-four of the final book, "The Sailing of the Swan," the poem continually picks up and metamorphoses image clusters and ideas. Allusions to Merlin's imprisonment by Nimue, for example, run throughout the poem, subtly shifting meaning in different contexts. Swinburne said he was "stimulated" by the music of Wagner when writing *Tristram of Lyonesse*, and his statement is not surprising, for even more than in "Hesperia," *Erechtheus*, or "On the Cliffs," the verse reverberates with the continually present, continually metamorphosing leitmotives of Wagnerian opera. [5] Further, the metaphoric identification of man's attributes with the natural world, which reflects his experiential perception of a "Thou" in nature, could not be clearer. John D. Rosenberg notes the "erotic interpenetration of nature and man"; [6] indeed, all of nature is alive with man's life, as almost any passage in

[4] *Swinburne: An Experiment in Criticism* (Chicago, 1972), pp. 159–67.
[5] *Letters*, I, xxxi.
[6] John D. Rosenberg, ed. *Swinburne: Selected Poetry and Prose*, p. xiv.

the poem would serve to illustrate. Tristram, moreover, is, like
Swinburne, a singer—and, like Swinburne's, his resurrection in
song corresponds with nature's resurrection in spring. He and external nature merge in the great cosmic song:

> And the spring loved him surely, being from birth
> One made out of the better part of earth,
> A man born as at sunrise; one that saw
> Not without reverence and sweet sense of awe
> But wholly without fear or fitful breath
> The face of life watched by the face of death;
> And living took his fill of rest and strife,
> Of love and change, and fruit and seed of life,
> And when his time to live in light was done
> With unbent head would pass out of the sun:
> A spirit as morning, fair and clear and strong,
> Whose thought and work were as one harp and song
> Heard through the world as in a strange king's hall
> Some great guest's voice that sings of festival.
> So seemed all things to love him, and his heart
> In all their joy of life to take such part,
> That with the live earth and the living sea
> He was as one that communed mutually
> With naked heart to heart of friend to friend.
>   [IV, 68–69]

That the narrative is, in some sense, a myth of the creative poet
should be clear from this passage—in which Tristram strikingly
resembles the Swinburne of "On the Cliffs"—but it becomes un-
ambiguously clear later in the poem, when the birth of the poet in
"Thalassius" is recapitulated in terms of Tristram:

> And like the sun his heart rejoiced in him,
> And brightened with a broadening flame of mirth:
> And hardly seemed its life a part of earth,
> But the life kindled of a fiery birth
> And passion of a new-begotten son
> Between the live sea and the living sun.
>   [IV, 139]

His heart, like the spiritual life of the poet of "Thalassius"—or of
"By the North Sea"—is born of the union of sea and sun.
    The significance of the myth in *Tristram of Lyonesse* becomes even

clearer when we recall that the sea consistently represents the world
of process and the sun symbolizes thought and poetry for Swinburne. Tristram's development in the poem is primarily a growth
toward acceptance of cyclical change, and the poem itself modulates
from a celebration of love in the "Prelude" to a remarkable prolonged antiphonal celebration of fate in "The Sailing of the Swan."
Fate, moreover, is merely another word for *change*:

> Fate, that was born ere spirit and flesh were made,
> The fire that fills man's life with light and shade;
> The power beyond all godhead which puts on
> All forms of multitudinous unison,
> A raiment of eternal change inwrought
> With shapes and hues more subtly spun than thought,
> Where all things old bear fruit of all things new
> And one deep chord throbs all the music through,
> The chord of change unchanging. . . .
>
> [IV, 144]

Fate and change, as changeably unchangeable as the sea, must be
acknowledged before love or art can be made, for "Fate that was
born ere spirit and flesh were made" is the one thing which must
preexist "Love, that is first and last of all things made" (IV, 7). For
those who accept and merge with change and process, for those
who participate in the cosmic song of universal change, life is "no
discord in the tune with death" (IV, 144); immortality may be
gained in song. The burden of the "Prelude," as well as of "The
Sailing of the Swan," is that passionate lovers, become one with the
cycles of nature, are resurrected by generations of singers just as
organic growth is resurrected in spring or the day in the dawn—
"short-lived things, long dead, live long / . . . in changeless change
of seasons" (IV, 10) because singers revive them. The one absolute
necessity is that man recognize change as law and consequently
recognize that life and death are one:

> If life were haply death, and death be life;
> If love with yet some lovelier laugh revive,
> And song relume the light it bore alive . . .
>   . . . . .
> Might he that sees the shade thereof not say
> This dream were trustier than the truth of day.
>
> [IV, 146]

It must be noted at some point that Swinburne's myth of cyclical return in song makes him the most prolific user of the prefix *re* the language has ever known—just as Hardy, tormented by his agnosticism, was the most prolific user of *un*, and Wordsworth, pioneering the subconscious, the most persistent user of *under*. The importance of this passage, however, is its emphatic statement of the truth and life of the imagination—made possible by a clear recognition of mortality.

According to Kerry McSweeney, "A Nympholept" and "The Lake of Gaube" rise above "Thalassius" and "the mediocrity of so much of the poetry that was to come" because they "emphasize the difficulty and danger of direct confrontation with nature, the terror it inspires, and the difficult struggle to put aside those things that keep the poet from fully surrendering himself to the natural world."[7] This is, as we have seen, true also of "On the Cliffs," "By the North Sea," and *Tristram of Lyonesse*, but McSweeney is right in noting that the element of fear and terror is more pronounced, more central, in the later poems. "A Nympholept," perhaps Swinburne's most perfect mythopoeic poem, is overtly concerned with the problem of overcoming fear of natural law, of change. The poem's ostensible deity, Pan, simply represents all of the natural world; like all of Swinburne's gods, he is man-made, created only by the soul's "strength to conceive and perceive [him] . . . / With sense more subtle than senses that hear and see" (VI, 142). Pan's wife, the natural complement of nature, is *change*, and the fear of the poet springs from a recognition of the inseparability of the two:

> No service of bended knee or of humbled head
> May soothe or subdue the God who has change to wife:
> And life with death is as morning with evening wed.
>   [VI, 143]

The central question, which immediately follows this perception, is whether hope, inspired by the beauty of the sunlit scene, is stronger than fear: "And yet, if the hope that hath said it absorb not fear, / What helps it man that the stars and the waters gleam?" (VI, 143). The vision, the actual seizure (*-lepsy*) by the nymph, immediately ensues, and though this is never made explicit, the nymph seems to be none other than Pan's wife, change itself, for she is described as a

---

[7] McSweeney, "Swinburne's 'Thalassius,'" p. 54.

strange oscillation between shadow and light (death and life)—as
change is frequently described in Swinburne. Recognition of the
nymph transforms fear to delight:

> I sleep not: never in sleep has a man beholden
>   This. From the shadow that trembles and yearns with light
> Suppressed and elate and reluctant—obscure and golden
>   As water kindled with presage of dawn or night—
>   A form, a face, a wonder to sense and sight,
> Grows great as the moon through the month, and her eyes embolden
>   Fear, till it change to desire, and desire to delight.
>   [VI, 144–45]

Fear is conquered by a euphoric acceptance of natural process—the
poet achieves a mergence with the All, which he had thought could
come only with death:

> I lean my face to the heather, and drink the sun
>   Whose flame-lit odour satiates the flowers: mine eyes
> Close, and the goal of delight and of life is one:
>   No more I crave of earth or her kindred skies.
>   [VI, 146–47]

The sleepless, unsatisfied urge of romanticism, the recognition that
"Our lives and our longings are twain," which had preoccupied
Swinburne since the first series of *Poems and Ballads*, is finally
brought to an end in the ecstatic embrace of "A Nympholept."

As in "By the North Sea," acceptance of mortal limits paradoxically leads to immortality, for the oblivious union with nature, a sort
of death into the life of process, suddenly makes the poet realize his
own power to create meaning. After the embrace, he asks, significantly: "My spirit or thine is it, breath of thy life or of mine, /
Which fills my sense with a rapture that casts out fear?" (VI, 147).
And in the closing lines he realizes that the nymph is of earth, the
ecstasy caused by his imagination, and that the power of the mind
brings heaven to earth:

> Heaven is as earth, and as heaven to me
> Earth: for the shadows that sundered them here take flight;
> And nought is all, as am I, but a dream of thee.
>   [VI, 148]

Even more clearly than in *Tristram of Lyonesse*, the final resolution is an affirmation of solipsistic creation from the void. Recognizing that he makes his own God, his own hope, his own passionate embrace and his own heaven, the poet celebrates the power of his imagination. The presiding deity of this poem is not Pan at all, but Apollo, the sun god and the singing god, whose rays pervade the noon landscape and unify poet, nature, and nymph in their splendor. The opening stanza sets the scene beautifully:

> Summer, and noon, and a splendour of silence, felt,
>   Seen, and heard of the spirit within the sense.
> Soft through the frondage the shades of the sunbeams melt,
>   Sharp through the foliage the shafts of them, keen and dense,
>   Cleave, as discharged from the string of the God's bow, tense
> As a war-steed's girth, and bright as a warrior's belt.
>   Ah, why should an hour that is heaven for an hour pass hence?
>   [VI, 133]

The concluding question indicates that the poet is not content merely to accept that his life and desires are twain, but the solution to his problem is implicit in the six preceding lines. The shafts from the God's, Apollo's, bow cleave—the word is used in the same sense as in "On the Cliffs"—all things into glorified unity. In an earlier poem, "Pan and Thalassius" (1889), Swinburne had used the myth of the singing contest of Pan and Apollo to suggest that the worshipers of nature, like Midas, are sadly mistaken. Thalassius, "seed of Apollo," given the final response in the lyrical dialogue, expresses the reasons for the superiority of Apollo. Pan has asserted that he is "All," but Thalassius answers:

> God,
> God Pan, from the glad wood's portal
>   The breaths of thy song blow sweet:
> But woods may be walked in of mortal
>   Man's thought, where never thy feet
>   Trod.
>
> Thine
> All secrets of growth and of birth are,
>   All glories of flower and of tree,

> Wheresoever the wonders of earth are;
>   The words of the spell of the sea
>   Mine.
>
> [III, 233]

Apollo occupies the "spirit within the sense"—an oft-reiterated phrase in late Swinburne—exalting man above nature by incorporating "mortal / Man's thought" in his song. At a more sophisticated level "A Nympholept" also recreates the contest between Pan and Apollo. The Wordsworthian joy in the unity of nature at the beginning of the poem results from a perception of a bond between heaven and earth, Apollo and Pan. The sun's rays, as in "By the North Sea" and many other poems, draw all things into harmony. The vision, however, does not reinforce this idea of unity; it shatters it, for the vision is of a shadow that separates the sun's rays from the earth, Apollo from Pan:

> What light, what shadow, diviner than dawn or night,
>   Draws near, makes pause, and again—or I dream—draws near?
>
> [VI, 144]

Only when the divorce of sun and earth is complete, at the end of the poem, does the poet advance beyond Wordsworthian joy to a new conception of man in nature:

> Heaven is as earth, and as heaven to me
> Earth: for the shadows that sundered them here take flight;
>   And nought is all, as am I, but a dream of thee.
>
> [VI, 148]

The poem ends where it began, with a blissful, sun-soaked nature, but on a new level, for the poet has seen that the mind of man is necessarily separated from nature by the shadow of mortality and that the perceiving mind *creates* the harmony of man and earth. He comes, by virtue of his vision of the sundering shadow, to realize that the Apollonian mind is not only separated from nature but creates nature. In the beginning, the poet, Midas-like, celebrates "the one God, Pan," and it is only through immersion in process and recognition of change that he comes to the element missing from the All—the power of man's thought.

The recognition in "A Nympholept," "Pan and Thalassius," and a

host of other late poems of the superiority of Apollo over Pan
clearly establishes Swinburne's main line of divergence from
Wordsworthian romanticism. Nature to him is not a great healer,
but is, as it was to Tennyson and the other Victorians, "red in tooth
and claw." His success in salvaging the visionary nature poetry of
romanticism from the Victorian pragmatism that had ruined it for
his contemporaries makes Swinburne unique in his period. Arnold,
Mill, and others could praise Wordsworth and his fellow romantics
even while knowing, sadly, that harmonious union with nature was
no longer possible. Swinburne alone both saw the impossibilities of
pantheism and was able to continue to see nature as imaginatively—mythopoeically—as his predecessors. Swinburne alone was
able to fuse the truths of romanticism and Victorianism, the earlier
generation's belief in the life of nature and his own generation's
knowledge of nature's brute, impersonal carnality. In Nietzschean
terms, Swinburne has recognized the need to incorporate Dionysian fear and ecstasy into a complete mythic view.

Swinburne was typical of his age in his preoccupation with the
subject of personal immortality, but as "A Nympholept" and, even
more emphatically, "The Lake of Gaube" illustrate, he was uniquely
successful in dealing with the agnostic's traditional fear of death.
More explicitly in "The Lake of Gaube" than anywhere else in his
poetry, Swinburne is concerned with the fear of mortality that destroys the Wordsworthian joy of childlike immersion in nature. The
salamanders that live near the lake, "living things of light like flames
in flower" (VI, 297), represent this total communion with sun-
soaked nature—the communion finally achieved in "A Nympholept"—but

> Fear held the bright thing hateful, even as fear,
>   Whose name is one with hate and horror, saith
> That heaven, the dark deep heaven of water near,
>   Is deadly deep as hell and dark as death.

[VI, 298]

As in "A Nympholept" again, the fear is overcome by an ecstatic
embrace of the terror—here, more explicitly death than change.
The poet plunges into the waters of death:

Death-dark and delicious as death in the dream of a lover and dreamer may
   be,
It clasps and encompasses body and soul with delight to be living and free:
Free utterly now though the freedom endure but the space of a perilous
   breath,
And living, though girdled about with the darkness and coldness and
   strangeness of death:
Each limb and each pulse of the body rejoicing, each nerve of the spirit at
   rest,
All sense of the soul's life rapture, a passionate peace in its blindness blest.
                                                [VI, 298–99]

Complete surrender to the deathlike state, an experience in life of
the oblivious mergence sought in so many of the early poems,
makes him realize that death is not a negation of life but a fulfillment and that acceptance of death eliminates the fear of process
which inhibits freedom. Comparing "The Lake of Gaube" with the
"Hymn to Proserpine," Kerry McSweeney has succinctly summarized Swinburne's maturation to this point of acceptance: "Death
is no more a longed-for oblivion, a release from meaningless imprisonment in mutability. It is rather something intimately a part of
man's relation to nature; a culmination, not an escape."[8]

The comparison with the "Hymn to Proserpine" is instructive in
other ways. We recall that in the earlier poems the depths of the sea
represented the changeless void of death, the surface the perpetually shifting semblance of mortal life. In 1867 Swinburne had found
consolation for mortality in contemplating the eternality of the
void, the end of strife, but had found no instruction as to how he
might best live out his days in the sun. In "The Lake of Gaube" he
does not contemplate the void, he experiences it; his consolation is
not philosophical but experiential, emotional, mythopoeic. After
the experience he can return from the void to the ever shifting
surface and live without fear; after the plunge into the depths he can
return to swim on the surface, in the full light of the sun, and
participate in the "sense of unison" (VI, 297) of all living nature.
The salamander is significant because, being amphibious, it
can live both on land and in water and because, according to legend, it can live through fire. In other words, the salamander lives

[8] "Swinburne's 'A Nympholept' and 'The Lake of Gaube,'" *Victorian Poetry*, 9
(1971), 214.

in harmony with all the elements, with nothing to fear from any of them. The swimmer, half in the water and half out, with the sun above him and the depths below, is in a precisely analogous state, a state of total surrender to the forces of the external world. The result, even more emphatically than in "A Nympholept," is that life and death are as one:

As the silent speed of a dream too living to live for a thought's space more
Is the flight of his limbs through the still strong chill of the darkness from
    shore to shore.
Might life be as this is and death be as life that casts off time as a robe,
The likeness of infinite heaven were a symbol revealed of the lake of
    Gaube.

[VI, 299]

The diver is completely at one with the cosmic song of nature. At a precisely analogous moment in *Tristram of Lyonesse* after Tristram has plunged into the sea, the metaphor of the cosmic song is explicitly evoked:

each glad limb became
A note of rapture in the tune of life,
Live music mild and keen as sleep and strife.

[IV, 139]

Like Tristram and like the salamanders, which are described earlier in the poem in terms of song (VI, 297), the diver becomes a chord in the universal harmony.

The lesson of "The Lake of Gaube," the cure Swinburne sets forth for the agnostic agony of the nineteenth century, is that surrender to the flux of experience, nurture of the whole self in the whole of nature, makes philosophical doubt irrelevant. The final section of the poem, after the description of the exhilarating plunge into elemental nature, begins with an agnostic litany:

Whose thought has fathomed and measured
    The darkness of life and death,
The secret within them treasured,
    The spirit that is not breath?
Whose vision has yet beholden
    The splendour of death and of life?

[VI, 300]

Wordsworthian romanticism does not ask such questions. Swinburne's contribution to the poetic succession is his incorporation of philosophical doubt into his myth and his triumphant affirmation of man's ability to make meaning. The answer vouchsafed for his question is, paradoxically, silence:

> Deep silence answers: the glory
>   We dream of may be but a dream,
> And the sun of the soul wax hoary
>   As ashes that show not a gleam.
> But well shall it be with us ever
>   Who drive through the darkness here,
> If the soul that we live by never,
>   For aught that a lie saith, fear.
>
> [VI, 300]

All of this recapitulates, with heightened awareness, the implicit lessons of "Hesperia," "By the North Sea," and "A Nympholept," that acceptance of our mortal part is the basis of creativity and that in creation from the void lies our salvation. Swinburne believed he had much in common with Blake, and so he had, but on the crucial question of the self in relation to nature, they disagreed entirely. Blake based his myth of the imaginative self entirely on a rejection of the natural, generative self, rhetorically asking of his mortal part in "To Tirzah," "Then what have I to do with thee?" Swinburne's answer, had he understood the poem aright (he did not) would have been *everything*: his own myth of imagination is based on the reality of experience—experience which tells him that freedom and peace are found in surrender of the self to cyclical change.

The uniqueness of Swinburne's myth in the late nineteenth century can best be appreciated by comparing it with the faith of the wholly antithetical but eminently Victorian Browning. Swinburne's final consolation lay in his belief—confirmed, he felt, by experience—that death would liberate him from the strife of time, Browning's in the Christian belief in personal immortality. Browning's last thoughts on the subject of death are set forth in the last stanza of the "Epilogue" to *Asolando*, published, ironically, on December 12, 1889, the day of his death. With the bravado of the true believer—both in Christianity and the Protestant work ethic—he exhorts us to

> Greet the unseen with a cheer!
> Bid him forward, breast and back as either should be,
> "Strive and thrive!" cry "Speed,—fight on, fare ever
>   There as here!"[9]

For Browning, as for most Victorians—from Carlyle to the Evangelical Protestants to the Utilitarian industrialists—the lot of man was ever to work and to strive; but reaching the goal was unthinkable, for in fulfillment the purpose, the strife of humanity, would be ended. Even after death, Browning insists, man must "fight on" as he fought in life. As we have seen, the early Swinburne had felt the same way, rejecting sterile completion in such poems as "Hermaphroditus" and asserting the need for perpetual striving until death. It is a mark of his development that in the late poetry he was able to find complete fulfillment in life, to find the joy Wordsworth had thought could only be known by the child.

For Swinburne, unlike Browning, life was not to be a continual kicking against the pricks in order to prove the integrity of the individual; rather it was to be a complete surrender to and immersion in the flux of nature. The Wordsworthian child knows the freedom of wild animals, bounds over the mountains like a roe; Swinburne at the end of his life, knew the same joy: "As a sea-mew's love of the sea-wind breasted and ridden for rapture's sake / Is the love of his body and soul for the darkling delight of the soundless lake" (VI, 299). The mythopoeic impulse in Wordsworth and Coleridge had died out when the moments of childlike rapture in nature had ceased to come, and their legacy to the Victorians had been the meager comfort that years bring the philosophic mind. Swinburne's distinction, as the finest of the heirs of romanticism, was to begin with the shattered vision of Wordsworth, the division of soul and sense, the philosophic mind, and work his way back to harmonious interpenetration of the self in nature. He utterly reversed the romantic process of growth from vision to philosophy, completing the cycle from fall to redemption by incorporating and subsuming the philosophical mind in his final vision. McSweeney, characterizing "A Nympholept," accurately describes the balance of

---

[9] "Epilogue," *The Complete Poetical Works of Browning*, ed. Horace E. Scudder (Cambridge, Mass., 1895), p. 1007.

philosophy and experiential joy in both that poem and "The Lake of Gaube": "None of the awareness of human limitations and of nature's separateness from man . . . is forgotten or negated here. It is for the moment transformed, because of the speaker's acceptance of it, into something positive and joyous."[10] Swinburne remained, contemplatively, agnostic while becoming, experientially, religious and mythopoeic. The fear he overcame in "A Nympholept" and "The Lake of Gaube" was the fear fostered on romanticism by rationalism.

The complete fusion of the self in nature is the first requirement of mythopoeic art, and "The Lake of Gaube" is as much a parable of the artist as a description of the loss of selfhood in the elements. In another late poem, "By Twilight," Swinburne clearly stated the absolute irreducible base of his myth:

> the supreme
> Pure presence of death shall assure us, and prove us
> If we dream.
>
> [III, 263]

In "The Lake of Gaube" the supreme presence of death verifies the dream of man's significance and makes possible the perpetuation of dreams, of myths. The description of the diver's return to the surface suggests, in the light of Swinburne's Apollonian myth, a return to creativity: "And swiftly and sweetly, when strength and breath fall short, and the dive is done, / Shoots up as a shaft from the dark depth shot, sped straight into sight of the sun" (VI, 299). He becomes as a shaft from the bow of Apollo returning to the quiver, revivified by acceptance of death. The lines recall the description of the unifying shafts of Apollo in the first stanza of "A Nympholept" and analogous descriptions in "On the Cliffs" and "By the North Sea." The salamander, whom the swimmer comes to resemble in his ability to live in joy in all elements, has been described by Meredith B. Raymond as "the manifestation of art" because he is a "living synthesis of two worlds, the universal, eternal world and the particular world of man."[11] This is true, but, even more significantly,

---

[10] "Swinburne's 'A Nympholept' and 'The Lake of Gaube,'" p. 211.

[11] "'The Lake of Gaube': Swinburne's Dive in the Dark and the 'Indeterminate Moment,'" *Victorian Poetry*, 9 (1971), 195.

the description of the salamander as a "flamelike tongue" suggests the Pentecostal image of the Holy Spirit, as a tongue of flame, coming to strengthen the apostles at a moment of doubt and fear. Swinburne, always rivaling the Christian myth, is creating a natural Pentecost, a trial by fire, in which doubt and fear are ousted and the soul is strengthened. Bolstered by a return to the elements, he is ready to sing again.

Just as "A Nympholept" and "The Lake of Gaube" are, in a sense, poems about art without ever mentioning art, so are dozens of the other late nature poems that have been dismissed as mere scene painting because readers have never realized that the myth of poetry and Apollo, arduously developed in other poems, unostentatiously pervades them. It would be impracticable—and redundant—to examine all of these lyrics, but it is worth while to glance at a few stanzas taken from Swinburne's last volume of lyrics, *A Channel Passage and Other Poems* (1904). Immediately following "The Lake of Gaube" in this volume is an exquisite trilogy of poems that has been all but ignored by critics. "The Promise of the Hawthorn," "Hawthorn Tide," and "The Passing of the Hawthorn" do not merely describe the budding, blooming, and drooping of a flower but the joy of man and nature in the changeless change of the eternal song:

A new life answers and thrills to the kiss of the young strong year,
And the glory we see is as music we hear not, and dream that we hear.
From blossom to blossom the live tune kindles, from tree to tree,
And we know not indeed if we hear not the song of the life we see.
                                                                [VI, 305]

The experiential verification of the dream of the song once again overrides the rational doubts. All of nature is alive and singing, and the perceiving poet is singing in complete harmony:

ever the sight that salutes them [flowers] again and adores them
        awhile is blest,
And the heart is a hymn, and the sense is a soul, and the soul is a song.
                                                                [VI, 308]

Part of the reason for neglect of these poems, no doubt, is that the myth of poetry is evoked, at times, in words difficult of comprehension to one not already well versed in it:

Music made of the morning that smites from the chords of the mute world
    song
Trembles and quickens and lightens, unfelt, unbeholden unheard,
    From blossom on blossom that climbs and exults in the strength of the
        sun grown strong,
    And answers the word of the wind of the spring with the sun's own
        word.

[VI, 305–6]

Such verse has been condemned as facile word-music—"a tale of little meaning tho' the words are strong"—but for one who has read Swinburne carefully, they are highly charged with significance. Finally, in neglected lyrics of as late a date as "Hawthorn Tide," Swinburne was still capable of such verbal tours de force as the description of a bank of flowering hawthorn as "One visible marvel of music inaudible" (VI, 309). As in "Hesperia," written some thirty years earlier, the dazzling harmony of synesthetic imagery still asserts a harmony of the senses that is purely a creation of the poet. Swinburne's language, as much as ever, if not more, is charged with metaphor to bring about a fusion of the soul and sense of man and the soul and sense of nature.

Two other poems included in *A Channel Passage and Other Poems* indicate the extent to which Swinburne drew comfort from his myth. He wrote "The High Oaks: Barking Hall, July 19th, 1896" at his mother's birthplace in celebration of her eighty-seventh birthday; Lady Jane Henrietta Swinburne died in November 1896, and he added an elegiac companion piece, "Barking Hall: A Year After." The first of the poems, a lovely evocation of the landscape, is filled with the images and ideas we have come to associate with the mature myth. The consolation for mortality is so prominent that even this poem sounds like an elegy:

Here we have our earth
Yet, with all the mirth
Of all the summers since the world began,
All strengths of rest and strife
And love-lit love of life
Where death has birth to wife,
And where the sun speaks, and is heard of man:

> Yea, half the sun's bright speech is heard,
> And like the sea the soul of man gives back his word.
>
> [VI, 342]

Nature is alive with the love and speech of man; the sun and the sea, life and death, are in unison and all is alive and at peace. According to Edmund Gosse, the death of Swinburne's mother was a devastating blow: "The grief of her son was overwhelming, and it may be said that this formed the last crisis of his own life." [12] It is of the greatest significance that Swinburne turned for comfort to the landscape, fulfilled of love and of song—including his own song of a year before. His lament for his mother begins as a celebration of wind, sun, and change:

> Still the sovereign trees
> Make the sundawn's breeze
> More bright, more sweet, more heavenly than it rose,
> As wind and sun fulfil
> Their living rapture: still
> Noon, dawn, and evening thrill
> With radiant change the immeasurable repose
> Wherewith the woodland wilds lie blest
> And feel how storms and centuries rock them still to rest.
>
> [VI, 346]

The "sundawn's breeze"—a potent image in view of the myth—is different, "more heavenly," because the fulfilling force of "wind and sun" have added his love and his song to the scene. Change, which carried off his mother, is accepted and seen as a mere part, an ornament, of changelessness, "the immeasurable repose." All is in harmony with the light of the sun; change itself is "radiant." As in "A Nympholept" and "The Lake of Gaube," however, the affirmation at the beginning must be earned in the course of the poem, must describe the pain of grief, the pain of knowing that the dead live only in our dreams. The last stanza returns to the consolation of the first, with greater impact because it has absorbed all of the pain of the intervening stanzas:

---

[12] *The Life of Algernon Charles Swinburne* (New York, 1917), p. 177.

Night and sleep and dawn
Pass with dreams withdrawn:
But higher above them far then noon may climb
Love lives and turns to light
The deadly noon of night.
His fiery spirit of sight
Endures no curb of change or darkling time.
Even earth and transient things of earth
Even here to him bear witness not of death but birth.

[VI, 348]

Love, born of the "transient things of earth," lives on in the eternal. The borderline between life and death is wholly eradicated and all change, leading to rest, is to be celebrated.

That much of Swinburne's late poetry is elegiac should not be surprising. His personal myth, evolved in response to his own fears of mortality, is perfectly adapted to the genre of consolation. He arrived slowly and arduously at a myth of "Art that mocks death, and Song that never dies" ("A Death on Easter Day" [V, 235]), and it was fitting that he should use it to mock death. Because a large part of the myth was concerned with the ability of the poet to fulfill the world with meaning by joining the cosmic Apollonian song of all generations of singers, it was fitting also that most of Swinburne's elegies should be about fellow poets. *Poems and Ballads* (Second Series), the volume in which the myth of poets and poetry is first fully set forth, consists largely of celebrations of dead singers, as do all the subsequent collections of lyrics. In mourning poets dead and gone, Swinburne not only paid tribute to them but expressed his own faith. The poignant "In Time of Mourning," written after the death of Hugo in May 1885, is short enough to be quoted in full, and will serve as a perfect example of Swinburne's use of the elegiac mode:

"Return," we dare not as we fain
Would cry from hearts that yearn:
Love dares not bid our dead again
Return.

O hearts that strain and burn
As fires fast fettered burn and strain!
Bow down, lie still and learn.

> The heart that healed all hearts of pain
>   No funeral rites inurn:
> Its echoes, while the stars remain,
>   Return.
>
> [III, 258]

The lesson is simple—the singer's heart never dies because the echoes of his song ring down the ages. The poem ties in perfectly with the idea of the eternal Apollonian song, the everlasting succession of poets and the immortal life of man, both aggregate man and the individual man, Victor Hugo.

The form of this simple little tribute exactly corresponds to its content. It is a roundel, a form enormously congenial to Swinburne, in which a word or phrase from the first line is caught up and used as a refrain. In this case the echoing of the word "return" rings in the perpetual returns of Victor Hugo, his heart redeemed in each succeeding poet who takes up his song. The song and the heart are metamorphosed in each return, of course, because the note of the new singer is added and the context of the song is changed. Hugo becomes Swinburnian Hugo. The roundel perfectly reflects this process of metamorphosis, this *repetitio ad differens*, because the refrain, like the poet's song, is transformed in the changing context. In "The Roundel" Swinburne beautifully characterizes the effects of the form,

> As a bird's quick song runs round, and the hearts in us hear
> Pause answer to pause, and again the same strain caught,
> So moves the device whence, round as a pearl or tear,
>   A roundel is wrought.
>
> [VI, 161]

The answer of song to song is the basis of Swinburne's myth and the answer of image to image, thought to thought, and line to line the basis of much of his best art. The echo system of *Erechtheus*, the calling of image to image in "On the Cliffs," and the recurring leitmotives of *Tristram of Lyonesse* all reflect, on a larger scale, the poetic concerns that led Swinburne to the roundel.

The principle of modulating echoes appears to form the basis of most of Swinburne's beliefs about lyric form. Relatively early in his career he had been able to accept and praise the free verse of

Whitman, but as his myth of poetry developed and his own attitudes about poetic form hardened, he came to insist on the need for rigid structures in lyrical verse. He emphatically insisted on the need for rhyme, for example, and was adamant on the importance of a fixed, repeating stanza form. Irregular odes, such as Wordsworth's "Intimations Ode," suffer from the "lawless discord of Cowley's 'immetrical' irregularity" and a "lack of ordered rhythm and lyric law." Even Coleridge and Shelley, in Swinburne's opinion the greatest English lyricists, "could not do their very best when working without a limit and singing without a law."[13] Stanzaic regularity in his own verse, which made possible the sort of dazzling antiphonal variation of "By the North Sea," reflects a general tendency of Swinburne's lyrics to continually repeat sounds and thoughts, subtly shifting the implications. Most of his best lyrics, in fact, follow a circular pattern, returning in the end to the thoughts expressed at the beginning, but with a more profound understanding. As we have seen, "On the Cliffs," "A Nympholept," "The Lake of Gaube," and "Barking Hall" all return in their closing lines to qualify and reaffirm the initial vision. The pattern is particularly significant in Swinburne both because it formally exhibits his belief in a continual expansion of the soul in the constant accumulation of song and because the final, qualified vision of his closing stanzas is almost always an assertion of man's solipsistic creation rather than of unqualified faith in external verities. The very form of these lyrics, a continuing modulation of song, is a microcosm of history as Swinburne perceived it. Man begins with unquestioning faith, falls into a period of doubts and speculation, and emerges triumphant in his own power to create. Significantly, the form is based on the Christian paradigm of fall and redemption only to refute Christian faith with the assertion, best expressed in the last stanza of "A Nympholept," that earth and heaven are one and the same, that it is all a matter of perception. The two poems written in tribute to his mother, "The High Oaks" and "Barking Hall," provide an informative example of the value of poetic form to Swinburne. The complex nine-line stanza, apparently invented for the first poem, is

[13] "Wordsworth and Byron," *The Complete Works of Algernon Charles Swinburne*, ed. Edmund Gosse and Thomas James Wise, XIV (1926), 224.

repeated in the second so that the elegy reverberates both the form and the content of the birthday tribute. Swinburne's recurrent use of standard forms throughout his career, in fact, is designed to echo the songs of earlier poets in the same way as "Barking Hall" is to echo "The High Oaks." A poem, Swinburne felt, could become a part of an earlier poem by being an antiphonal response to it. In a letter to D. G. Rossetti he wrote that "of all things I like (not repetition but) antiphony—if there be such a word—in poems— two notes struck in the same key—two companions mutually responsive and reinforcing."[14] Swinburne is here discussing two poems by one author—like his own "Hymn to Proserpine" and "The Last Oracle"—but the principle would apply as well to two poems by different authors. "On the Cliffs," for example, is an antiphonal response to Whitman's "Out of the Cradle Endlessly Rocking." Formally, from his earliest experiments in pastiche to his resurrection of Greek and Elizabethan tragedy to his late use of highly formalized structures like the roundel and sonnet, he is self-consciously harmonizing with the eternal voices of the Apollonian song. Even his meters, as in "Sapphics" and "Hendecasyllabics"—or more subtly, in "On the Cliffs," where he adopts the rhythms of "Lycidas"—are often chosen to strike in the same key with a certain past singer or song.

Swinburne's astonishing gift for parody—"a kind of miracle of 'negative capability,'" Cecil Lang has called it—is, in a more profound way than one might expect, indicative of the nature of his genius. His parodies exhibit not only his "unsurpassed *maestria*," but also his uncanny ability to enter into the creative process of another poet.[15] They are, in their own way, antiphonal responses to Swinburne's victims, pitched in precisely the same key. That the parodies are perfect echoes of form and ghastly distortions of content reflects yet another of Swinburne's aesthetic beliefs—the importance of a harmonious fusion of form and content. It was because he so clearly saw the need for such fusion that he so clearly saw the absurdity of separating the two, and it was on the basis of such a separation in the poems of his victims that he chose them. The division of soul

[14] *Letters*, II (1959), 100.
[15] Ibid., I, xv; Gosse, p. 267.

and sense, for example, in the bodiless philosophizing of Tennyson's "The Higher Pantheism"—

And the ear of man cannot hear, and the eye of man cannot see;
But if we could see and hear, this Vision—were it not He?[16]

—is only slightly exaggerated in Swinburne's antiphon, "The Higher Pantheism in a Nutshell":

Body and spirit are twins: God only knows which is which:
The soul squats down in the flesh, like a tinker drunk in a ditch.

[V, 384]

The parodies, like everything else Swinburne wrote, from his mythopoeic poetry to his translations—also miracles of negative capability—reflect his two central aesthetic beliefs: all poems are conditioned by and responsive to other poems, and form and content in poetry are, ideally, inseparable.

It is altogether fitting that this discussion of Swinburne's poetry, which began with an analysis of his concept of form, should in the end, like a Swinburnian roundel, return to its beginning in an altered context. Swinburne's paradoxical insistence on the all-importance of form, his unabashed aestheticism, and his equally emphatic insistence on the importance of thought can now be resolved. Thought, in Swinburne, rarely means contemplative or philosophic meditation but rather designates the emotional and artistic truths of creative poetry, part of the collective soul of man, and has a set form, a defined body, that cannot be neglected. Further, though it may seem that mythopoeia should be a spontaneous reaction, uninhibited by arbitrary rules, to the whole life in nature, it must be remembered that, for Swinburne, the life in nature is the soul of man, the soul of man is poetry, and poetry is form. His mythopoeic creation and his myth are based not on perceptions of a chaotic nature but on perceptions of a nature vivified and "fulfilled" by the highly structured Apollonian song.

Finally, for Swinburne, form *is* thought. His vision is extraordinarily solipsistic, for he believes only in what he perceives, knowing

---

[16] "The Higher Pantheism," *The Poetic and Dramatic Works of Alfred Lord Tennyson*, ed. W. J. Rolfe (New York, 1898), p. 274.

all the while that "nought may be all," and the formal structures he employs are those that are best adapted to fill space, as it were, and cover the abyss of meaninglessness. The roundel, which typifies Swinburne's ideals of form, demonstrates more clearly than any form I know—except perhaps the triolet—that even words have no genuine, verifiable meaning outside the context which the individual, solipsistic intellect provides. The word "return," used three times in the elegiac roundel for Victor Hugo, has three distinct meanings. Swinburne believed in poetry more than he believed in anything else, but even poems, he knew, had different meanings at different times to different people. "On the Cliffs" shows that Sappho's song is immortal, but also shows that it has no single meaning to all men—that it, like Christianity, cannot be used as a universal verity on which to base a faith. Thus it is the form, the beauty, of Sappho's song that is carried on the wind, not its message or moral, and because it is the beauty of the song which uplifts and inspires Swinburne, it is the form which is, for him, the meaning.

Perhaps the most outstanding of Swinburne's many unusual qualities was his ability, perhaps unique, to make a virtue of solipsism. He was a born rebel who could not simply accept another man's creed, and his belief that no creed was externally verifiable, except by individual experience, not only encouraged but compelled him to create his own myth. Yet he was, nevertheless, following in the footsteps of Shelley. A final example of his poetic revisionism, his revision of Shelley's "Adonais," will serve to show both his essential romanticism and his atypically cheerful but typically Victorian solipsism. Like so many of Swinburne's late poems, "Adonais" is an elegy for a poet, and, like so many of Swinburne's early poems, it rejects all received myths of consolation to arrive at a longing for oblivion, a return to the All. In the most famous stanza of "Adonais" Shelley wrote:

> The One remains, the many change and pass;
> Heaven's light forever shines, Earth's shadows fly;
> Life, like a dome of many-coloured glass,
> Stains the white radiance of Eternity,
> Until Death tramples it to fragments—Die,
> If thou wouldst be with that which thou dost seek!
> Follow where all is fled!

As in Swinburne's early elegy "Ave atque Vale," the main consolation appears to be escape from the insignificance and suffering of
mortality. In the final stanza of "Adonais," however, Shelley moves
in the direction of a Swinburnian myth of poetry. The breath of
Urania, which had vivified Keats's song, now descends on him and
unites him in spirit with Adonais:

> The breath whose might I have invoked in song
> Descends on me. . . .
> . . . . .
> I am borne darkly, fearfully, afar;
> Whilst, burning through the inmost veil of Heaven,
> The soul of Adonais, like a star,
> Beacons from the abode where the Eternal are.[17]

Shelley's poem, like many of Swinburne's, rejects received
mythologies, acknowledges and accepts death, and then seeks consolation in a mythopoeic conception of an eternal song of man—the
breath of Urania for Shelley, the Apollonian song for Swinburne.
Yet though Shelley accepts death in "Adonais," he is not able to
overcome the fear of it; and though he acknowledges mortal limits,
he does not give thanks for them.

Swinburne's poetic revision of "Adonais," found in the final book
of *Tristram of Lyonesse*, definitively establishes his point of departure
from Shelleyan romanticism. After claiming that song will "relume
the light [love] bore alive," Swinburne continues with a summation
of his agnostic creed:

> If aught indeed at all of all this be,
> Though none might say nor any man might see,
> Might he that sees the shade thereof not say
> This dream were trustier than the truth of day.
> Nor haply may not hope, with heart more clear,
> Burn deathward, and the doubtful soul take cheer,
> Seeing through the channelled darkness yearn a star
> Whose eyebeams are not as the morning's are,
> Transient, and subjugate of lordlier light,
> But all unconquerable by noon or night,

---

[17] "Adonais," ll. 460–66, 487–88, 492–95, *Shelley: Poetical Works*, ed. Thomas
Hutchinson, corrected by G. M. Matthews (Oxford, 1970), pp. 443–44.

Being kindled only of life's own inmost fire,
Truth, stablished and made sure by strong desire,
Fountain of all things living, source and seed,
Force that perforce transfigures dream to deed,
God that begets on time, the body of death,
Eternity: *nor may man's darkening breath,*
Albeit it stain, disfigure or destroy
The glass wherein the soul sees life and joy
Only, with strength renewed and spirit of youth,
And brighter than the sun's the body of Truth
Eternal, unimaginable of man,
Whose very face not Thought's own eyes may scan,
But see far off his radiant feet at least
Trampling the head of Fear. . . .

                         [IV, 146–47, emphasis mine]

Swinburne, far more than Shelley, emphasizes the impossibility of knowing absolute truth but affirms that the truth which thought cannot find may be created by emotional, experiential conviction, may be "stablished and made sure by strong desire." Though the lovers of *Tristram of Lyonesse* are irrevocably destined for death, the intensity of their passion, "life's own inmost fire," is sufficient to cast out fear, which, significantly, Swinburne goes on to equate with the received myth of Christianity. Shelley had discarded received myth to embrace his own agnostic mythmaking, but he never achieved enough conviction to cast out fear or to apprehend that the lack of external verities made man's life more, not less, meaningful. For Shelley the negative connotations remain in the statement that life "Stains the white radiance of Eternity." Swinburne's fundamental divergence from his romantic predecessors is apparent in his conscientious elimination of negative connotations from this simile. The white light of eternity is, as we have repeatedly seen, only a euphemism for the void of eternity, and for Swinburne the breath that stains the glass does not disfigure it but only makes life and joy visible to the soul. Man's breath, in Swinburne a symbol of both life and song, is all that has meaning because it is all man can know. Thus Swinburne's final poetic creed, though hopeful, is no facile optimism but a call for unblinking acceptance of death and pain and continual strife to live intensely and create continually. His insistence on agnostic mythmaking both as an aesthetic and ethical necessity was, in practice, no less than a challenge to himself to overcome solipsistic fears through incessant creation of myths, to fulfill the empty universe with meaning. No poet ever set himself a harder task, no poet ever worked so long and faithfully at achieving his ends, and no poet ever succeeded so fully at creating his own consolation in a bleak and cheerless world.

Conclusion

SWINBURNE'S MYTH OF poetry as the perpetuation by individual
singers of the eternal Apollonian song fits in neatly with the recent
emergence of critical interest—both in literature and the graphic
arts—in *influence* as something more than pedantic source hunting.
The modern notion that museums should be laid out, without separate rooms, as one continual wall on which works of art can be
chronologically arranged to allow viewers to see them in the context of all that has influenced them, and all they have influenced, is a
sort of graphic representation of the eternal song. The standard of
critical judgment becomes the place and prominence of the work in
the stream of influences:

Along the path that defines our access to the work, each work of art has
ancestors, or as Gadamer has phrased it, is the answer to a question which
we must discover in the prior history of art. . . . It must be as Fried has put
it "radical" and "fecund"; it must account in a deeply critical way for its past
and become seminal for the future. The two define its "place" and it is
place that is the essence of intelligibility. Its presence as a work depends on
our knowledge of its horizons.[1]

This study has been predominantly concerned with the ways in
which Swinburne was "radical," with his "deeply critical" revision of
romanticism, his brilliant adaptations of those romantic ideals that
remained tenable in the latter half of the nineteenth century. We
have seen how Swinburne retained Blake's respect for the holiness
of man while rejecting his Christian mysticism, how he retained the

---

[1] Philip Fisher, "The Future's Past," *New Literary History*, 6 (1975), 596.

ever unsatisfied urge of Byronic romanticism while rejecting Byronic posing, and how he adapted the pantheism of Coleridge and Wordsworth to remove any sense of an informing divinity other than man. Finally, we have seen how he modified the Shelleyan ideal of agnostic mythmaking by placing greater emphasis on poetic faith and less on the pains of skepticism.

Swinburne was radical, in fact, in ways that most of his contemporaries were not. The great concern of the romantic poets had been to replace the Christian God, who had been separated from the truth of experience by eighteenth-century theism, with a myth of redemption that had a stronger hold on the imaginative and emotional life of man. The fundamental problem with romanticism was that the myths generated were the products of individual experience and had no external verification. From Arnold to Carlyle to Mill, the Victorians decried the lack of objectivity of the solipsistic myths of the romantics. Poems of the individual imagination could not stand up to the scrutiny of what Arnold called "disinterested objectivity." The hallmark of romanticism had been faith in the truth of experience and the creation of the imagination—"I am certain of nothing," said Keats, "but of the holiness of the Heart's affections and the truth of Imagination." [2] The hallmark of the Victorian period was "disinterested objectivity," which denies the validity of individual perceptions and, therefore, of intuition and faith. The romantic period, in other words, was characterized by faith, the Victorian by doubt. Just as the problem of the romantics had been the death of the Christian God, so, in a very real sense, the problem of the Victorians was the death of romanticism. Abstract empiricism took the place of intuition, and men like Arnold and Clough strove always to be *reasonable* above all. Clough's poetry represents a steadfast refusal to mythologize, and Arnold, stubbornly resisting the tendency to mythologize, perhaps disastrously undernourished his poetry. Tennyson, the most Victorian of the Victorians, wanting desperately to believe in personal immortality, struggled all his life to reconcile faith and reason, and Browning, though believing absolutely in the truth of intuitive knowledge, rarely felt free to speak in

[2] *The Letters of John Keats*, ed. Hyder Edward Rollins (Cambridge, Mass., 1958), I, 184.

his own voice—to defend a belief by reference to his own feelings. Swinburne was unique among the major Victorian poets in facing up to the romantics imaginatively and critically. He alone was truly radical.

The argument against Swinburne, however, has always been that he is merely radical, that he is not "fecund." Samuel Chew's comment that he "founded no school" and that he "was not . . . the sunrise of a new era of poetry, but the flaming sunset of Romanticism" reflects the prevailing belief that he was somewhat anachronistic, a throwback to earlier days who somehow didn't belong in the late Victorian period.[3] Yet Swinburne, very much a man of his time, confronted the crucial problems of the late nineteenth century as directly as any of his contemporaries, and the answers he found are at least as viable today as those of his more highly acclaimed brethren. The sole fruits of his fecundity, it has commonly been supposed, were the epiphenomenal decadent and aesthetic movements. While it is true, however, that in their exaltation of art, their flouting of convention, and most of all in their solipsism, these movements follow in Swinburne's wake, it is equally true that they run counter to his central poetic faith. Even when obeying Pater's injunction to lose the self in experiential mergence with beauty, the aesthete separates the work of art from life. Art, for the aesthete, lends joy to the moment but not meaning, genuine religious feeling, to life. The aesthetes were, in fact, fundamentally unlike Swinburne because they exalted the observer rather than the creator of art and therefore were to a certain extent necessarily detached and disinterested.

Swinburne is in the mainstream of the Apollonian song not so much for his contribution to aestheticism as for his continuation of the romantic tradition. He was able to reconcile modern rationalism and solipsism with romantic faith by insisting—as did William James—that reality is what we experience, not just what we can empirically prove. Swinburne inherited his agnostic mythmaking from Shelley, modulated it, and passed it on in altered form—with a greatly increased realization of solipsism and man's dependence upon himself—to the greatest of his disciples, Thomas Hardy. Even

---

[3] *Swinburne* (Boston, 1929), p. 302.

more emphatically than Swinburne Hardy believed that the only certain truth that exists outside the human mind is that chance and change rule the universe. In the obvious sense that his poetry is essentially dramatic, whereas Swinburne's is generally bardic, Hardy is a very different type of poet. But his explanation for his dramatic style suggests an underlying affinity: "Unadjusted impressions have their value, and the road to a true philosophy of life seems to lie in humbly recording diverse readings of its phenomena as they are forced upon us by chance and change."[4] Swinburne insisted on the sovereignty of the perceiving mind, attributing to poets the power to create and impose meaning; Hardy simply democratized the idea, using dramatic characters and dramatic situations as Swinburne had used poets and poetical situations—to avoid describing a merely personal view of life. Both poets wanted to write about life in a meaningful way, but since there is no external principle which lends meaning to life, since all meaning is in the eye of the beholder, Hardy's purpose was to see from as many different perspectives as possible.

The comparison with Hardy helps to illustrate how Swinburne's poetry is, in spite of its cheerless and often bleak skepticism, a consoling and ultimately life-enhancing experience. The knowledge that man is part of no great scheme of things, no vast universal order, does, in some ways, make him seem utterly insignificant, but Hardy, following and democratizing Swinburne, carried this understanding to its logical extreme, realizing that if each man creates reality by imposing meaning on what would otherwise be chaos, each individual becomes all-important. Vast indifferent nature, unfeeling fate, and all metaphysical abstractions become, in this light, insignificant because meaningless. Hardy's faithful representation of "unadjusted impressions" exalts the individual and the individual's ability to survive in this meaninglessness. Like Shelley's, and even more like Swinburne's, Hardy's poetry shows that man's consolation for existence lies in his ability to create ideals to believe in. The idea that consolation is to be found in the solipsistic construction of illusory comforts, odd though it may sound thus baldly stated, is the explicit subject of the poem "On a Fine Morning," which asks the

[4] Preface to *Poems of the Past and Present*, in *The Complete Poems of Thomas Hardy: New Wessex Edition*, ed. James Gibson (London, 1976), p. 84.

question, "Whence comes Solace?" The answer is that it comes not from seeing life as it really is

> But in cleaving to the Dream,
> And in gazing at the gleam
> Whereby gray things golden seem.

To make the concept even clearer, Hardy provides an example of such cleaving:

> Thus do I this heyday, holding
> Shadows but as lights unfolding,
> As no specious show this moment
> With its iris-hued embowment;
> > But as nothing other than
> > Part of a benignant plan;
> > Proof that earth was made for man.[5]

For Hardy, as for Swinburne, knowledge and belief are separated. The delusory comforts that both poets affirm do not involve permanent illusions but are based on a fundamental recognition of the miseries of existence. Hardy's poetry perfectly illustrates what we moderns can hope to learn from Swinburne: by confronting wretchedness directly, we can surmount it by a willed act of consciousness, by an affirmative use of that faculty which separates us from elemental nature and supplies our only meaning. Wordsworthian romanticism, which seeks union with nature, has been completely transcended by an insistence that we find consolation in mortality, not in intimations of immortality. To accept any hypothesis about a vast design for man, both Swinburne and Hardy knew, is to deny his only real significance, his ability to create meaning.

Swinburne is in the center of the path that leads from Shelley to Hardy; he is in the mainstream because he kept mythopoeia alive in English verse. He is in the path that leads away from the passive acceptance of received myth, in the path that leads to Lawrence, who, in conscious memory of Swinburne, rejected Christ, "that pale young man," for a new primitivism.[6] He is in the tradition that leads not to the garnering of fragments of a lost wholeness, as in Eliot and

---

[5] Ibid., p. 93.
[6] "Give Us Gods," *The Complete Poems of D. H. Lawrence*, ed. Vivian de Sola Pinto and F. Warren Roberts (New York, 1964), p. 437.

even more clearly in the imagist poets, but to the preservation of old myths and the creation of new ones from the chaos of modern life, as in Joyce's *Ulysses*, where Swinburne is invoked frequently, in many of O'Neill's plays, in Wallace Stevens's poetry, and even in Yeats's myth of the cycles of history. Swinburne is, in a sense, the link between the first English romantics, who perceived mythopoeically, and the modern romantics (as they may be called) who perceive first the void, the meaningless chaos, and then actively impose mythic meaning upon it. His development—from unthinking acceptance of earlier modes, through disillusionment and rebellion, solipsism and denial, and finally to creative affirmation—perfectly reflects the development of the most viable of literary traditions: a tradition that paradoxically rejects the passive acceptance of received doctrine while insisting on the metamorphic renewal of old myths, a tradition that insists on radical and fecund reinterpretation, a tradition, in short, that insists on the creative continuation of tradition itself as the one certain bulwark against meaninglessness.

Index

Index